SOLVING FOR PROJECT RISK MANAGEMENT

"Once you have realized that risk management is the formal communications methodology for identifying, quantifying, and mitigating the threats and embracing the opportunities within your projects, the next wise step is to analyze them. There is no better person to explain that analysis and solve for project risk management than Christian Smart. I would encourage all project professionals to study this book."

Dale Shermon
Qinetiq Fellow, Council member and Fellow of the
Association of Cost Engineers (FACostE); author of
Association for Project Management Body of Knowledge
(7th ed.); and editor of *Systems Cost Engineering*

"As a leader in the Integrated Program Management community, I believe that we often lack the understanding and awareness of the impact that risk and uncertainty have on a program. As such we are often at a loss on how to handle risk and the mitigations that can be applied. Dr. Christian Smart brings the reader into his world by helping them understand the intricacies and nuances of risk management. This book is a chat with a leading expert in the field who will make you feel comfortable with risk complexities and the best approach to manage them."

Neil Albert
CEO, NFA Consulting, LLC, and Vice Chair,
Integrated Program Management Division of the
National Defense Industrial Association (NDIA)

"Dr. Christian Smart is an acknowledged leader in the field of project risk management. In this book he introduces and develops sophisticated concepts in ways that are accessible to every reader from expert to novice. His broad experience and deep understanding of this field are on display as he illuminates events that people face in their daily lives. The book helps us better understand current issues that have a risky content—and reading Dr. Smart's book we realize that most of life can be understood from a risk standpoint."

David T. Hulett, PhD, FAACE
author of *Practical Schedule Risk Analysis* and
Integrated Cost-Schedule Risk Analysis

"A no-holds-barred book on understanding and managing risk, *Solving for Project Risk Management* conveys the ugly truth about cost and schedule risk and offers effective ways to evaluate and manage risks. Christian Smart tells a story that's easy to read and understand, a must read for those responsible for managing complex projects or telling project managers what they absolutely need to know about the cost and schedule risks of their projects."

Rick Collins
Technical Director, Technomics, Inc., and President,
International Cost Estimating and Analysis Association

"I have long admired Christian Smart's wisdom and ability to explain concepts to project managers and others that need real understanding and solutions. This book exemplifies his ability to teach difficult concepts. Its humor and delightful stories provide decades of project management wisdom, lessons learned, and actionable information in a must-read way. I will quote this book for years to come."

Dan Galorath
founder, Galorath Incorporated, and author of
Software Sizing, Estimation, and Risk Management:
When Performance Is Measured, Performance Improves

"All projects have uncertainties and *Solving for Project Risk Management* provides project managers with the tools needed to identify key vulnerabilities and take steps to mitigate them before they can jeopardize the success of the undertaking. The author offers the background and history of how risks impact the cost, schedule, and technical success of ventures and how human tendencies cause us to overlook risks and be overconfident. Most important, it provides workable ways to assess risk, calculate confidence levels, and manage risks in order to enable project success. This is the best book on this topic that I have seen—it should be required reading for all project managers!"

Joseph Hamaker, PhD
former NASA Senior Executive and senior
cost analyst, Galorath Federal

"I have been lucky to know Christian since the early days of his exemplary career. Christian is a relentless innovator that has used his Applied Mathematics PhD to develop a plethora of useful models. No doubt all professionals in cost estimating will welcome the publication of this book summing up all of Christian's research on risk. Many of the concepts addressed in this book have been appraised by our professional cost estimating community as testified by the numerous Best Paper Awards he has collected over the years. Christian's research work is rigorously supported with facts and numbers. It results in solid work that the reader may use with confidence. The readers will find powerful tools in this reference book to handle projects cost and schedule risks.

More than any other, Christian Smart will have brought us the possibility to open our eyes and to conduct our large projects in a more intelligent and effective way. I hope that everyone will take this chance."

Herve' Joumier
Senior Advisor, European Space Agency

SOLVING FOR PROJECT RISK MANAGEMENT

SOLVING FOR

UNDERSTANDING THE CRITICAL

PROJECT RISK

ROLE OF UNCERTAINTY IN

MANAGEMENT

PROJECT MANAGEMENT

CHRISTIAN B. SMART

McGraw Hill

New York Chicago San Francisco Athens London Madrid
Mexico City Milan New Delhi Singapore Sydney Toronto

1 2 3 4 5 6 7 8 9   LCR   25 24 23 22 21 20

ISBN   978-1-260-47383-4
MHID   1-260-47383-X

e-ISBN   978-1-260-47384-1
e-MHID   1-260-47384-8

Library of Congress Cataloging-in-Publication Data

Names: Smart, Christian, author.
Title: Solving for project risk management : understanding the critical role of
    uncertainty in project management / Christian Smart, Ph.D.
Description: New York City : McGraw Hill, 2020. | Includes bibliographical
    references and index.
Identifiers: LCCN 2020026092 (print) | LCCN 2020026093 (ebook) | ISBN
    9781260473834 (hardback) | ISBN 9781260473841 (ebook)
Subjects: LCSH: Project management. | Risk management.
Classification: LCC HD69.P75 S563 2020 (print) | LCC HD69.P75 (ebook) |
    DDC 658.4/04—dc23
LC record available at https://lccn.loc.gov/2020026092
LC ebook record available at https://lccn.loc.gov/2020026093

For Glenda and Miles
In memory of Mom, Nanny, and Pa

CONTENTS

ACKNOWLEDGMENTS

I have a PhD in Applied Mathematics. My decision to pursue a career in industry rather than academia required me to take a risk that has paid significant dividends over the past 20-plus years. The focus of my studies was not probability or risk management. Rather, my education in risk and uncertainty took place on the job. My first significant work in this subject was developing a cost risk capability for a NASA and Air Force cost model. Leading this project brought me into direct contact with Drs. Steve Book and Paul Garvey, whose papers, books, seminars, and conversations served as my initial education in the field of project risk management. Dr. Book's knowledge, humor, and outstanding writing and presentation skills continue to inspire me. I also learned much from Tim Anderson and Ray Covert.

My intuition had always led me to believe that conventional approaches to risk management underestimated the true degree of hazards in projects, particularly the consequences of adverse events. In this regard, I was glad to see that Nassim Taleb's *The Black Swan* confirmed my suspicions. This encouraged me to conduct my own research. My self-education continued by studying actuarial approaches to risk. Actuaries have the most sophisticated and mature approach to risk management. The application of their methods to my work spurred me to write several conference and peer-reviewed journal publications about risk, which form the basis of this book. In reading Norman Augustine's book *Augustine's Laws*, I realized that all the problems with project management risk I had discovered on my own he had written about years before. This confirmed my findings and made me realize that these problems were not new but had occurred for decades.

My experience is in Department of Defense, NASA, and aerospace programs. Stephen Isaacs at McGraw-Hill suggested I broaden the scope. Upon doing a little research, I discovered that my findings applied to all types of projects. I have found the works of Bent Flyvbjerg, John Hollman, and Edward Merrow to be especially enlightening in this regard.

Throughout my career, I have found the guidance and encouragement from my friends and colleagues Dr. Joe Hamaker, Douglas Howarth, and Andy Prince to be especially helpful. Joe has been a huge influence on my thinking. Andy encouraged me to present at conferences, and Doug urged me to write a book. Joe, Andy, and Doug are gifted writers and presenters, and I have learned much from them. I have also benefited from supportive management over the years, notably Dan Galorath, Brent Heard, Bob Hunt, Bob Packard, and Gary Pennett. I admire their combination of acumen and ethics and strive to follow their example. I appreciate Dan's and Bob's support for the book.

My wife, Glenda Smart, helped with the initial editing of my writing. I appreciate her input as well as her patience and support for the nights and weekends I spent putting together the initial manuscript.

INTRODUCTION

Before its launch, the *Titanic* was touted as being unsinkable. Its tragic maiden voyage in 1912 is a realization of risk, which is the possibility of a hazardous event. Risk has a variety of dimensions that can be broken into two distinct categories: technical and resource. Technical risks are those that threaten the performance of a system. Resource risks are those that present the possibility of cost increases or schedule delays. When technical risks are realized, they result in system impairment or even outright failure. The occurrence of resource risks leads to additional cost and/or longer schedules.

There are some notable examples of technical risks. These include the Space Shuttle disasters in 1986 and 2003; the nuclear disasters of Chernobyl in 1986 and Fukushima in 2011; and the oil spills from the *Exxon Valdez* oil tanker in 1989 and the Deepwater Horizon drill in 2010. Not all technical failures are catastrophic. For example, the Hubble Space Telescope was put into space with a primary mirror that was polished to the wrong shape. It was a problem that took years for NASA to fix with servicing missions. A recent example of a disastrous system failure is the Boeing 737 MAX aircraft, which experienced fatal crashes in 2018 and 2019. This failure culminated in the indefinite grounding of the plane. While technical failures occur from time to time, resource issues are a far more common occurrence. Most projects do not experience significant technical issues, but the vast majority suffer from cost overruns and schedule delays. In some industries, such as aerospace and defense, more than 80% of projects experience cost overruns, and 90% experience schedule delays. Average cost growth for development projects exceeds 50%, and one in six more than doubles in cost. This imbalance of risk between technical and resources is due to a lack of attention to the issue of resource planning and management. This book has been written to address the issues of risk management of resources—the importance of addressing and planning for risks, the common problems encountered in resource risk management, and ways these can be fixed. Throughout we will also address technical risk, especially its connection with resource risk. The two have a strong connection, as technical problems typically have significant resource impacts. While many of the issues and solutions we discuss also apply to technical risk, the focus of this book remains resource risk.

The most well-known examples of big cost overruns and long schedule delays are for large projects. The absolute dollars and years spent on these complex systems can be enormous. When NASA began planning the successor to the Hubble Space Telescope, which is now called the James Webb Space Telescope (JWST), it convened a meeting of managers, scientists, engineers, cost estimators, and other program professionals to determine how to design a system with a price tag of $1 billion or less. In inflation-adjusted dollars that amounts to approximately $1.5 billion. Despite the initial plans for JWST to cost less than Hubble, JWST is much more complex. It has a bigger mirror that is in a folded-up configuration when launched and then unfolds in space. JWST will be outside of a low Earth orbit after it is launched. Current launch capabilities for astronauts are only to low Earth orbit, so there is no option to repair it once it is launched. The planning for JWST started in 1996 with an expected launch in 2007. There was a significant amount of cost and schedule growth from program initiation. This resulted in a program replan in 2005. In 2010, JWST was called the "Telescope That Ate Astronomy"[1] because it was consuming a large amount of the space science budget. As a result, other astronomy objectives could not be achieved due to lack of available funding. As of March

2020, the planned launch date was in 2021, a 14-year delay and the expected program costs exceed $9.7 billion, a more than sixfold increase from the initial plan.[2] Programs with this amount of cost growth often get cancelled. However, sometimes even problem programs, when they are high priority, continue onward.

Even though resource risks are most prominent in large projects, significant cost and schedule growth often occur in more mundane endeavors. For example, in 2004, the City of Huntsville, Alabama, signed a contract for construction of a 1,100-bed addition to the local jail for $25 million. The initial schedule was to complete this effort in three years. However, the city called a halt to construction after an inspection discovered cracks in the support beams. Due to these findings, it terminated the contract with the builder. The city then hired another company to finish the project. These actions led to significant delays and cost increases. The addition was eventually finished in May 2010, three years behind schedule.[3] Also, the city and the original builder sued each other. This resulted in the City of Huntsville spending another $3 million in legal expenses and paying the original contractor an additional $2 million. The total cost of the project exceeded $80 million,[4] more than triple the initial contract. Even though it might appear that such a project should be simple, jails require sophisticated components such as electronic locks and security systems with which average building contractors may not have experience. The City of Huntsville did not vet the contractor before awarding the contract but merely went with the lowest bid from an out-of-town company that had never worked with the city. As this example reveals, cost overruns and schedule delays can occur in what may appear to be simple building and infrastructure projects.

Understanding risk is challenging. The second law of thermodynamics states that entropy, which is the level of disorder in the universe, is always increasing, unless there is some intervening action that occurs to stop it. My son once tossed a plate from our dinner table. When it hit the floor, the plate shattered. The plate was in one piece on the table only moments before and was nice and orderly. An intervening action would have been to catch the plate as it fell off the table. There was nothing to be done to make the plate more orderly, but there are plenty of opportunities, especially in the hands of a small boy, to quickly make things messier. Entropy is a complicated process. The famous physicist and mathematician John von Neumann once stated that no one really understands entropy.[5]

Similarly, risk is a difficult concept to grasp. It too always seems to be increasing everywhere. Like a dinner plate on a table, there is little that can change, if anything, to make it better, but many ways things can go wrong. There are many more ways for costs and schedules to increase than to decrease. This includes all kinds of projects—aerospace, defense, infrastructure, construction, and many others. Some projects are inherently riskier than others, but all projects bear some resource and technical risk. A former NASA colleague of mine once wrote, "without some intervening action chaos will eventually rule project management."[6] To guard against risk, much more "intervening" action is needed, especially in the measurement and management of risks. This does not mean that we should not take risk. Risk-taking is as American as apple pie. Walter Wriston, the CEO of Citibank/Citicorp from 1967 to 1984, noted in the 1980s that society had become averse to risk to the point it had become another four-letter word. He argued for risk-taking by stating, "The driving force of our society is the conviction that risk-taking and individual responsibility are the ways to advance our mutual fortunes."[7] However, that does not mean we should take risks blindly. We need to understand the risks we face and use that information to make rational decisions. Not doing so has led private companies to take too few risks and government organizations to take too many. Private companies, faced with bankruptcy if they take on too much risk, often err on the side of risk avoidance in the absence of proper risk management. By contrast, government organizations, which lack incentives to avoid hazards, often take on too much risk.

The term "black swan" is often used to refer to unpredictable events that have extreme consequences.[8] Risk management often ignores them. Due to their significant consequences, plans should be made to deal with black swan events. The phenomena that lead to such events have the property that no matter how severe the consequences of such events in the past, it is only a matter of time before an even worse one occurs in the future. Reducing their impact requires careful consideration, fast action, and even over-reaction. For example, during the COVID-19 pandemic, Taiwan swiftly acted early in the outbreak in January 2020 to shut its borders and require people to wear face masks.[9] As a result, by May 2020, the island nation had only 440 confirmed cases of infection and six deaths. Normalizing for population, Taiwan had only 18 cases per million people, tiny compared to the global average of 513, which translates to only 0.3 deaths per million people, compared to 35.3 globally.[10]

Current risk management practice is a fantasy conceived of optimism and willful ignorance. I have firsthand experience with this in my profession. I have worked as a consultant with NASA and the Department of Defense and have served as a government employee at a Department of Defense agency. During my time as a civil servant, I worked closely with project managers and senior leaders, including several generals and admirals. I have had an inside view of how decisions are made. Project managers do some things extremely well. They ensure the development, production, and operations of complex systems, and those systems work as designed most of the time. Many projects involve solving hard engineering problems. You know the saying, "It doesn't take a rocket scientist"? Well, sometimes it does. Government weapon systems and aerospace programs are examples where many rocket scientists are needed. Many other organizations in a variety of fields, such as infrastructure, mining, and chemical processes, also require sophisticated engineering. All these organizations have detailed, sound approaches to the technical planning process. However, most of the time, these same projects lack solid resource planning. Instead, resource risks are routinely ignored and lack proper consideration. Planning for the resources required by a portfolio of systems is poorly done and extremely shortsighted. Alas, to many project managers, risk is often just another four-letter word.

This book is written with the intention to provide information that can help fill the risk management void that exists in project management practices. The common occurrence of large cost overruns and long schedule delays provides overwhelming evidence of significant cost and schedule risk in most projects. It also demonstrates that in general this risk is not being managed well. The case for quantitative analysis of risk for projects is made. There are several problems with the current state of practice because even when risk is quantitatively assessed, it is not done well. Several of these issues are addressed, and ways to fix them are provided. Risk does not need to be just another four-letter word. It is an important part of project management. When managed correctly, it can be used to make smarter decisions and help ensure project success.

CHAPTER 1

Show Me the Data

The Enduring Problems of Cost Growth and
Schedule Delays

Gottfried von Leibniz was a German polymath who lived in the seventeenth and early eighteenth centuries. Two of his most well-known contributions include coinventing differential and integral calculus and his philosophy of optimism. Leibniz believed that we live in the "best of all possible worlds."[1] This was lampooned by the French writer, historian, and philosopher Voltaire, who caricatured him as Professor Pangloss in his novel *Candide*. Throughout the novel Pangloss suffers from a series of misfortunes. Among other calamities, he is enslaved on a Turkish ship and almost executed by the Inquisition. Despite this, Pangloss remains optimistic. This gave rise to the term "Panglossian," which means extreme optimism, especially when faced with misfortune.[2] One of the chief sources of cost and schedule risk, as we shall discuss in this chapter, is a Panglossian outlook on the part of project managers. Just like the professor with an always sunny outlook even when storm clouds threaten, project management as a profession has refused to face the

1

reality that we live in a hazardous world. The evidence for this is the abundance of cost growth and schedule delays for a wide variety of projects.

Cost and schedule growth reflect changes in dollars and time from one point to a later point. A program budgets for $100 million, but the final actual cost doubles to $200 million by completion. A program plans for a three-year schedule, but it takes nine years instead. Growth is calculated based on the increase in cost or amount of time divided by the earlier cost or amount of time, respectively. To express a number in percentage terms, it is multiplied by 100. For example, in the case of the increase from three years to nine years, the increase is 6/3 = 2, or 200%.

Cost growth and schedule delays are systemic and enduring issues. Many projects in a wide variety of industries regularly experience them. Depending on the application, average cost growth ranges from 30% to 50%, and it is much higher in many cases. For most endeavors, at least one in every six projects more than doubles in cost from initial projections during the development phase. In accordance with the adage that time is money, schedule delays are also significant. Depending on the type of project, in percentage terms schedule delays can average just as much and sometimes more than cost increases. These two interrelated problems have been consistently high for decades with little change over time.

When you see the word *average*, you probably think about a likely or expected outcome. An average represents the central tendency of a data set. In statistics, three different kinds of averages are commonly used: the mean, median, and mode. These values have a significant impact on our treatment of risk, so they are the most meaningful measures for our purposes. For a discrete set of points, the *mean* is the sum of data points divided by the size of the data set. Just like the center line on a road, the *median* is the 50/50 point. Half the outcomes are greater than the median, and half are less. That is, there is a 50% chance of a result less than the median, and a 50% chance of a result greater than the median. The *mode* is the most likely occurrence. When data points are evenly spread in a symmetric pattern around the average, these three measures are all the same. For example, given the five data points {1,2,3,4,5} the mean, median, and mode are all 3. This is because the data points are symmetric about 3. Given the seven data points {1,1,2,3,5,10,20}, the mean is $(1 + 1 + 2 + 3 + 5 + 10 + 20)/7 = 6$. The median is 3 since there are three data points {1,1,2} that are less than 3 and there are three data points {5,10,20} greater than 3. The mode is 1, since there are two occurrences of 1 in the set, while all the other numbers occur only once. When we refer to the word *average* in this chapter, we will be referring to the mean because it considers the large cost and schedule risks. The second set of data points {1,1,2,3,4,10,20} is *skewed*. That is, the largest numbers are farther away from the average than the smallest numbers. We see this often in practice in projects.

The cost of a project can never be less than zero; it cannot be cheaper than free. Schedules cannot be negative, as time travel is impossible. However, both cost and schedule can increase significantly, as there is no true upper bound. Also, while it is possible that in some cases a project will discover an opportunity for savings, there is a built-in asymmetry. More can go wrong than can go "right." As a result, cost is more likely to grow than shrink. Even if a program manager finds savings, he or she will likely not turn in the savings but rather find ways to spend the money on the project. It is typically the case that, once money is allocated, it will be spent. This is often referred to as the "money allocated is money spent" (MAIMS) principle.[3]

Note that the problems of growth and delay are distinct from the issues that some projects cost too much and take too long to develop. For example, the government is infamous for overpaying for simple items, such as $10,000 for a toilet seat cover.[4] The subject of this chapter is increases in cost and schedule from one point in time to another. For development projects, the beginning point is typically the beginning of detailed design. Some organizations, such as NASA, start tracking cost and schedule before that point. The earlier the point in time a project starts tracking growth and delays, the greater the uncertainty and the greater the likelihood of growth and delays, but a fair starting point for a baseline is when preliminary designs are in place so that a project has a good sense of scope. Figure 1.1 displays a general timeline that applies to all projects.

Figure 1.1   Timeline of Project Phases

Initial Planning → Development → Production → Operations → Disposal

Some organizations have their own names for these phases, but the phases in Figure 1.1 apply to all projects. Initial planning is the start. Depending on complexity, this could be a short period or a long period affected by factors such as the use of advanced technologies, as some of the time for initial planning could be used for necessary technology development. Once initial planning is complete, the development process begins. This involves engineering work, along with building prototypes and conducting tests. At some point during development, production begins. Production does not apply equally to all endeavors, and to some, it does not apply at all. Weapon systems typically produce in quantities numbered in the hundreds and thousands. NASA satellites typically involve the production of one unit, as do infrastructure projects such as a bridge, tunnel, road, or dam. Software projects do not produce a tangible product at all. Endeavors that do not result in a physical product or those that produce one unit may consider any production to be part of the development phase. Once a product has been developed and produced, it needs to be operated and maintained. This can occur over a long period such as years or even decades. This is typically the longest phase and often consumes the largest amount of cost and time in the life cycle of project. At the end of their useful life, a tangible, non-software product will need to be disposed of or destroyed.

When measured from the beginning of development, the phase with the greatest amount of cost uncertainty is often development, so many studies of cost growth focus on this phase. However, it is not always the case that development has the greatest amount of risk for cost increase. If the product is a new configuration that is not like anything in the past, the operation and production phases can be risky as well. For example, the Space Shuttle was a radical departure from previous launch vehicles, such as the Saturn V that preceded it. The initial plans called for the Shuttle to operate much like a conventional airplane with one flight per week. However, this was wildly optimistic as it never flew more than nine times in one year. This low flight rate, combined with the complexity of the system itself, caused operations costs per flight to be much higher than initial projections. Production cost increases can be driven by errors in forecasting production quantities. When multiple units are to be produced and it takes years to develop a design, it is hard to accurately forecast quantities to be produced. The number of units produced is an important driver for production costs, as it is inversely correlated with the average unit cost. In most cases, there is a large fixed cost associated with manufacturing. When more units are produced, this cost can be spread over more units, which results in lower average unit cost. When fewer units are produced, this fixed cost is allocated across fewer units, thus raising the average unit cost.

IT ALWAYS COSTS MORE AND TAKES LONGER THAN YOU THINK

Cost increases and schedule stretches are commonplace for many different types of projects. Megaprojects—those that cost billions of dollars—are often the focus of growth studies.[5] However, most projects, regardless of size, experience cost and schedule increases. A recent NASA study showed average cost growth for 133 development programs was equal to more than 50% across a wide range of small to large projects, from those that cost tens of millions of dollars to those that cost billions.[6] See Figure 1.2.

Figure 1.2   Actual Cost of NASA Missions Compared to Initial Estimates

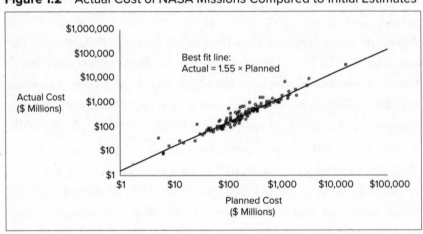

The equation in Figure 1.2 is simple. Take the planned cost and multiply it by 1.55 to get the best estimate of actual cost. This simple line explains more than 95% of the relationship between the planned and actual costs. Note that the scale of the graph in Figure 1.2 is on a log scale, which means that orders of magnitude—1, 10, 100, etc.—are equally spaced. This is necessary to properly visualize data that varies over a wide range. This simple analysis is not intended as a Band-Aid to fix cost growth, as there is a significant amount of variation around the line that is diminished by the log scale. It is intended as an illustration that both small and large projects experience significant cost growth. The variations like those in Figure 1.2 have consistently been at this level for not only NASA but also Department of Defense missions since the 1960s. I have also analyzed schedule growth for these types of missions, and the average schedule delay ranges from 27% to more than 50%. Norman Augustine, former Army official and former CEO of Lockheed Martin, one of the largest defense contractors in the United States, noted that the cost for development programs grows on average by 52%, which he called the "Las Vegas Factor of Development Program Planning"[7] as this is the amount estimates would need to increase in order to ensure that the project (akin to a casino in this analogy) will break even.

Cost overruns get much attention, but schedule delays are important as well because time is a valuable resource. Augustine also noted that in his experience schedules for development projects grew by 33% on average, which he termed the "Universal Fantasy Factor."[8] Douglas Hofstadter, a cognitive scientist, noted that there were predictions in the early days of computer chess that it would only be 10 years before computers could play chess as well as the world champion. Claude Shannon, a mathematician who developed information theory, was an early pioneer in the field. He published a paper on programming a computer to play chess in 1950. Hofstadter noted that 10 years after that there was an update to the prediction, which was that in another 10 years computers would surpass the best human chess players. The point in time at which computers became superior to the best humans in chess always seemed to be 10 years away. This example led Hofstadter to coin the eponymous Hofstadter's Law: "It always takes longer than you expect, even when you take into account Hofstadter's Law."[9] However, there are often exceptions to such laws. Garry Kasparov, world chess champion from 1985 to 2000, predicted in 1990 that it would be at least 10 years before a computer could beat the best human chess player in a match. Kasparov would make a good project manager, as he was optimistic. His forecast was off by three years. In 1997, the IBM computer program Deep Blue defeated Kasparov in a six-game chess match.[10]

To understand why Hofstadter's Law holds (with the occasional exception for overconfident chess grandmasters), consider a thought experiment that most everyone can relate to—the daily commute to work. At one time, my daily commute by car to work ranged anywhere from 25 minutes to more than an hour. The typical, or most likely, commute time was around 35 minutes. Two factors that drove this time were when I left my house and the amount of school traffic. If I left my house early enough, I would avoid school traffic and many other commuters, and I could make it to work in 25 minutes. Also, during the summer and school holidays, like Christmas and spring break, my commute was also about 25 minutes regardless of when I left home. However, there were other events that would slow me down. For example, road construction along my route to work happened occasionally and would slow my commute. I also crossed a train track going to work, and sometimes would have to wait on the train. A significant part of my route was along an interstate, and occasionally there were wrecks that slowed my commute. My longest commute was over an hour—a car had crossed the median at a high speed, hitting another car head-on, and caused two deaths. My commute was typically 35 minutes. Only so many things could speed up my commute, but there were many events that could slow me down. The things that could go right were lack of school traffic and leaving for work earlier or later than usual. The things that could and did sometimes go wrong included waiting for a train crossing, a stalled car along the route, a car wreck along the route, someone stopped by a police officer for speeding, me being stopped by a police officer for speeding, road construction along the route, and school traffic, including bus traffic, being heavier than usual for some reason. It is much harder to overestimate the amount of time it takes to get to work than it is to underestimate because there are so many more things that can happen to increase the time than to decrease it. As a result, schedule growth, like cost growth, is highly skewed to the right (or upside).

Not only do development endeavors take longer than planned on average, they are rarely completed on time. I have discovered in my experience that schedule underruns are rare, and schedule slips are even more likely to occur than cost growth. C. Northcote Parkinson was a twentieth-century British naval historian and author of 60 books. Today, he is best remembered for Parkinson's Law, which states that work expands to fill the time available.[11] Rather than finish early, projects typically use any spare time to continue system development such as doing additional testing to ensure that the system works correctly.

SHOW ME THE DATA

A few years ago, I compiled a data set of development cost growth for 289 NASA and Department of Defense programs and projects.[12] The minimum cost growth was −25.2% for a super lightweight version of the Shuttle external tank. The negative number means that cost underran the initial budget by approximately one-quarter of the initial budget. One in six missions reported actual costs that were lower than the initial plan. The maximum cost growth among the missions studied was 474.8% for the Comanche helicopter program, which was eventually cancelled before development was completed. The average cost growth for all missions was 52.0%. This value is the same as Augustine's Las Vegas Factor that we discussed earlier. Most missions experienced relatively small amounts of cost growth—half experienced growth less than 30%, with some missions experiencing extreme amounts of cost growth. One in six missions had cost growth equal to or in excess of 100%, which means cost at least doubled. See Figure 1.3 for a graphical summary.

Figure 1.3   Summary of Cost Growth Data for 289 NASA and Department of Defense Development Programs

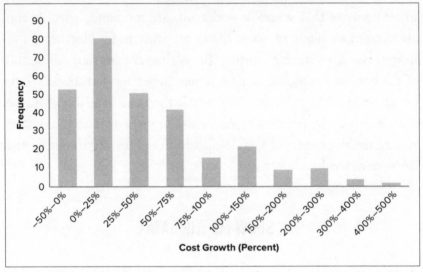

Several years ago, I collected data on development schedule delays for 98 NASA missions.[13] There was only one schedule underrun. This was for a well-managed in-house effort. It was an Earth-orbiting spacecraft that observed the time variation of a variety of x-ray sources, including black holes. Eight other missions were completed on time, which means more than 90% of the schedules had some amount of delay. The average delay was 38%. Ten percent of missions doubled or more in length of time. The longest delay was for the Ulysses program, a joint NASA and European

Space Agency mission to study the sun. Figure 1.4 displays a summary of this data as a histogram.

Figure 1.4 Summary of Schedule Delay Data for 98 NASA Missions

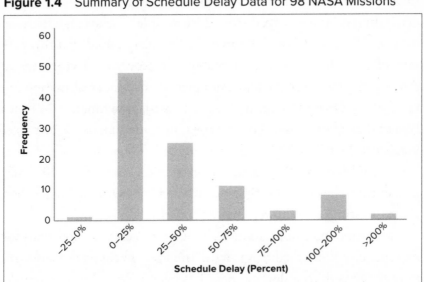

Schedule delays are common in defense projects as well. A study of tactical aircraft (*tactical* is used to denote shorter-range weapons such as jet fighters) found an average 7% delay in length of development and 25% in production. A study of tactical missiles found an average 52% increase in development schedules and a 53% increase in production schedules.[14] Another study of a variety of weapons systems found an average development schedule delay equal to 27.5%, with 9 of 10 missions experiencing increases in schedules.[15]

Cost overruns and schedule delays are not limited to aerospace and weapons systems development projects. Bent Flyvbjerg, a professor at Oxford, has been studying the issue of cost growth for large infrastructure projects for many years. He calls these large endeavors megaprojects. He has studied a variety of different types—rails, bridges, roads, and tunnels, including the tunnel under the English Channel that connects England and France. In a large study of 258 transportation infrastructure projects, approximately 90% experienced cost growth. The average cost growth, depending on type, ranged from 20% to 45%. The average increase in schedule ranged from 23% to 45%. Flyvbjerg found that this pattern of growth has been remarkably stable over a 70-year period. Among the more spectacular examples of cost underestimation are the Sydney Opera House, with actual costs approximately 14 times higher than those projected, and the Concorde supersonic airplane, with cost 12 times higher than predicted. When the Suez Canal was completed in 1869, actual construction costs were 20 times higher than the earliest estimated costs and three times higher than the cost estimate in the year before construction began.[16]

Software and information technology projects are notorious for extreme cost and schedule growth. The average change in software requirements during development has been reported to average 1% to 2% each month and can be much higher.[17] This means that the longer the project, the more requirements will change. For a 5-year project, on average, requirements will increase between 80% and 220%. For a 10-year project, this range is 230% to 980%. A commonly used metric for measuring the scope of a software project is called equivalent software lines of code (ESLOC). The number of lines of code is a count of the lines in the text that make up the instructions in a computer program. ESLOC represents new software lines of code to be developed plus some fraction for integrating those previously developed. This metric is closely correlated with the cost of a software project. For military applications, a study of 131 data points found 51% average growth in ESLOC during development and that 16% more than doubled.[18] Another, smaller study for military missions showed similar programs averaged 49% ESLOC growth, with approximately 20% at least doubling in cost.[19] A large survey of thousands of software and information technology development projects has tracked cost growth and delays from 2000 to 2008, finding that average cost growth ranged from 43% to 56%, average schedule delays ranged from 63% to 84%, and 24% of these kinds of projects failed.[20] New oilfield projects experience significant cost growth as well, with 30% experiencing overruns in excess of 50%.[21]

Hydroelectric power generation from dams often experiences significant cost growth and schedule delays. Dams require complex engineering and geological studies, as the amount of water contained can impact fault lines and cause seismic activity. Cost growth for these systems ranges on average from 24% to 96%, and schedule delays average 27% to 44%.[22]

The Olympics may have the worst record of all for cost growth of any project type. From 1968 to 2016, the average cost overrun was 156%. Almost half reported cost overruns in excess of 100%. The largest overrun was for the Montreal Olympics in Summer 1976—the final cost was more than eight times the initial plan.[23] The date for an Olympics is set well in advanced. Unlike most other projects, there have been no schedule delays in the past. This could be a factor in why the cost overruns are much higher than for other types of endeavors. However, the 2020 Summer Olympics planned for Tokyo was postponed in March of that year due to the COVID-19 pandemic. A schedule delay for an Olympics is unprecedented, and a risk no one could foresee—just as it always costs more and takes longer than you think, it is always riskier than you think.

Table 1.1 summarizes cost and schedule growth across several industries.

The averages for cost and schedule growth among industries varies from 20% for roads to 156% for the Olympics. Average schedule delays range from 0% for Olympics prior to 2020 to 84% for information technology and software projects. All projects experience regular, recurring cost and schedule growth. Cost overruns occur

Table 1.1 Comparison of Cost and Schedule Growth Across Several Industries

	Olympics	Software/ IT	Dams	NASA/ DoD	Rail	Bridges/ Tunnels	Roads
Average Cost Growth	156%	43–56%	24–96%	52%	45%	34%	20%
Frequency of Occurrence	10/10	8/10	8/10	8/10	9/10	9/10	9/10
Frequency of Doubling	1 in 2	1 in 4	1 in 5	1 in 6	1 in 12	1 in 12	1 in 50
Average Schedule Delay	0%	63–84%	27–44%	27–52%	45%	23%	38%
Frequency of Schedule Delay	0/10	9/10	7/10	9/10	8/10	7/10	7/10

in 80% or more of projects, and schedule delays occur in 70% or more of projects, regardless of industry, as shown in the table by frequency of occurrence. The frequency of doubling is an important statistic.[24] This indicates how often projects have more than doubled in cost from the initial plan. For every industry, except roads, this is a relatively common occurrence, ranging from one in every 2 projects to one in every 12. These wide ranges make it difficult to grasp the true magnitude of risk and make basic statistics not useful for its analysis. I gave a presentation on risk at a workshop. When I discussed that the average cost growth for military and aerospace projects has historically been in excess of 50%, someone in the audience said that if you look at how many projects experience that much growth, it is much lower. That is true, as we mentioned earlier due to skewness, 50% of military and space projects experience cost growth less than 30%. He considered this latter figure as evidence that, most of the time, projects "get it right." I do not consider 30% cost growth to be getting "it" right, especially for billion-dollar programs, but that is not the point. Risk has two dimensions—likelihood of occurrence and consequence. Consequence is the more important of the two, but less appreciated, due to our innate need to be "right." What causes trouble is the programs that more than double in cost. While they are not the majority, their growth is large enough to make a difference. We can be right 90% of the time, or even more frequently, but get wiped out by a blowout program that doubles, triples, or quadruples in cost. We will expound on this idea in later chapters.

IT'S EVEN WORSE THAN IT APPEARS

Ideally, growth in cost and schedule should be measured holding everything else constant, or what economists call "other things being equal." However, that is impossible to do as performance is not fixed. When project managers find that their costs are growing and it is taking longer to accomplish work than planned, they may not always have the luxury of getting more money or more time. In such cases, the project either must stop work, which could mean cancellation, or it must cut scope to live within its means. In a canceled project, most if not all the work done is wasted. In some cases, technology development or part of a project can be transferred to another. Regardless, much time and effort are wasted when projects are cancelled. For example, hundreds of millions of dollars were spent on developing the cancelled Ares I launch vehicle, part of NASA's Constellation program to replace the Space Shuttle. Cutting scope happens frequently and is one way that projects often cope with cost and schedule growth. A program may have originally planned to fly five scientific instruments on a satellite but, when faced with pressure to keep costs reined in, may instead fly only three. Thus, the true risk is under accounted for in the actual cost and schedule growth data as the scope is not held constant. Without this option, programs would experience even greater cost overruns and even longer schedule delays. A satellite can remove a scientific instrument and still conduct at least part of its mission. Software can cut out features and still be worthwhile. A road project may plan to widen two lanes to six, but due to overruns may only be able to expand to four. In my experience with NASA and military projects, I have firsthand anecdotal evidence that development projects frequently cut scope to try to deal with overruns in money and time. The impact of this is that the risk management problem is even worse than is indicated by the numerous studies on cost and schedule growth. That is because the value of the delivered project is less than planned. Projects often end up paying more but getting less. This problem is not limited to aerospace and weapons systems: large infrastructure projects that cost billions of dollars, typically referred to as megaprojects, are criticized for frequent poor performance.[25]

The Ulysses space mission is a prime example of such a project. It was named after the Latin for Odysseus, the hero of Homer's Odyssey. The Ulysses spacecraft took a long voyage to study the sun. This was a joint project between NASA and the European Space Agency (ESA). The initial plan was to use two spacecrafts. One spacecraft was to be developed by each of the two agencies. Development started in October 1978, with a planned launch of both spacecraft on the Space Shuttle in February 1983. This was only 52 months. While four years and four months seems like a long time, the average development schedule for a NASA mission is 60 months.[26] This average includes both Earth-orbiting and planetary spacecraft. Simple Earth-orbiting spacecraft can be developed, built, and launched in a few years, but deep space missions typically take much longer—a decade or more. Cassini, a mission to Saturn, took 110 months to develop, build, and launch, and Galileo, a mission to Jupiter, required 135 months. This latter mission, like Ulysses, was originally planned to be much shorter in terms of development time, only 43 months. Galileo's schedule tripled in length during development.

The original plan for Ulysses was for NASA and ESA to each pay for the development of their respective spacecraft. NASA was to pay for the launch aboard the Shuttle. To save money in fiscal year 1982, NASA delayed the planned launch. Congress cut the budget for the program. This caused NASA to cancel the development of its spacecraft. The result was a loss of half the instruments planned for the mission. However, NASA paid for the launch and for a radioisotopic thermal generator, a type of power source that uses a radioactive material often used on long duration planetary missions. The launch was again delayed by the Space Shuttle *Challenger* incident. The overall costs, excluding the mission operations costs, decreased slightly from the initial plan, but this is hardly a good deal, as the mission lost half its scope as a result![27]

Another case of a (potentially) successful project that has significantly cut scope is the California High-Speed Rail (CHSR). The initial goal of this state government-funded project was to provide bullet train transportation with 520 miles of track from San Francisco to Los Angeles, with several stops. In 2008, planning began. Initial projections for cost were $40 billion, with completion planned for 2028. A one-way fare for one ticket from Los Angeles to San Francisco was expected to be priced at $55. One year later, the project was expected to cost $98.5 billion with a completion date in 2033, and a one-way ticket from the City of Angels to the City by the Bay was expected to cost $95. The section of the project where construction began, a 119-mile path in California's Central Valley between Madera and Bakersfield, was initially expected to cost $6 billion. Estimates for that rose to $7.8 billion in 2016. It increased again in 2018 to $10.8 billion. Of this latter $3 billion increase, $600 million was for reserves, so at least some attention was paid to risk.[28] Estimates for the total project continued to fluctuate over the period from 2009 to 2019. The latest estimate published in early 2019 was $77 billion, almost double the initial forecast.[29] On February 12, 2019, the governor of California,

Gavin Newsom, announced a significant scope reduction in his state-of-the-state address. Governor Newsom said the new scope of the project was restricted to a 171-mile stretch from Merced to Bakersfield. This includes the initial 119-mile track from Bakersfield to Madera, plus a 52-mile track from Madera to Merced.[30] This smaller scope endeavor is projected to cost $12.4 billion. Plans also include the use of low-speed Amtrak trains rather than bullet trains.[31] California Highway 99 travels directly between Merced and Bakersfield. The distance is 165 miles, and the drive time is projected as two hours and 26 minutes. A high-speed train could make the trip in about an hour, saving about one-and-a-half hours compared to a car trip. A $12.4 billion investment is a lot of money to provide fast trips between Bakersfield (population 380,000) to Merced (population 80,000). Unless this is eventually followed by completion of the original scope, this mega project will be a mega waste of time and money. This is a good example of the sunk cost fallacy. The California government has already spent a large sum of money, but it is never rational to continue with a project simply because a lot of money and time have already been devoted to it. Despite the irrationality of making decisions based on sunk cost, behavioral economists have noted its frequent occurrence.[32]

The pharmaceutical wholesaler FoxMeyer's attempt in the mid-1990s to implement a new enterprise resource planning system is an example of a project that suffered cost overruns and schedule delays. It not only failed to perform up to expectations, it drove the company to bankruptcy! At the time it started the project, FoxMeyer was an established, large enterprise with annual sales in excess of $5 billion. FoxMeyer's mainframe system needed replacement. The company decided to replace this with a (then) newly emerging business software product called enterprise resource planning (ERP). This type of product unifies all processes with a company into one system. It replaces separate products for different departments such as logistics, sales, and production with one single software product.

The company was also expected to receive additional business from a major new client, so it needed to be able to handle this additional workload. The company expected to save $40 million in annual operating costs once the new system was in place.[33] The project began in 1993. The company invested $65 million and planned to complete implementation in 18 months. While initial testing of the system indicated that it could handle the increased workflow, it turned out it could only process 10,000 orders a day compared to the legacy mainframe system's capacity of 420,000. Despite the new product's limitations, FoxMeyer's leadership refused to abandon the new product and continued to try to make the new system work. The cost rose to $100 million and the schedule slipped. In 1996, the company filed for bankruptcy.[34] This information technology endeavor not only suffered from cost growth and schedule delays, but the technical performance was so abysmal that management's refusal to abandon it took down the company.

SUMMARY

We have shown that cost and schedule growth are consistently high across a wide range of projects. This has been the case for a long time and shows no signs of slowing. Not only is the track record bad, it is even worse than the historical data indicates. That is because in many cases technical performance is reduced in order to mitigate cost and schedule problems. Projects spend more, take longer, and achieve less than planned. The next chapter discusses the key reasons for cost and schedule growth.

CHAPTER 2

Here We Grow Again

Why Cost Increases and Schedule Delays Occur

I am from the southeastern United States. My entire family is from that part of the country dating back several generations. This region is known for colorful stories and expressions, and my family was no exception. My parents and grandparents related everything to stories. In school, especially early in college, I discovered that I needed to learn to move beyond thinking in stories and instead make deductions based on logic and facts. I later learned, in trying to communicate my work to other people, that I could draw on my family's storytelling background. I found that I could get my point across better as a narrative rather than as a dry set of facts and figures. In the last chapter, you got the college version of cost growth and schedules. We talked about the statistics of these phenomena—who, what, when, and where. In this chapter, we will talk about the why, and in relating stories about cost and schedule growth, provide a deeper understanding of these phenomena.

Cost and schedule growth occur due to numerous reasons. These can be delineated into internal and external factors. Internal factors are those the project controls, and the external ones come from outside the project. Some can be included in both, but I will place them in the more appropriate category. Internal factors include:

- Optimism
- Planning
- Execution
- Errors in estimation
- Schedule, cost, and technical misalignment

External factors include:

- Constant change
- External dependencies
- Black swans

This is not an exhaustive list, but it covers many of the issues that occur. One reason resource risk is more severe than technical risk is that all these factors impact resources, but not all influence system performance or technical requirements. A planning risk is that an emerging technology that is going to be used will not be mature when needed. This impacts technical performance, cost, and schedule. However, some sources of growth, such as reductions in quantities, will not directly affect technical performance, but they will increase the average cost of production items. We next discuss each of these sources of risk and provide specific examples to illustrate them. On close examination, most projects experience several on the list, but we will highlight instances where a project's cost, schedule, or performance suffered because of the issue.

THE CULT OF OPTIMISM: DON'T DRINK THE KOOL-AID

One of the key reasons for increases in cost and schedule from a project's inception to its completion is optimism, as mentioned at the beginning of Chapter 1. Plans for programs should include what is most likely to happen and prepare for adverse events. Instead, programs tend to budget for the best case possible. This makes it almost certain that the outcome will cost more than planned. The psychologists Daniel Kahneman and Amos Tversky noted this tendency, which they termed the "planning fallacy."[1] The devotion to optimism in the project management profession is so extreme that I liken it to a cult. One of the most infamous cult leaders in modern history was Jim Jones. He founded the Peoples Temple cult in Indiana in the 1950s and in the late 1970s relocated to Guyana, a small country in South America. There he founded a city he named Jonestown. After a Congressional delegation came to investigate reports of human right abuses, the cult murdered them, along with some cult members who wanted to leave. This culminated in a mass suicide where more than 900 people drank a cyanide-laced drink that was like Kool-Aid. Blindly following the planning fallacy optimism promulgated by project managers and other senior leaders is said to be "drinking the Kool-Aid."[2] Unlike the members of the Peoples Temple cult, however, optimism is alive and well in project planning. Even though the problems of cost and schedule growth occur repeatedly, project managers maintain their positive outlook. This is like Charlie Brown and the football. Each fall, Lucy van Pelt plants a football on the ground and invites Charlie to kick it. He initially declines, recalling what has occurred in the past. Lucy tells Charlie this time is different. Charlie tries to kick the football, but the outcome is the same as always. Lucy pulls away the football just before Charlie can kick it, and he falls flat on his back.

I have experienced this optimism firsthand. A program where I once worked had a 40% test failure rate. This was to be expected as it was for a development program with challenging objectives. Some failures are bound to happen. The problem is that costs to address them were not budgeted. When I asked management about their reserves in case a test was not successful, I was told that the program did not "plan for failure, it planned for success." As these failures required significant time and money to investigate, their optimism ensured ineffective risk management. This led to inefficiencies because when failures occurred, money had to be reallocated from other projects.

An example of optimism in practice is the STEREO (Solar Terrestrial Relations Observatory) space mission. STEREO consisted of two almost identical spacecraft that were launched into orbits around the sun. One was ahead of the Earth's orbit, and the other was behind it. These two different views enabled stereoscopic imaging of the sun. The satellites that were launched in 2006 bore little resemblance to the initial concept put forth in 1997 by the program's Science Definition Team. The final spacecraft weighed more than three times as much as initially planned. The data rates, storage, and power requirements grew significantly. Not surprisingly, the cost and schedule also grew by substantial amounts. The schedule slipped by two and a half years, from 40 months to 70. The initial cost estimate of the system was $249 million. To account for risks, the program added 20% to this value and budgeted for $299 million. However, the cost almost doubled again from this seemingly conservative value to $551 million by the completion of development and production.[3]

Project managers have an incentive to be optimistic. They need to put forth a positive attitude. This assures their management that things are going well and will continue to do so. In many cases, a program with a realistic initial estimate would never have been approved. In public endeavors, such as infrastructure, satellites, and weapons, most of the work is done by a private company, a contractor. Contractors also have an incentive to be optimistic. North American Aviation used to be a leading defense contractor. Through a series of mergers and acquisitions over the years, it is now a part of the Boeing Corporation. The president of North American Aviation in the 1950s, J. L. Atwood, noted that there is an incentive to bid low on development contracts to win both the development and production work. There is little, if any, competition after development. From the contractors' point of view, a development contract competition is basically an auction for the monopoly rights to produce and operate the system. The bulk of the life-cycle cost is in operations, followed by production. Thus, the development work is a buy-in for the real payoff in production and sustainment.[4]

The propensity for contractors to bid low to get the work, only then for costs to grow significantly, has been called "Bid 'em low; watch 'em grow."[5] Most development contracts for publicly funded projects are cost-plus. In this type of arrangement, the government pays the contractor for the cost that it incurs, plus some fee for profit. The contractors have an incentive to bid low to get the work, knowing that there will be no penalty when costs grow. As their profit is a percentage of the total cost, the higher the cost, the more they profit. This is a rather perverse incentive. Not all contracts are cost-plus, but development projects typically have a great deal of unknowns. Contractors are leery of signing up for fixed-price contracts knowing they could lose money. Fixed-price contracts remove the risk to the government and are used in government contracting primarily for low-risk items, such as the production of an item after several lots have been purchased. Fixed-price contracts are not always a good deal for the government, either. As the contractor bears all the risk, fixed-price bids may cost the government more as they include not only potential profit but also contingency to cover risk.

J. L. Atwood also noted that assumptions are subject to optimistic bias. This drives the forecasts to be low.[6] This is the planning fallacy of Kahneman and Tversky, documented two decades before the professors wrote about it.

Prospect Theory and Project Management

Optimism is so prevalent among project managers that there must be a logical reason for it. It can be explained by the application of psychology to economics. Daniel Kahneman and Amos Tversky, of the planning fallacy we just mentioned, are also responsible for one of the most widely cited academic papers in the field of economics.[7] They made a simple observation that has been used to explain a variety of phenomena and performed experiments to verify that their theories hold true in practice. Economists have long recognized that when it comes to financial gains and losses, people do not just react to the amount gained. They have different responses depending on the amount that they have. Economists coined the word *utility* to measure the satisfaction derived from money. A central assumption is decreasing marginal utility, which means that every additional dollar increases utility, but at a decreasing rate. For example, an extra $1,000 means much more to someone making $10,000 a year than someone making $1,000,000 a year. This was the standard approach to utility theory for 200 years. Kahneman and Tversky discovered that changes in utility also depend on whether the amount is a gain or a loss. People react differently to losses than gains. Kahneman and Tversky called this prospect theory. They noted people are risk averse when faced with prospective gains, but risk seeking regarding prospective losses. Most people, when faced with an uncertain outcome, will be conservative when it comes to a gain. They prefer a sure thing over something that has the same expected outcome but is uncertain. For example, one option would be to gain $100 with certainty. The other option would be to toss a coin. If the coin comes up heads, you get $200. If the coin comes up tails, you get $0. Which option do you prefer? Even though the average outcome is the same for both options, more than 70% prefer the sure gain to the gamble. However, suppose the situation is reversed. You are faced with a sure loss of $100, or a coin toss where you either lose $200 or lose $0. Do you still prefer the sure thing, which in this case is a loss equal to $100? Even though the average of both alternatives is the same, about two-thirds of people prefer the gamble to the sure loss. Thus, losses are more painful than gains are pleasurable.[8]

Many projects are public in nature—weapons systems, roads, bridges, dams, satellites, and so on. The project managers in these cases are serving the government's interest. Their projects will not make a profit, but the outcome will be a significant contribution that does not have a specific dollar value attached to it except for the cost. Cost is a dollar amount that ranges from some lower positive bound to a potentially high value. The reference point is what the project manager initially believes the cost will be. In my experience, this will be formed in one of two ways. One is that initial rough-order-of-magnitude estimates from contractors are solicited before projects develop their own internal estimate. This will be a low amount, for the reasons we have discussed. The second way is that projects may develop their own internal estimates independent of contractors. However, these estimates, while independent of the contractors, are not independent of the project. They are tainted by internal optimism. These estimates will incorporate a host of rosy assumptions, such as reuse of existing parts and no issues with implementing advanced technologies. Any dollar amount less than this reference point is considered a gain from the program manager's point of view. Any dollar amount more than the reference point is considered a loss. A cost estimate that comes in above that reference will be a painful experience to be avoided. This will result in risk-seeking behavior and provide an incentive to cling to the lower reference value for as long as possible. However, increases from these initial reference points will occur as contractor proposals and later, more thorough and more detailed internal estimates will both be higher than initial optimistic estimates.

THE (NOT-SO) BEST LAID PLANS OF PROJECT MANAGERS: PROBLEMS WITH PLANNING

Issues with planning are common. The decision to use immature technologies occurs during this stage. Developing technologies is often expensive and is a key driver of cost and schedule growth. This could be due to optimism in some cases, but at times organizations undertake cutting-edge projects that entail significant technical, schedule, and cost risk. For example, NASA's charter is to advance science. To do this, it must assume risk to do things that have never been done before—one current project is considering using nuclear-powered rockets to send humans to Mars. However, the advanced technologies under consideration should be critically examined to see if they are needed. If so, the program should plan to spend time and money developing these technologies before starting detailed design. The adoption of not-quite-ready technologies during the development phase often leads to significant increases in cost and schedule. Using historical program experience, studies have been done to assess the penalty in terms of percentage cost growth. This is a striking amount. For example, starting a program using a key technology that has only been demonstrated as a proof of concept will likely lead to cost increasing by a factor of two or more.[9]

A lack of technical definition up front is another all-too-common occurrence that leads to both technical problems and resource growth. Programs are initiated before enough detail is worked out. This results in an increase in technical requirements during development, which in turn leads to an increase in cost and schedule. Some of the changes are due to fixes, as the initial design will not work. For example, in 2004, NASA embarked on the Constellation program. Constellation was intended to provide access to space once the Space Shuttle program ended, to return humans to the Moon by 2020, and ultimately to send a crewed mission to Mars. One of the launch vehicles involved putting a crewed capsule atop a modified version of a large boosting rocket used on the Space Shuttle. This was the Ares I launch vehicle, which was planned to launch astronauts into orbit with the Orion crew capsule. This type of configuration was unprecedented. The use of mature technologies in new configurations also requires technology development, an underappreciated fact that leads to the underestimation of the amount of technology development required for projects.[10] The Shuttle rocket had four segments. The new system would modify this to be longer, adding a fifth segment. The initial assumption was that this new rocket would benefit from significant heritage. This meant that less design work would have to be done. Less design work would save money in development. I developed some of the initial estimates for this rocket. We later learned in working with experts that any time you open a solid rocket motor casing to make a change, the result is a complete redesign. Updating the estimate to reflect this one change increased it hundreds of millions of dollars. It was also discovered during the design of the rocket that it would create significant vibrations, requiring a change to incorporate dampeners. These design changes lengthened the schedule and increased cost. As a design matures, these kinds of details come to light, requiring more work than planned. As the saying goes, the devil is in the details.

The Sydney Opera House is an architectural wonder, but it was a project planning nightmare. The preliminary design was selected based on a competition. Initial estimates of cost and schedule were $7 million in local currency and four years. In one of the worst cases of cost and schedule overruns in recorded history, the final cost was $102 million in local currency, and the schedule lengthened to 14 years. The seeds for this enormous increase were planted during the planning stage. The problem was that there was no plan, at least not a detailed one. The initial plan was based on incomplete design drawings and surveys of the construction site. Construction started before a detailed design could be completed. There was also no official project manager. Leadership consisted of an informal collaboration between the architect and the head of construction. The architect was focused solely on fulfilling the design objectives and neglected cost and schedule concerns. During the project, the government increased requirements, leading to further cost growth and schedule delays. The architect was fired during the middle of the project. As he did not leave behind his designs, the replacement had to redesign the final structure based on the work done up to that point. Despite being a total failure from a project management perspective, it was eventually completed, and the project paid for itself.[11]

Set Up to Fail: An Example of How Projects Sabotage Their Success

Other times, projects are set up to fail at the outset by plans that lead to too much complexity. One large-scale endeavor I have worked on had a variety of issues, but a major reason for its failure occurred in planning. In the following discussion, I have avoided using the project's name and have changed the costs discussed to protect the guilty. It was a development program for a government agency and thus a cost-plus contract. Three contractors submitted their estimates for the cost of a major new program. The lowest of these three was $250 million. The cheapest this type of system has ever been developed for is three times this amount. The government's independent estimates were much higher than $250 million as well, between two and three times as much. Despite this, leadership funded to the lowest contractor estimate.

After this initial estimate, the organization decided to increase requirements. It made 10 significant changes. These changes included adding a flight test, four more test units, and a dedicated development lab. It also lengthened schedule by one year. The approach adopted was highly complex. It involved combining the best parts of the three contractors' legacy systems into a new system. It sounds like a good idea until you realize the complexities involved in the interactions of three large companies. This increased the complexity of communication and led to a triplication of activity. The Hubble Space Telescope experienced significant cost growth for a variety of reasons, including technical complexity, but one reason was that it had two lead contractors. Three is even more complex. One senior analyst with the Department of Defense mentioned to me that for a system with multiple lead organizations, he found that the cost increased at a rate equal to the square root. For example, with two organizations leading the work, the cost would increase by the square root of 2, which is approximately 1.41, or a 41% increase. With three, the cost would increase by about 1.73, or a 73% increase. Thus, using multiple lead contractors alone would likely result in a significant cost increase. Once the best-of-breed approach was established, it removed the impetus for the contractors to lowball the estimates, leading to a significant increase in planned cost.

After all these additions in the first year, the planned cost jumped to $450 million. Within the next month, the organization added additional component-level testing, more reviews, and another two years to the schedule. This increased the cost to $550 million. The contractors updated their estimate again the next month to $600 million. The government, frustrated by these increases, asked the contractor for a no kidding, not-to-exceed value. The contractors complied, providing an $800 million cost estimate. A year and a half after agreeing to go with the $250 million contractor estimate, the government again revised the schedule, raising the planned cost to $850 million. This is approximately a 250% increase in less than two years. A year later, the development schedule slipped by two years, increasing the cost by another $250 million to $1.1 billion. At this point, the program had already experienced a greater than fourfold increase in cost and was still far from completion. Cost growth for development programs is back-loaded as most of it occurs once the detailed "critical" design for the program is completed. This effort had not even passed that point. The project failed this review, signaling even more cost growth ahead.

I conducted cross-checks for the program during this period. Using historical data from previous similar types of missions, the minimum number I was able to come up with was 50% higher than what leadership insisted the cost should be. The information I provided was likely on the low side, as it assumed similar requirements to previous programs, whereas this program was intended to be more capable and designed to be operated in harsher environments. The idea that a project manager can direct that costs be lower is a little like the story of the old king of England, Canute, who had his throne set along the shore of the sea and ordered the rising tide to stop and not get him wet.

After failing the design review, the schedule for the first test slipped seven years. Four years into the project, agency leadership admitted that the entire program would have to be reassessed. An independent review estimated the final cost at $1.6 billion, more than six times the initial plan. After an extensive review, the Pentagon cancelled the program six months later. Development of the capability would have to start over, replaced with a competition that should have been held in the first place. As of March 2020, the program restart was still in the planning stages.

NOT ALL PROJECT MANAGERS CAN BE ABOVE AVERAGE: PROBLEMS WITH EXECUTION

I used to listen to Garrison Keillor's radio program *Prairie Home Companion* on National Public Radio. I particularly enjoyed his "News from Lake Wobegon" segments, stories about a fictional small town where Keillor said all the children are above average. Like these young people, the project managers and contractors who work for them have always been considered above average by themselves and their management. While I wish that were true, statistically it is impossible. Often, cost, schedule, and performance issues are caused by poor program execution.

One of the initial concerns with complex aerospace programs was the quality of contractors, particularly in a competitive environment. John Glenn, the first American astronaut to orbit the Earth in 1962 on the Friendship 7 mission, is said to have remarked, "As I hurtled through space, one thought kept crossing my mind— every part of this rocket was supplied by the lowest bidder."[12] This type of thinking led to the government establishing oversight in the disciplines of systems engineering and project management. Systems engineering helps ensure everything works together as whole. Project management includes not only the direct leadership but also support functions that provide information critical for decision making, such as cost estimating and schedule analysis.

Together, systems engineering and project management make up a large percentage of the total cost of the development of a system. For some types of projects, the average is 40% in addition to the cost to design the system, and it is sometimes much higher than the average. The discipline of system engineering is heavily embedded in government bureaucracies and is an integral part of the government acquisition process. Both the government and its contractors use systems engineering. The cost involved in the actual product itself is termed direct cost. The cost of oversight, which includes systems engineering and program management, is indirect cost. In a bureaucratic system, the ratio of indirect to direct costs can be large. The ratio is larger for systems that are complex or have had design issues. When a technical issue arises, the root cause should be investigated and fixed. But the tendency is to add additional oversight, more tests, and more paperwork. The staff doing the direct work on the system have to interact with the indirect functions. The more oversight, the more frequently the staff who are designing and building the final product must stop to answer questions and provide data about their work. This increases cost and lengthens schedule.

Once additional project surveillance is established, it rarely diminishes. Bureaucracy, like entropy, always seems to be increasing. One instance where I have seen this occur was an extremely challenging technical project. Every problem that arose resulted in more oversight. It eventually reached the point that for every hour spent building the system, 10 hours were spent on checks, paperwork, and other support tasks. There may be others that are worse, but this is the most extreme instance I've encountered so far. Bureaucratic issues do not just affect the government. In working for large corporations, I have found them to be government-like in their procedures and policies. As we live in an era of giant corporations, these issues afflict much of the private sector as well.[13]

Sometimes projects fail because those responsible for doing the work are not capable. Two examples of poorly executed projects are attempts to upgrade the Department of Motor Vehicle (DMV) computer systems in California and Washington. In 1987, the state of California began its project. It solicited a bid from only one contractor, leading to higher cost from the start. The contract was for $27 million over five years. In 1990, tests indicated that the new system was slower than the legacy system. The project was cancelled in 1994, more than two years after the system was planned to be in place. Estimates of final cost ranged from $44 million to $49 million, a 62% to 81% overrun. Audits of the project conducted later concluded that the California DMV had broken laws and violated regulations. In 1990, the Washington State DMV began its project to automate the process to register vehicles and renew licenses. The initial plan was for $16 billion to be spent over five years. The project was cancelled in 1997 after state legislators discovered it would have six times as much in annual operating costs compared to the legacy system. At that point, $40 million had been spent with an estimate to complete the project of $67.5 million.[14]

Incompetence has many causes. Otherwise capable professionals who have no background in an industry can wreak havoc when they are put in charge of a complex undertaking. When the Newfoundland and Labrador province of Canada embarked on a major hydroelectric project, the leaders selected were from the oil and gas industry. None had hydroelectric project experience. The firm selected to build the powerhouse for the project had no past history with working in northern and remote environments. During the course of the project, management had to be replaced, and the powerhouse contractor was fired. As of early 2020, the cost had grown from $6.1 billion (local currency) to $12.7 billion. The project was also three years behind schedule when the COVID-19 pandemic slowed progress to a crawl, signaling more cost growth to come.[15]

ERRORS IN ESTIMATION

The Joint Strike Fighter, a jet combat aircraft also known as the F-35, is a program that has a long and troubled history. It has had its share of delays and cost overruns. The F-35 has three variants, one each for the Air Force, Navy, and Marines. There is a great deal of commonality but some unique requirements for each service. For example, the Navy needs a plane that can take off from and land on aircraft carriers. The F-35 has been in the news frequently. As recently as 2017, its total life-cycle cost was projected to be $1 trillion, making it the most expensive program in the history of the Department of Defense. Shortly after his inauguration that year, the new President of the United States declared the cost for the program to be "out of control."[16]

The F-35 program began in 2001. The estimated initial cost for development was $34.4 billion. By December 2017, as development was in the end stages, the estimate had grown to $55.5 billion, approximately a 60% increase. The cost to produce the aircraft had likewise grown from $196.6 billion to $345.4 billion, a 75% increase. The total cost growth for development and production grew by $170 billion between 2001 and the end of 2017. The development schedule also stretched from a 10-year development to an 18-year development, an 80% increase. Estimates to operate the system over its life cycle grew by $200 billion. The total cost growth of the system is expected to be \$370 billion.[17] As a point of comparison, this is approximately the annual gross domestic product of Israel.[18]

The cost increase is due to several reasons. A critical problem was that some of the technologies planned for the design were not mature. As the design advanced, weight had to increase. That one change alone delayed the completion of development by 18 months and added \$7 billion to the cost of development. Another reason was concurrency between development and production—after flying one nonproduction representative aircraft, the program decided to start production. At this point, planned testing was less than 1% complete. Once costs continued to grow, the program decided to cut costs by cutting back on testing. This raised technical risk and the chance for schedule delays. In the Department of Defense, when a major program has cost growth of this magnitude, a series of evaluations is triggered. The program was assessed and considered for cancellation. The program survived but underwent a major restructuring to mitigate additional risk. The concurrency issue was never resolved.[19] After the F-35 entered the operations and sustainment phase, there were issues affecting the reliability and maintainability of the aircraft. This included a shortage of needed spare parts and limited repair capacities at depots. In 2018, the upgrades to the depots needed for F-35 were six years behind schedule. This resulted in average repair times equal to 172 days, twice what was planned.[20]

Another source of cost growth for the program was an under accounting for inflation. Inflation is a fact of life. Over time, prices for goods and services tend to increase. This used to be a much bigger concern. Annual inflation rates for consumer goods from the late 1960s to the early 1980s were much higher than they are today. However, government-produced indices understate true inflation. The Department of Defense produces annual inflation guidance that must be used in adjusting for inflation. Once a signed contract is in place, inflation rates are negotiated and included as "forward pricing rate agreements." As these are more in line with reality, they are higher than the annual inflation indices produced by the government. In my experience, they are often double. The best practice in accounting for this is that, once contracts are in place, costs should be estimated using the signed forward rate price adjustments rather than the government index. This means automatic cost growth once contracts are signed, as the government index is used for estimates before contracts are in place. If not incorporated, it will continue the underestimation, masking the true cost growth until it is corrected. In the case of F-35, the program kept using old labor rates and adjusting them with government-produced inflation indices for a decade rather than use the negotiated forward rate pricing agreement. The result was a significant underestimation of the effects of inflation on labor cost.

HASTE MAKES WASTE VS. TIME IS WASTING: COST, SCHEDULE, AND TECHNICAL MISALIGNMENT AND FUNDING CONSTRAINTS

My maternal grandfather once told me that his grandfathers each had diametrically opposed philosophies of life. His maternal grandfather's motto was "Haste makes waste," while that of his paternal grandfather was "Time is wasting." My grandfather said he found these diametrically opposing views to be confusing, but I have found a way to reconcile these seemingly two contradictory statements. The two mottos are both true depending on the circumstances. The resolution of this paradox will be revealed by examining the relationship among time, cost, and performance.

Having good grasps on cost, schedule, and technical characteristics are all key for project success. These interconnections are like a three-legged stool. If they do not all align, the project will have serious challenges. This misalignment occurs during both planning and execution. Poor planning up front leads to problems during execution. If the planned schedule is too short for a complex program, that will lead to costly delays. If the projected cost is too low, that will lead to overruns. If the planned technical requirements do not reflect the program's realities, that will increase cost and lengthen schedule. If the cost is too high and/or schedule too long relative to technical requirements, the project will find a way to fill up the spare time (recall Parkinson's Law) and spend the extra money (recall MAIMS), leading to a waste of resources. In execution, changes to schedule, either compressing or expanding the schedule, will result in a cost increase. There is a great deal of fixed cost that is paid every year on a contract regardless of the work that is accomplished. If the time lengthens, that fixed cost will occur over a longer period, increasing the total project cost. If a schedule can be shortened, it would seem reasonable that cost would be reduced. On the contrary, tight schedules are difficult to achieve as the act of trying to do more tasks in parallel and quickly ramp up activities has proven to be costly.

An illustration of the effects of pushing the boundaries of the interrelationships was a NASA policy in place for much of the 1990s called "faster-better-cheaper." In 1992, Dan Goldin was appointed by President George H. W. Bush as the NASA administrator. He had previously spent 25 years as an engineer and executive for an aerospace contractor. Goldin served as head of NASA for nine years. During his tenure, he instituted the faster-better-cheaper policy. This was a response to two factors. In the 1980s, there were several costly missions, including the Hubble Space Telescope, that consumed a large part of the agency's overall budget. Internal NASA studies found a systematic, increasing trend in the complexity of missions, with concomitant increases in cost. In the late 1980s, "NASA was in danger of pricing itself out of business."[21] The other factor was budgetary. NASA's budget grew dramatically in the 1960s to support the Apollo program. Afterward, its budget shrank in the 1970s but grew again in the 1980s. However, in the early 1990s, the space agency's budget, in inflation-adjusted terms, peaked in 1991. Over the next 10 years, after adjusting for inflation, NASA's overall budget shrank by more than 20%. Given a ceiling that was moving downward in terms of purchasing power and a trend of greater complexity in missions, something had to give. Faster-better-cheaper placed an emphasis on executing small missions with fewer instruments, at a lower cost, and over a shorter time period.

Smaller spacecraft can be built in less time and are less expensive than larger spacecraft. Many of the small spacecraft launched in the 1990s and early 2000s only had one scientific instrument, whereas larger spacecraft often host multiple scientific instruments. On a cost-per-pound basis, the reduction in size reduces cost for straightforward designs that use existing technologies. However, many NASA missions use the latest technologies and do not always neatly fit within this paradigm. Some of the small spacecraft built in the 1990s achieved lower costs and shorter schedules by taking on more technical risk. Reviews and extensive tests needed to ensure mission success were often forgone, leading to a higher risk of mission failure. For most satellites, there is no option to fix hardware issues after they are launched, so they need significant testing to ensure that they will work as designed.

Two studies in the early 2000s analyzed the trade-offs among cost, schedule, mission complexity, and mission success. The first of these illustrated the correlation between lack of time and resources and failure in terms of relative complexity. Examining a few dozen missions, researchers found that there was a positive trend between cost and complexity, and that the failed missions in the 1990s were all highly complex. They did not have enough time or resources compared to the amount the trend line would indicate.[22] See Figure 2.1.

Figure 2.1 Cost vs. Complexity and the Triangle of Death

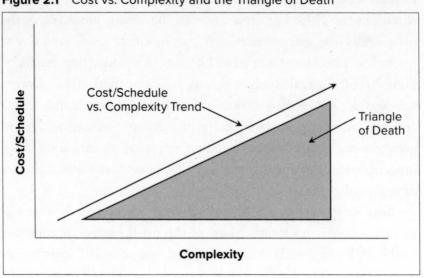

In Figure 2.1, the average cost vs. complexity trend line is shown, along with a triangle in the bottom right. For a given complexity, the trend provides the average cost associated with that level of complexity. The triangle indicates a cost or schedule that is lower than average for a given level of complexity. That means that not enough resources are applied for that level of complexity. The study found that all nine failed missions included in the study were below the line, in the "triangle of death." Also, all the impaired missions, which included a variety of partial failures that either prevented complete mission success or made it more challenging, could be found in this area as well. All the missions on the line or above it succeeded. However, below the line, the failure rate was high, approximately 50%. A model I developed for NASA's Goddard Space Flight Center predicted the probability of mission success using cost, schedule, technical, and programmatic parameters as inputs. It was able to predict that many of the mission failures that has occurred in the 1990s were indeed too cheap and did not have enough schedule to support mission success. It was used by NASA to determine when budgets might be too small or schedules too optimistic for a planned mission.[23]

While the faster-better-cheaper emphasis on cutting costs was a good goal, it was not balanced with a consideration of risk. It was also done without consulting with cost estimators or schedule analysts, who could have helped effectively calculate the benefits of going to smaller missions and provided realistic projection of savings under faster-better-cheaper, allowing for an effective trade-off of risk/performance, cost, and schedule. Instead of soliciting input, the lead cost estimator at NASA Headquarters was banished to another center after Goldin was confirmed as NASA administrator. NASA did not have a cost estimating lead at its headquarters until after Dan Goldin left the organization. The tools developed at the end of the faster-better-cheaper era were helpful in determining the cost, schedule, and performance trade-offs to help NASA effectively balance affordability with risk. Every project should consider these trade-offs. If they are not in alignment, replanning is in order.

A prime example of an unbalanced three-legged stool is the Boeing 737 MAX. This aircraft was grounded in 2019 after two crashes that resulted in a total of 346 deaths. Investigations found that to compete with its rival Aerobus, Boeing cut costs in order to maintain its production schedule. New flight-control software that was critical to system safety did not have sufficient controls to prevent a fatal crash.[24] Commercial air travel is typically much safer than automobile transportation. However, Boeing's decision to risk performance in order to prevent cost and schedule from increasing ended up compromising safety, leading to additional cost and longer schedules. As of March 2020, it was estimated that this issue will cost the aerospace company at least $18.7 billion.[25]

In addition to the planning phase, significant changes to any of cost, schedule, or performance during execution will lead to problems. Once a program begins, a schedule delay will cause cost increases. If the schedule is stretched due to funding constraints, external factors, or other reasons, there is a certain amount of personnel who will work on that project until it is completed. A longer schedule will mean that this fixed set of personnel will charge to the project for a longer period, increasing the cost.

An example of a schedule increase causing a cost increase is one that I am familiar with from personal experience. It was a small bridge replacement that occurred just outside my old neighborhood several years ago. The original schedule for the work was mid-June to mid-September and was projected to cost $930,000. However, the original plan was to use prefabricated sections that could be transported and dropped in to serve as the primary structure for the bridge replacement. The state Department of Transportation decided after work began that this was not sufficient. A retaining wall of reinforced concrete had to be added. This one change increased the schedule six weeks, a 50% increase, and added $140,000, a 15% increase.[26] This is the "time is wasting" effect.

Since longer schedules involve higher costs, it might be reasonable to think that shorter schedules are better. The optimism that affects cost also affects schedule, so initial schedules are likely on the optimistic side. Trying to compress an already optimistic schedule is difficult and, in some cases, impossible to achieve. Compressing a schedule will lead to people working overtime, which costs more. It also leads to cutting corners, which often results in more mistakes. Once discovered in testing and checkout, this will require rework to fix the errors. Trying to do things in a hurry can also result in lower reliability or safety, as with the Boeing 737 MAX. There will be a higher chance that the product will not work as designed or fail to work altogether. While stretching the schedule is costly, it is even more costly to compress it. It has even been called the costliest action possible.[27] In these instances "haste makes waste" applies. A

notable example of schedule compression occurred during the Space
Race of the 1960s. In 1961, President John F. Kennedy announced
an ambitious program to send humans to the moon by the end of
the decade. NASA employees and the firms working for NASA
worked long hours and six-day workweeks to develop the technology necessary. The program spent, in current dollars, approximately
$300 billion to meet President Kennedy's goal.[28]

Accelerating schedule increases the likelihood that there will be
concurrency between designing the product and building it. This
means that there will be attempts to start manufacturing hardware
before the design has been completed and vetted. As we mentioned
earlier, this affected the F-35 fighter jet program. Studies have
shown that concurrency between development and production are
common. According to Government Accountability Office (GAO)
testimony to Congress in 1990,[29] 6 of 34 major weapons systems
were found to be highly concurrent since operational testing started
as soon as the initial production decision was made. Eleven other
projects were found to have a smaller amount of concurrency. The
B-1B bomber is a prime example. In an extreme example of the problem, development and production for the avionics subsystem started
at the same time! There were costly attempts to fix this system, but
it still did not meet performance expectations. In a 2016 report, the
GAO found 16 programs in the production phase experienced development cost growth, some as high as 45%, due to concurrency. Five
of these projects experienced growth because of deficiencies due to
unresolved design issues before the start of production. The others
were due to additions to capability, which means that requirements
were unstable.[30]

Knight Capital was a leading financial services firm. In 2012,
it rushed into production new software intended to help individual
investors receive better prices on stock trades. The new program is
believed to have been test code not ready for full use.[31] A bug in the

software caused Knight Capital to buy millions of shares in more than 100 stocks in less than an hour. This temporarily inflated these stock prices. When prices dropped, the firm sold them at lower values, losing more than $400 million.[32] The firm was rescued from bankruptcy by a merger with another firm.[33]

Denver International Airport's planned automated baggage handling system was another system that suffered from extreme schedule pressure. The project, if it worked as designed, would have cut aircraft turnaround time significantly for the new airport that was built in the 1990s. It required 17 miles of track, five miles of conveyor belts, 3,500 baggage carts, a network of more than 100 computers to control the flow, and complex software to provide the instructions. Construction of the airport started in 1989 with a planned opening date for the airport in 1993. However, a contract for the baggage handling system was not signed until April 1992. The initial planning for the system took place in only three working sessions between the city and the contractor. The planned opening date for the airport slipped to 1994, which put pressure on the baggage handling project to complete in two years. Similar but much simpler systems had previously been installed in the San Francisco and Munich airports in two years. The additional complexity meant that two years was an impossible goal for the Denver project. Struggles in completing the project delayed the opening of the airport by 16 months, which cost the City of Denver an additional $560 million. In order to open the airport, the baggage handling system had to be scaled back significantly. It was used in one concourse for one airline, and only for outgoing flights. The maintenance costs were higher than for a manual tug and trolley system.[34]

Another factor that causes costs to increase is budget constraints. Paradoxically, not enough funding can increase cost. Programs have a natural ebb and flow. Development programs start small, ramp up, reach a peak, and then ramp down as the development nears completion. See Figure 2.2.

Figure 2.2 Phasing of Cost for a Development Program

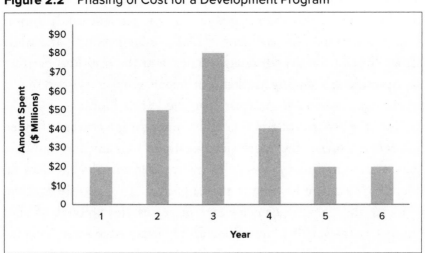

One of the results of all the early optimism is that too many projects are started, leading agencies to hit funding constraints because they are trying to do too many things at once. A frequently overlooked reason for cost growth is that many organizations often try to do too much with too little. The underestimation of initial costs for projects leads to starting new ones without full consideration for their later cost. The initial up-front cost of a project is quite small, then cost grows each year until it reaches its peak effort, typically around the middle of the schedule, and then it decreases again. If a program cannot ramp up to its natural peak, the schedule stretches to the right, leading to additional costs. As a colleague of mine once said, it is cheap to conceive a child, cheaper than the cost of preventing pregnancy. Couples are often in the situation that they become pregnant without taking into consideration the cost of raising a child.[35] This is one consequence of a lack of planning and proper portfolio management within government agencies.

Also, over time, budgets for public projects fluctuate. Projects plan years into the future—unexpected decreases in the total amount of funding available will lead to funding constraints during development. This often happens to government-funded projects. For example, Department of Defense budgets wax and wane depending on the overall budget deficit and the priorities peculiar to a presidential administration. For instance, military spending is often higher when a Republican is in the White House.

Another source of funding constraints for government-funded projects is Congress. Congressional staff ask so many questions and get so far down in the weeds of many programs that it takes an inordinate amount of time to pass a budget. This also slows down work at the defense agencies and increases the amount of staff needed to answer these questions. In my experience, every government agency requires a team of several people whose sole job is to serve as liaisons between the agency and questions brought forth by various other government organizations such as Congress. Partly as a result of this bureaucracy, only seven times since 1945 has Congress passed a budget on time. This is approximately once every 10 years. As of July 2020, the last time Congress passed a budget on time was in 1997.[36] If Congress does not pass a budget before the end of a fiscal year, it must either pass a continuing resolution or shut down the government. While the government occasionally shuts down for a few weeks before either passing a budget or a resolution, what typically happens is that a continuing resolution to continue spending at the previous year's levels is enacted. Between 1976 and 2019, there were 21 government shutdowns.[37] This results in several inefficiencies. Contracts for new developments cannot be signed under a continuing resolution, so contract awards are often delayed. Continuing resolutions for part of or even all of a fiscal year have become a norm. All these factors lead to additional cost and lengthened schedules. In my experience, Congress also meddles with specific project funding, causing disruptions to schedules and leading to increases in cost.

The relationship among the amount of funding and time required relative to performance also needs to be considered. Figure 2.3 illustrates this relationship. This relationship is derived based on a combination of experience and data from previous studies.[38]

Figure 2.3 Relationship Between Performance and Cost and Schedule

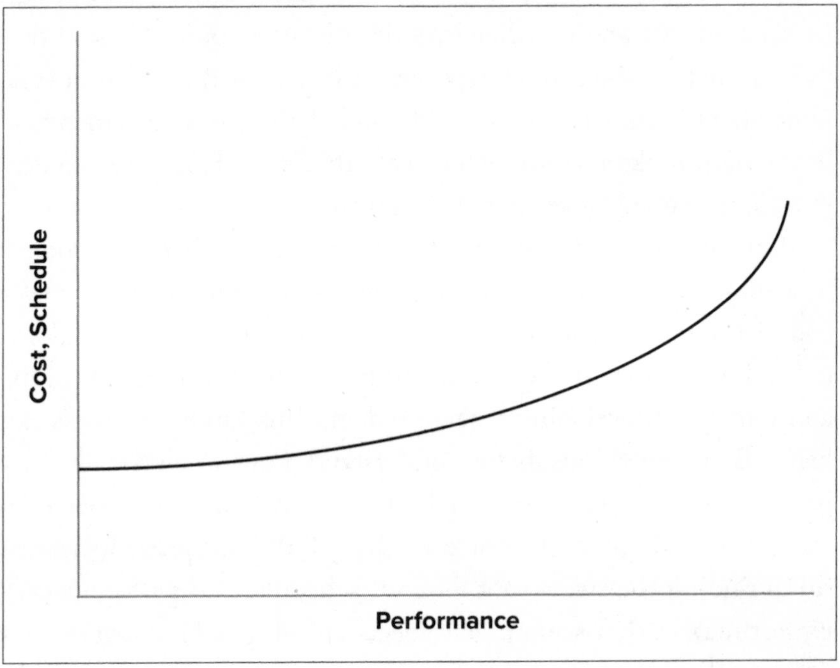

In Figure 2.3, some amount of time and money is required to achieve a minimum level of performance. As performance increases, so do cost and schedule. At the highest levels of performance—at the right end of the curve—there is what economists call diminishing marginal returns. In this area of the curve any additional improvement is extremely expensive and time prohibitive. Organizations that do not make a profit or loss, such as the Department of Defense and NASA, are often at the right end of the curve. Sometimes that performance is needed but not always. The impact of requirements on cost and schedule should be considered. If requirements can be reduced slightly while saving a significant amount of money, this should be taken into account. As one Army general told me, "If you can get where need to go in a Volkswagen, why buy a Mercedes?" I once heard a NASA senior executive tout the performance of a recently launched spacecraft. It had overrun its planned cost and schedule by a significant amount. He said that did not matter, since after a spacecraft is launched, all that anyone remembers is its performance. He added that no one remembers how long it took or how much it cost. This attitude is unfortunately prevalent in many government organizations.

On the other hand, when private firms invest their own money in a project, they can be too risk averse and may be at the lower end of the graph. They could likely improve their product and sell it at a higher price if they were willing to invest a little more time and money in developing a new product. This kind of analysis can help all organizations better understand how to optimally mix performance and resources. Helpful initiatives were conducted in the 1990s and the first decade of the 2000s that proved successful in finding the sweet spot for cost, schedule, and performance.[39] Unfortunately, they seem to have been a passing fad for government projects. The emerging field of multidimensional economic analysis that considers these interrelationships can be used.[40]

OBSOLETE ON ARRIVAL:
THE PROBLEM OF CONSTANT CHANGE

We live in a constantly changing world. Large projects, which take years, and even decades to complete, can become obsolete by the time they are completed, if not before. Venice, Italy, is a beautiful city that attracts throngs of tourists. Its 150 canals mark one of its most distinctive features. The city's future is threatened by climate change and the accompanying rise in sea levels. The city began a project in 2003 to protect itself from this threat. Initial estimates for cost and schedule were 1.6 billion euros and eight years. In 2014, the project, already three years behind schedule, was halted due to a corruption scandal.[41] As of early 2020, the project is expected to be completed in 2021 and cost 5.1 billion euros.[42] Even once it is delivered, the project will not provide all the protection that Venice needs. Due to changes in the climate since the project began, it is obsolete already, before completion.[43]

Moore's Law: The Exponential Growth in the Advancement of Technology

A specific challenge that affects resource and technical performance of projects is the exponential growth in the advancement of technology over time. In 1965, Gordon Moore, cofounder of the Intel Corporation, observed that the number of components in an integrated circuit doubled every year. He expected this trend to continue for the next 10 years. In 1975, he revised the doubling to every two years. That trend, known as Moore's Law, has continued ever since. There were concerns in the 2010s that it would not continue.[44] However, in 2017, Intel announced that it could keep Moore's Law going using hyperscaling technology.[45] Hyperscaling technology enables computer chips that measure in the range of 10 nanometers, which is 10 billionths of a meter (by comparison, the width of a human hair is 75,000 nanometers). Moore's Law remained unbroken in 2020.[46] It is an example of exponential growth. Complex projects take several years and, in some cases, decades to develop. Those that take a decade or more to develop are technologically out-of-date by the time that they enter production, unless new technologies are incorporated during this process. This involves changes in requirements. Changes in requirements involve additional scope and time and hence additional costs. One area where this issue manifests itself is in follow-on programs. For example, observation, communications, and weather satellites need occasional replacements. Ideally, the blueprint from previous designs could just be built to print. However, because of the rapid change in technology, this is not possible. Many of the specialized components for these systems are built by small companies. Once the next block of satellites is built these small firms may be out of business. Also, the technology in some cases may no longer be available. It would be like trying to procure a cathode-ray tube television in the current era of flat-screen TVs. In my experience, these follow-on efforts usually require complete redesigns.

EXTERNAL DEPENDENCIES

Modern projects are complex. They require interactions and inter-dependencies with numerous other projects. Most have inputs provided from outside the project that are needed to complete development and to conduct manufacturing. Any disruption in another organization that supplies a critical component for a project will cause the project's schedule to slip. For example, automobile manufacturers rely upon other firms to supply a variety of parts. If a key supplier of one of these has a labor strike, there will be a schedule delay in car or truck production. An increase in cost or schedule delay for an outside supplier will raise the cost and/or lengthen the schedule of a project.

Predicting Demand: High Reward, High Risk

A specific type of external dependency that drives cost growth is overestimation of demand. In most manufacturing situations, the average cost of a product is a decreasing function of the number of units produced. As people work on a task, they learn to do it better and more efficiently. The result is that successive units are produced in less time and with less effort, which lowers cost. Advances in technology also reduce manufacturing costs over time. This phenomenon, called learning, has been observed to occur across a wide range of manufactured goods, including missiles, refrigerators, aircraft, and semiconductors. Manufacturing also tends to have excess capacity. I have experience with this phenomenon in public projects,[47] but it is common across all industries in the United States. The overall average capacity utilization rates range from 70% to 90% between 1967 and 2011 and fluctuate around an average equal to 80%.[48] This means additional units can be built with the existing plant and labor. Typically, the fixed costs to run these concerns are much higher than the cost to add an additional unit, and as most firms are not operating near their limit, additional units can be added with little additional cost. This is known as the rate effect. The impacts of learning and the rate effect are that the greater the output, the lower the average cost. The reverse is also true. As quantities decrease, the average unit cost increases. For example, if the fixed cost to produce a system is $6 and the cost of building a single unit is $1, the average cost for three units is ($6 + $1 × 3)/3 = $9/3 = $3. If the number of units produced increases to six, then the average unit cost drops to ($6 + $1 × 6)/6 = $2.

External dependencies in the supply chain aside, projects control their supply. However, they have no control over the demand for their product. Organizations have to forecast demand. As the end product typically requires years of development before it can be produced, there is significant uncertainty in future demand. When firms project demand well, they can profit tremendously. A good case of successful forecasting is Texas Instruments. This semiconductor firm foresaw a growing demand for its product. Based on their experience with learning, management expected that costs would decrease as they produced more of their product.

Texas Instruments priced aggressively, below its then-current production costs, in the belief that it would eventually make a profit as production continued. This proved to be an effective strategy. With low prices, the company dominated the market, driving out competition. With a bigger share of the market, Texas Instruments increased its profit.[49]

When projects overestimate the demand for their product, the outcome is higher average costs. Firms that produce weapons systems for the government can pass this cost along to the government. A classic example of a system whose unit costs have increased dramatically from initial plans at least in part due to quantity reductions is the Navy's Littoral Combat Ship (LCS). (Littoral means the area near the shore.) The LCS was planned to be cheap and with modular capability allowing for a range of applications including minesweeping and above- and below-surface warfare. The initial plan was to purchase 55 ships at $220 million each, but as of early 2020, the cost of the first 32 was expected to be $655 million each.[50] Part of this is due to reductions in quantities, but other important factors contribute to this growth. One is that in the initial plan, two different designs were to be completed by two different contractors. One design would be selected and built. Instead, the Navy decided to produce both designs. This increased production costs as the large fixed cost to produce two different designs is double that required for one. Operating costs also increased due to increases in crew sizes.[51] In addition to the large cost overruns, the development schedule tripled from three years to nine. Technical requirements were cut to try to contain cost growth, which led to performance shortfalls. The primary surface vehicle missile was cancelled. The modular approach also had to be abandoned.[52] The F-35 program mentioned earlier also had unit costs increase substantially due to cuts in production quantities. To mitigate the large overruns, leadership cut planned production by 400 aircraft. As a result, the cost per aircraft doubled from the initial plan of $69 million to $141 million.[53]

When projected demand falls short of reality, commercial firms are not always able to pass along higher average cost to their customers. The Airbus A380 is a large, double-decker aircraft. In the late 1990s company leadership wanted to build a mega-jet that would have even greater capacity than rival Boeing's 747. They expected demand from airlines for international travel. At the time, the prevailing paradigm for air travel was the hub-and-spoke system, where travelers are routed from nearby smaller airports to a central hub for travel to a more distant destination. Airbus projected this system would continue to generate a need for large jets for international travel. Management also believed there would be economies of scale in ferrying more passengers in one large plane, especially to remote locations such as Australia. Instead, the industry shifted to a more point-to-point system for both international and domestic travel, causing airlines to purchase smaller aircraft. Demand was initially expected to exceed 1,300 airplanes, but Airbus sold less than 300.[54] The development schedule proved to be too aggressive—the A380 had concurrency in design and production, which led to schedule slips. Private firms do not provide full transparency into their profits and losses, but analysts believe the cost of developing the A380 likely more than doubled from initial estimates of $11 billion to $25 billion.[55] This could have been more than offset in production, but that proved to be unprofitable. The market would not bear the high cost of the complex double-decker, and the company lost money on every order. In 2019, Airbus announced it was stopping production of the white elephant.[56]

Waiting Is Hard—and Expensive

A specific example of an externality that can cause a schedule slip is launch vehicle availability. Satellites must be launched into space. A problem with a launch vehicle can lead to its unavailability when needed. This may require the satellite to be put into storage. Satellites cannot just be stuck in a closet and then pulled out and dusted off when the launch vehicle becomes available again. Clean room storage, which is costly, is required to avoid contamination. Several Earth-orbiting satellites and planetary spacecraft were planned for launch on the Space Shuttle for the 1986–1988 period. The Space Shuttle had a major catastrophic failure in early 1986 with *Challenger*. This required a redesign of the solid rocket boosters, and the Space Shuttle was not launched again for two and a half years. All the satellites and spacecraft affected had cost growth as a result. One of the programs negatively affected by the *Challenger* incident was the Hubble Space Telescope. Originally estimated to cost $1.6 billion in current year dollars, the cost eventually grew to approximately $6 billion, a 275% increase, nearly four times the initial estimated cost. In addition to the cost growth, there was a technical flaw in the primary mirror when Hubble was first launched. It was polished to the wrong shape, leading to less useful observations until the issue was corrected three years after launch by astronauts aboard the Space Shuttle.

The Hubble Space Telescope suffered from several sources of traditional cost growth, including funding constraints, launch vehicle delays, and underestimation of time and resources necessary to develop the requisite technology. One of the key factors that led to a low initial estimate was optimism by management. Historical data indicated that the optical instruments, the structures that house these instruments, and the fine guidance sensors needed for a precision telescope like Hubble were expensive. Management picked the lower historical cost data points that backed up their desire for a lower cost, ignoring the higher cost data points. There were complexities induced by having two different NASA centers running the project. Also, as mentioned previously, two different contractors were charged with developing the telescope. The program planned to use existing hardware, which did not happen. An insufficient number of spare parts was included in the initial estimate, so these parts had to be added later, at extra cost. Hubble was planned for a launch on the Space Shuttle in 1986. However, when the Space Shuttle *Challenger* catastrophic failure occurred, the Hubble had to be put in storage. The cost of clean room storage was $6 million a month.[57]

BLACK SWANS

Sometimes extreme events occur that few can foresee. One example is the COVID-19 pandemic of 2020. The fast spread of this new virus had tremendous health risks. Its rapid spread in the early part of the year disrupted economic activity around the world and overwhelmed healthcare system capacity. The 9/11 terrorist attacks in New York and Washington in 2001 were the worst terrorists attacks in the history of the United States, resulting in thousands of deaths and billions of dollars of property damage. The Fukushima Daiichi nuclear incident was the result of a one-two punch combination of a large earthquake and an ensuing tsunami. These kinds of events, termed "black swans,"[58] are unpredictable and have a huge impact. These are typically not accounted for by programs. The term has come to be overused and is often used to refer to any project with a large cost overrun and/or schedule delay. Its use should be reserved for those unusual events, like the ones mentioned here.

SUMMARY AND RECOMMENDATIONS

Cost and schedule growth are enduring and ubiquitous phenomena. For many decades and across a variety of industries, they have been consistently high and occur in most projects. Technical issues abound as well.

A variety of factors drive cost and schedule growth. One of the primary ones is optimism. The way to combat optimism is to conduct independent estimates and cross-checks of program plans. In the absence of an independent estimate, looking at how much similar past programs have cost without making any adjustments for optimistic assumptions can help.

Smart planning up front can help reduce the odds of cost and schedule growth. Balancing all three legs of the stool—cost, schedule, and performance—is important. Maturing technologies before starting design can help reduce technical, cost, and schedule risks.

More attention from senior management on cost and schedule issues can also be beneficial. I have noticed that when budgets are increasing, accurate cost and schedule projections are not a leadership priority, since a program manager expects to get at least as much funding if not more the next year. However, when budgets are tight, accurate and reliable cost estimates are critical. Program managers want to make sure that they can achieve their goals within their given funding. Between 2011 and 2015, defense spending was significantly reduced, and senior leaders at the Pentagon focused more on controlling cost. Perhaps not coincidentally, cost growth in defense programs declined from 9.2% per year in 2011 to 3.5% in 2015.

Cost and schedule growth are evidence of large amounts of risk, as well as evidence that these risks are not effectively managed. Risk is a necessary part of every endeavor, not something to be taken lightly or avoided. However, projects need to recognize it, measure it, and plan for it. Quantitative risk assessment of cost and schedule, the subject of the next chapter, is an integral part of ensuring project success.

CHAPTER 3

Beyond the Matrix

The Cost and Schedule Risk Imperative

The German composer Carl Orff composed the classical music piece *O Fortuna* in the 1930s. It has appeared in a variety of film and television soundtracks, and in 2009, it was listed as the "most widely heard classical piece" in the United Kingdom.[1] The lyrics are from a medieval poem about the whims of chance. It compares luck to the phases of the moon, waxing and waning during its orbit around the Earth. The title is a reference to Fortuna, who is the Roman goddess of luck and is the origin of the word *fortune*. The operations of Fortuna are symbolized by a wheel, which she spins at random. This causes losses for some and gains for others, like a cosmic roulette wheel. As a result of the misfortune that they either suffered or saw happening around them, people in the ancient and medieval worlds appreciated the role of uncertainty. During the Middle Ages, people had an appreciation for risk, as the bubonic plague alone killed up to 60% of Europe's population.

In the modern world, we underappreciate the role of uncertainty and tend to be blind to risk. The Nobel Prize–winning economist Kenneth Arrow wrote, "Most individuals underestimate the uncertainty of the world . . . our knowledge of the way things work, in society or in nature, comes trailing clouds of vagueness."[2] The resistance to recognition of risk and uncertainty includes project management. As a colleague of mine aptly put it, "Project management types, especially, have a tendency to treat plans as reality."[3] We established in previous chapters the problem of significant cost and schedule growth. These widespread and enduring increases reflect the high degree of risk inherent in projects. If there were no recurring history of cost and schedule growth, there would be no need for resource risk analysis and management. The planning of such projects would be as easy as planning a trip to a local dry cleaner. Instead, the tremendous risk inherent in such projects necessitates the consideration of risk and uncertainty throughout a program's life cycle.

The mathematics of risk and uncertainty belong to the related fields of probability and statistics. Even among mathematicians, these topics are not regarded as highly as other, more traditional fields. The subject of risk is the stepchild of mathematics. The study of randomness arose in France and England in the seventeenth century. In France, it began with gambling. The mathematician Blaise Pascal was a friend of two gamblers who were obsessed with a dice game that was a forerunner to the modern gambling game craps. One of them asked Pascal how payment should be distributed if a dice game were interrupted before its completion. Pascal started a correspondence on the subject with his friend Pierre de Fermat, a judge who studied mathematics as a hobby. This exchange was the genesis of the study of probability.[4] In England, the study of statistics started with counting the different ways in which people died. One of the worst outbreaks of the plague occurred in England in 1603. This led to the collection of causes of mortality. These statistics listed on a weekly basis the number of children who were christened in the Church of England as well as the number of deaths, categorized by disease. The amateur statistician John Graunt used them to produce life tables showing the probability of surviving to a given age. He also used this data to estimate the population of London.[5] Perhaps the twin shady origins of the subject—gambling and death—led to a lack of respect for the study of statistics as a serious subject. David Mumford, a prominent mathematician who has won numerous awards, including the Fields Medal, one of the top prizes in mathematics, admits admonishing a student to not study statistics, as it is "all cookbook nonsense."[6] Mumford later changed his mind. In 1999, he wrote an article proclaiming that the new millennium would herald a dawning of an age of randomness.[7] This dawning has only begun with project management. As we will see, there is a long way to go until the sun fully rises.

One way to understand risk is to consider a lottery. These are a common form of gambling run by state governments in the United States. As of 2020, 44 states and three territories have lotteries. A popular variety is the 6/49 format. This type of lottery involves choosing six numbers from 1 through 49. If you choose all six numbers correctly, regardless of their order, you win the jackpot. The chance of this happening is roughly 1 in 13 million. By comparison, the chance of your being struck by lightning in the next year is 1 in 700,000. However, even though the chance is small, the payoffs for lotteries are large. The largest ever payout was a Powerball lottery in 2016 that had a winning jackpot equal to $1.6 billion. A lottery is an example of a gamble with a small downside. If you only buy a few tickets, that is all you can lose. However, it has a tremendous upside payout, albeit an extremely remote one. Starting a new project is also a gamble. Depending on the type of project, the payout could be profit or it could be a tangible good whose value is more qualitative, such as the advancement of national security. The potential downside could be bankruptcy for a private endeavor or major cost and schedule growth for a public project. This is like a reverse lottery. As we saw in Chapter 1, one in six programs doubles in cost from the start to the completion of development. This would be like risking a dollar with a one in six chance that you would have to pay another dollar to obtain the product. The chance of loss is relatively high, as are the consequences, making it an unfavorable gamble. Despite a poor track record in delivering projects on time and within budget, project managers display either an unwillingness or an ignorance of the role of risk in a project's success or failure. In his study of large projects, Oxford professor Bent Flyvbjerg attributes "inadequate deliberation about risk" to be a key contributor to the poor performance of projects.[8]

DEFINITIONS

We must define some basic terms for a discussion of uncertainty. *Probability* is a number that describes the chance that an event will occur. For example, if a fair coin is tossed, the probability that it lands heads up is 50%. A *point estimate* is one that does not consider risk; that is, it is a non–risk adjusted cost or schedule estimate. *Uncertainty* is the indefiniteness about the outcome of a situation. It includes both favorable and unfavorable events. The favorable events are also referred to as *opportunities* because they have the potential to result in saving time or money. *Risk* represents the unfavorable outcomes, as it represents the chance that cost or schedule will increase. *Cost risk* is a measure of the chance that, due to unfavorable events, the planned or budgeted cost of a project will be exceeded. *Schedule risk* is the chance that the planned schedule will increase in length. *Cost and schedule risk analysis* is a process of quantifying the cost and schedule impacts of unfavorable events.[9]

For example, cost risk is the probability that an estimate will exceed a specified amount, such as $100 million or $150 million.

Cost growth and cost risk are intrinsically related. Historical cost growth provides an excellent means for determining the overall level of risk for cost estimates. For example, if 90% of past programs have experienced less than 100% growth, we should expect that the probability is 90% that the increase in the actual cost as compared to the initial estimate should be less than 100%. Thus, cost growth is the impact of cost risk in action. See Figure 3.1 for a notional graph.

Figure 3.1   Risk (R) vs. Opportunity (O)

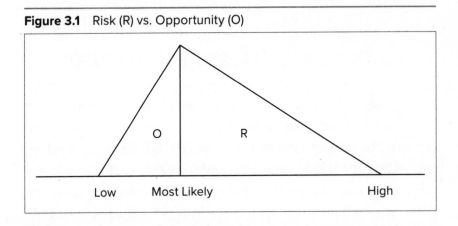

The height of the triangle in Figure 3.1 represents the relative likelihood of occurrence. The peak is the most likely value. The area to the right of the peak is the risk side of the triangle, marked with an R. It represents the probability and impact of events that will cause cost or schedule to increase. We have discussed many of these, such as optimism, in the last chapter. The area to the left of the peak represents opportunities for savings, marked O. We have seen in the cost growth and schedule delay data that most of the variation represents risk. The opportunities area is smaller than the risk/threats area. This means that there is greater risk of cost or schedule increasing than there is opportunity for savings, since, as we have mentioned, more can go wrong than can go right. As discussed earlier, when money is allocated, project leadership will find a way to spend the money and fill the time allocated. Thus, the likelihood of cost or schedule decreasing is low. The graph in Figure 3.1 is not to scale. The risk of increases is overwhelmingly larger than the opportunities for savings. The difference is so much bigger that we can almost equate risk with uncertainty. For these reasons, I use the terms "risk" and "uncertainty" interchangeably. Unfortunately, in my experience, most project managers focus only on the opportunities side and ignore the risk side.

THAT'S JUST MEAN: THE PROBLEM WITH AVERAGES

In the last two chapters we focused much of our attention on averages. However, there is much more to risk than averages. The seriously flawed and controversial book *The Bell Curve* by psychologist Richard J. Herrnstein and political scientist Charles Murray purported to demonstrate that the standard measure of intelligence, the intelligence quotient (IQ), is destiny.[10] This is a single number to which a great deal of meaning is attached. How can the complex and manifold phenomenon of human intelligence be represented by a single number? The developer of the IQ, Alfred Binet, admitted that intelligence cannot be accurately represented by IQ. He proposed the use of his test to identify students who were falling behind in order to help them, not categorize and rank different groups of people.[11] Just as intelligence cannot be measured with a single number, the cost or schedule of a project cannot be adequately measured with a single value.

The sport of baseball is a good example that more than just averages should be considered. Between 1900 and 2019, among players with at least 250 at bats in a season, the mean batting average has fluctuated around a value equal to .275. A .275 batting average means that a hitter gets a hit in 27.5% of his at-bats (this does not include reaching base by being walked or hit by a pitch).[12] There are long trends upward and downward that can last a few decades, but batting averages have fluctuated up and down over the years around this value. However, the variation around this mean value has not stayed constant. As measured by the standard deviation, the variation in batting average among batters has been declining steadily since the nineteenth century, when play began.[13] The last player to hit .400 or better was Ted Williams in 1941, when he hit .406 for the Boston Red Sox. The four players to come closest since have been Tony Gwynn, who hit .394 in 1994 for the San Diego Padres in a strike-shortened season; George Brett, who hit .390 for the Kansas City Royals in 1980, another strike-shortened season; Rod Carew who hit .388 in 1977 for the Minnesota Twins; and Larry Walker, who hit .379 for the Colorado Rockies in 1999. From 2000 to 2019, no one has had an average higher than .372. Miguel Cabrera had the highest batting average between 2011 and 2019, leading the American League with .348 in 2013.

Long ago, exceptional batters hit .400 or better. Due to less spread in the range of batting averages, the very best batters no longer hit .400 after World War II. Measured in terms of the number of standard deviations above the mean, George Brett's 1980 batting average of .390 can be considered more exceptional than any batter since Ted Williams's 1941 season. The declining trend in standard deviation is due to several reasons. Baseball has become accessible to a wider group of people. The sport has matured. Training methods have optimized over time, and with increases in salaries there is a financial incentive for players to play well. In 2019, the average major leaguer made more than $4 million a year.[14] As pitchers and batters improve, it gets harder to exceed the average. Just knowing that the average batter hits .275 only tells part of the story.

Sam Savage, in his book *The Flaw of Averages: Why We Underestimate Risk in the Face of Uncertainty*, focuses on the overreliance on expected values and the hazards it causes. Savage defines the term "Flaw of Averages" as "plans based on average assumptions are wrong on average." As he states succinctly, plans based on averages are destined to be "behind schedule, and beyond budget."[15] Savage cites several examples where the use of averages has led to disaster. One of these was the 1997 flood of the Red River, which flows through Minnesota, North Dakota, and southern Manitoba. Experts forecast that the flood would crest at 49 feet, which was based on an average of past floods. The dikes protecting Grand Forks were designed to withstand a flood crest up to 52 feet. When the flood crested at 54 feet, many people had to evacuate at the last minute and there were billions of dollars of flood damage.[16]

Stephen Jay Gould, an eminent biologist and author, devoted an article to this subject, titled "The Median Isn't the Message," which was published in *Discover* magazine in 1985. Gould wrote that the "average is an abstract measure applicable to no single person, and often largely irrelevant to individual cases."[17] In his book *Full House*, he goes even further, stating, "Our culture encodes a strong bias either to neglect or ignore variation. We focus instead on measures of central tendency, and as a result we make some terrible mistakes, often with considerable practical impact."[18] Gould had a personal connection to uncertainty. In 1982, he was diagnosed with a rare form of cancer. The "average" survival time after diagnosis was only eight months. This average was a median. Once Gould started looking into the disease, he discovered that the distribution is skewed much like the cost and schedule growth data we have discussed. For such distributions, the median is less than the mean, and there is a long right tail. There was much more to Gould's survival chances than just the median. Indeed, Gould lived another 20 years and died of a different cancer unrelated to his first case.[19]

Another important reason for incorporating uncertainty is that for many projects there may be few directly applicable precedents. Many endeavors are highly specialized. For these types of projects there are few historical precedents, if any, on which to base credible estimates of cost and schedule. Making predictions from small data sets is highly uncertain. A trend that appears to be significant for 10 data points could be random noise.[20] Some cutting-edge programs have no precedent at all.

Averages are useful. But we need to consider more than just the average, especially in the light of uncertainty. If we are going to incorporate uncertainty, why can't we just use a high estimate? Some fixed percentage could be added to every cost estimate for contingency. This was indeed an approach that was widely used at one point. Many projects add a fixed value, such as 20%, to a point estimate of cost or schedule for contingency. Adding a fixed amount in the range of 5% to 10% is still standard practice in construction projects.[21] However, a one-size-fits-all approach to contingency will not work. We may overfund some programs and underfund others. The ones with too much funding and time will likely find ways to spend the money and use all the time, leading to an inefficient allocation of resources. Risky development programs will likely need more than a relatively small fixed percentage for reserves. There is no substitute for a risk assessment for cost and schedule. We saw in the last chapter that projects often experience extreme amounts of cost growth. The average growth is 50%. Approximately one in six development projects more than doubles in cost from beginning to end. Given this wide variation, the representation of cost by a single number will not be enough. If we only use a single number to represent cost, we know that it will be wrong. We are better off being imprecisely right than precisely wrong.

BIG DATA EQUALS BIG DISTRACTION?

The advent of big data, as measured by the sheer amount of data available and the speed at which it is updated, is unprecedented.

I am a big fan of this movement. However, I have discovered that more information and new algorithms have largely provided better ways to produce averages, and as we have seen, averages can be problematic. As an example, a classic method that predicts an average is a trend line. We saw in Figure 1.2 in Chapter 1 what appears to be a close-fitting trend line between planned and actual cost. There is a strong correlation between planned and actual cost, but there is also a great deal of variation around it. The spread around the trend line, as measured by the standard deviation, is roughly 50%.

Newer methods used in the analysis of large data sets also have significant variation around their average predictions, but this aspect is often ignored. These methods have the potential to produce better estimates of risk and uncertainty, but this is often overlooked because of the focus on new and improved ways to calculate expected values. Risk needs to be kept in view, even when a large amount of information is available.

"TRUST NOT ALL YOUR GOODS TO ONE SHIP"

While still not fully appreciated, the notion that there is more to averages has been around for a long time. During the Renaissance, the humanist scholar Desiderius Erasmus compiled a list of proverbs whose title in English is *Adages*. These were largely drawn from ancient Greek and Roman sources. They included a variety of expressions commonly used today, such as "the blind leading the blind," "kill two birds with one stone," and "between a rock and a hard place." One that relates to risk is "trust not all your goods to one ship."[22]

When the disciplines of probability and statistics began in the seventeenth century, the focus was average outcomes. It was not until the eighteenth century that mathematicians considered that uncertain outcomes needed to be considered in their entirety, such as the variance around the expected value. Swiss mathematician Daniel Bernoulli lived in the eighteenth century and was part of a family that included several famous mathematicians. As a scholar, he may have even been familiar with the idea of not putting all your goods on one ship because he came up with a numerical example that illustrates this notion. Bernoulli's example explains the need to look at more than the expected value.[23] His example used a type of coin called a ducat. The ducat was a coin made of precious metals commonly used as a trade coin in Europe until the twentieth century.

In Bernoulli's example, a merchant owns 4,000 ducats worth of goods at home. He possesses another 8,000 ducats of goods in a foreign country. These goods can only be transported by sea, a perilous trip. Based on experience, half of all ships that journey across the sea do not reach their destination because of storms, pirate attacks, and other reasons. If the merchant has all his foreign goods sent home on one ship, there is a 50% chance that he will get his 8,000 ducats worth of goods. There is also a 50% chance that these goods will wind up at the bottom of the ocean, stolen by pirates, or perhaps even in the belly of a large white whale. Thus, after the voyage, there is a 50% chance that his net worth will be 4,000 ducats and a 50% chance that his net worth will be 12,000 ducats. The expected value is just the weighted average of these two values, which in this case is $(4,000 \times .50) + (12,000 \times 0.50) = 8,000$ ducats. (To keep things simple, assume that the cost of shipping the goods is zero.) However, suppose that the merchant decides to diversify his risk. He transports the goods in two ships, with half in each. Three different outcomes are possible. One is that both ships arrive safely, in which case his net worth is 12,000 ducats. Another is that only one ship makes it, in which case his net worth is now $4,000 + 4,000 = 8,000$ ducats. And the third possibility is that neither ship makes it safely across, in which case his net worth is only 4,000 ducats.

To determine the expected value of this approach, note that the 50% probability of the goods arriving safely is the same as the result of tossing a fair coin. Looking at the arrangement of two independent coin tosses, there are four possibilities, if you consider the order of the tosses. One is heads, then heads again. The second is heads, then tails. Next is tails, then heads. Lastly, there is tails, then tails again. Each one of these outcomes is equally likely since the probability of heads or tails on each flip is 50%. Let heads denote the event that a ship arrives safely, and tails denote the event that the ship is lost at sea. Since these events are all equally likely, and there are four of them, each has a probability of occurrence equal to 25%. That is, the probability that both make it is 25%. The chance that neither ship makes it is also 25%. The chance that only one ship makes it is 50%, since there are two equally likely ways this can happen—the first ship makes it, and the second does not, or the first ship does not make it, while the second ship arrives safely. Thus, there is a 25% chance that the merchant's net worth will be 4,000 ducats, a 25% chance that his net worth will be 12,000 ducats (both ships make it), and a 50% chance that his net worth will be 8,000 ducats (only one ship makes it). The expected value of his wealth is equal to the weighted average of these outcomes:

$$(4{,}000 \times .25) + (12{,}000 \times 0.25) + (8{,}000 \times 0.50) =$$
$$1{,}000 + 3{,}000 + 4{,}000 = 8{,}000 \text{ ducats.}$$

The expected value of both alternatives is the same, 8,000 ducats. This average, however, does not tell the entire story. In the first case, half the time the merchant has a net worth equal to 4,000 ducats, while in the second case, in three-quarters of the cases he has at least 8,000 ducats in net worth. The second case is preferable. You are better off not putting all your goods in one ship. See Figure 3.2 for an illustration of this.

Figure 3.2 Differences in Outcomes Between One and Two Ships

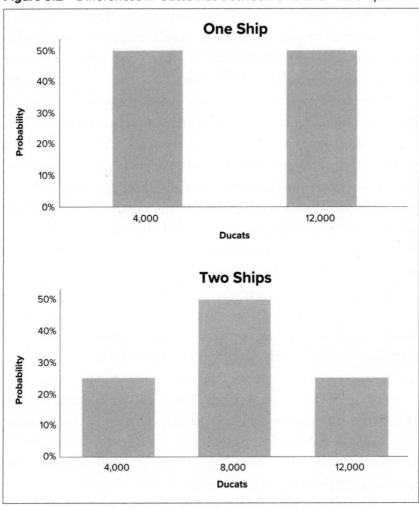

A PRACTICAL EXAMPLE OF COST UNCERTAINTY

The previous example provides some insight into logistics uncertainty for modern projects, although transportation in the modern world is much safer and more reliable. As a more concrete and contemporary example of cost uncertainty, consider a software-intensive project that is considering one of two options. For a critical piece of software, there is an existing commercial product that the company believes it may be able to integrate into the rest of the system. The firm can develop this on its own, but it would be more expensive than the commercially available alternative. However, attempting to integrate commercial off-the-shelf (COTS) software is risky. It can require significant testing. The integration can require significant software development to interface with the COTS system. The interfaces are often not well documented, making the integration more challenging, as it is often a trial-and-error process.

I have seen firsthand the difficulties in doing this. Early in my career, I worked on a project that required integrating COTS geometry software into a computer-assisted design software project. One of the challenges was decreasing the run time. Optimizing code to ensure the software runs efficiently is hard when not all of it can be manipulated. Partly due to the integration issues with this software, the product was ultimately not successful, and the project was cancelled. Problems with integrating COTS are widespread, and evidence provided by multiple studies shows that the hoped-for savings from using COTS is not often realized.[24] As an example, suppose that if the software capability is developed internally, the project will cost $120 million. If the COTS alternative is pursued, there are two possible outcomes. One is that everything goes well, and integration is simple and trouble-free. In this case, the project will cost $90 million. However, the probability that this happens, given all the evidence, is only 33%. If things do not go well, the project will end up costing $135 million, more than if the project had developed the software internally. The probability of this outcome is 67%. The expected value of both outcomes is the same, $120 million. However, if the COTS option is pursued, the probability is 2/3 that the project will cost more than that. Given that risk, the better alternative is to avoid the COTS option, but this can only be discerned if risk is considered. That information is not revealed by the expected value alone.

THE IMPORTANCE OF SCHEDULE UNCERTAINTY

As a practical project example that illustrates the problem with just considering averages in schedules, consider an aircraft refurbishment project. As these systems get older, they occasionally need significant renovation. A simplified version of the steps in this activity is illustrated in Figure 3.3.

Figure 3.3   Schedules Consist of Both Serial and Parallel Activities

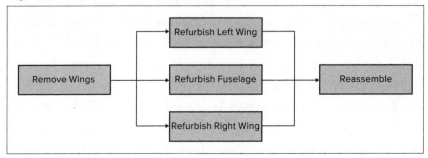

Adapted from Philip Fahringer, "The Flaw of Averages in Project Management," Project Management Institute Virtual Library, 2011

Figure 3.3 is a simple schedule network that shows which activities occur in sequence and which occur in parallel. Sequential activities, known as serial, occur one after the other. Each activity in a serial chain must be completed before the next can begin. Parallel activities are conducted at the same time. For parallel activities, all must be completed before that set of tasks is considered complete. The refurbishment begins by removing the wings of the aircraft. Once this is done, three actions are performed in parallel—the left-wing, fuselage, and right-wing refurbishment are all conducted at the same time. Once all these are finished, the wings are reattached and the overhaul is complete.

The cost of the activity is driven by the schedule. The longer the refurbishment takes, the longer the time staff are dedicated to working on the overhaul of the aircraft. A company bid on a project to refurbish a fleet of aircraft. The bid was based on the median time expected for each task. Wing removal and reattachment were each expected to take one week. The refurbishment of each of the three sections of the plane was expected to take five weeks. They added these times, deriving an expected schedule equal to seven weeks. For parallel activities, using averages leads to trouble. A delay in any one of the parallel activities causes the entire schedule to slip. As these are median times to complete, there is a 50% chance that any one of the parallel activities will take no longer than five weeks. For the total set of parallel activities to finish within that time, all three have to be completed within this five-week time period. This is like flipping three coins and having all three come up heads. Extending the discussion from the last example from two to three coins, the probability that this occurs is $1/2 \times 1/2 \times 1/2 = 1/8$. If this set of parallel tasks were done eight times, we would expect that only one would be completed on time. There is a $7/8 = 87.5\%$ chance of a schedule slip based on planning to the median time to complete any one of the three parallel activities. This example is based on an actual project; the numbers have been changed and the firm has been kept anonymous to protect the guilty. The firm won the contract to overhaul the aircraft. As expected from our analysis, the average time to turn around each airplane took longer than initially expected. The company lost millions of dollars as a result.[25]

BIG BETS AND FINANCIAL RUIN

There are numerous instances in financial markets where focusing solely on averages has led to tremendous losses, especially when leverage is used. In traditional investing, you cannot lose more than you invest. However, if you borrow some of the money needed to fund an investment, you are using leverage. This makes good investments more profitable, but it increases risk tremendously. Orange County, California's treasurer used municipal funds to make leveraged investments in bonds. This strategy worked for 20 years, earning the county better returns than the state of California's investment pool. However, in 1994, the county lost $1.5 billion and filed for bankruptcy.[26] The county treasurer later stated that he made investments based on what he foresaw as "most likely interest rates." This is how he said he achieved his remarkable results. He said that focusing on a "worst-case scenario" would lower investment returns.[27] This worked for a long time, but his failure to consider risk eventually resulted in catastrophe. In the 1990s, the hedge fund Long-Term Capital Management made superior returns by taking on leveraged bets. The investment advisors included two Nobel Prize–winning economists. However, in 1998, the firm lost $4.5 billion.[28] The hedge fund did not consider the risk involved in their excessive use of leverage. The financial crisis of 2008 was precipitated by large, highly leveraged investments based on the belief that the average past increase in mortgage prices would continue. Also, hardly anyone considered the added risk of the expansion of subprime mortgages.[29]

These examples demonstrate that in the face of uncertainty, you need to consider more than just the expected value. As we have seen in previous chapters, all projects have inherent cost and schedule risk, and this risk is typically significant. When uncertainty is high, understanding the variation about the average is critical to good decision-making.

RISK AFFECTS ALL PROJECTS

Risk is clearly important for private ventures. If a company is exposed to too much risk, it can go bankrupt. However, risk is often not appreciated for public projects. I was discussing risk with a friend. He said no one worried about risk for government endeavors because if they need more money, they can just go print some more. While it may be true that the government will not go out of business when cost grows or it fails to deliver a project on time, risk is just as vital for these ventures. To not consider risk wastes time and money. For example, in defense programs, a lack of proper risk management is a key reason the United States is lagging its rivals in the development and fielding of critical weapons systems, such as hypersonics. Hypersonic weapons travel more than five times the speed of sound and at a low altitude compared to traditional weapons, which makes them challenging to defend. Even though the United States has the world's largest defense budget by a factor of three, both China and Russia beat the United States in fielding hypersonic weapons. Russia deployed a hypersonic weapons with a nuclear payload, and China fielded one with a conventional payload in 2019. As of 2020, the United States was still developing this capability.

BEYOND THE MATRIX

A popular methodology used by many organizations to analyze cost risk is a matrix approach. This looks at the two critical dimensions of risk—likelihood of occurrence and consequence. It typically uses subjective input from experts to:

1. Determine the potential bad events, that is, the risks
2. Assign a likelihood of occurrence to each risk
3. Assign a consequence to each risk

The likelihood of occurrence represents the chance that an event occurs and is a probability between 0% (impossible) and 100% (certain). The consequences are usually expressed as a percentage of the total program cost. See Table 3.1 for an example of a typical risk matrix.

Table 3.1   Risk Matrix

Likelihood/Consequence	Minimal (C ≤ 10%)	Moderate (10% < C ≤ 20%)	Significant (C > 20%)
Likely (L > 80%)	Motor Performance		
Possible (20% < L ≤ 80%)		Test Failure	
Unlikely (≤ 20%)			Technology Not Mature

In Table 3.1, the likelihood of occurrence values are marked L, and the consequences are marked C. This notional project has determined three risks: Motor Performance, Test Failure, and Technology Not Mature. Motor Performance is assigned a Likely likelihood of occurrence with a Minimal consequence. Test Failure has been determined to have a Possible likelihood of occurrence with a Moderate consequence. Technology Not Mature has been assessed as being Unlikely to occur, but it is believed to have a Significant consequence if it is realized.

Matrices like that in Table 3.1 were designed for use in engineering to assess technical risk. They are used to identify hazards to system performance that must be mitigated during development and production. Once identified, a plan to remove these risks must be crafted and implemented. The matrices are updated at internal reviews at which the matrix provides information on the progress in lowering the likelihood and reducing the impact of these risks. This is the ideal use for such matrices. They should not be part of a quantitative risk assessment, but they provide leadership with a consistent and structured method to reduce technical risk. Unfortunately, this is not taken seriously enough by many engineers, as I have noticed a reluctance on the part of technical personnel to identify risks because of the amount of paperwork involved. I attended a review for one project that was experiencing technical issues but did not identify any technical risks.

The bigger issue with this matrix is when it is used to assess cost and/or schedule risk. This type of matrix is commonly used in a wide variety of projects but only for cost risk assessment. If the information in Table 3.1 is used for a cost risk analysis, the likelihood of occurrence values and the consequence percentages are used to determine an expected value for risk. Suppose the project cost estimate is assessed to be $100 million. The Motor Performance risk is in the Likely likelihood category, which ranges from 80% to 100%. The midpoint of this range is used, which is 90%. The consequence for this risk is in the Minimal category, which ranges from zero to 10%. The midpoint of this range is used as well (5%), for an expected risk impact equal to (.05 × $100 million) × 0.90 = $4.5 million. The Test Failure risk is treated similarly—its expected risk impact is equal to (.15 × $100 million) × .5 = $7.5 million. The Significant risk, Technology Not Mature, has a consequence in the greater-than-or-equal-to 20% category. Even though the consequence is assessed as being at least 20%, the value typically used to assess expected risk is the lower bound, 20%. This ensures a low bias. The Technology Not Mature expected risk impact is equal to (.2 × $100 million) × .1 = $2 million. The total of these three values is equal to $14 million. If this value is then used to establish reserves, it is only 14% above the point estimate. This value is typical for those obtained from these types of risk analyses. As we discussed earlier, just the immaturity of technology can double the cost, or more, so the use of this method significantly underestimates risk. As a result, it is not a credible way to assess cost risk when used by itself. A full probabilistic risk analysis is needed that accounts for multiple sources of uncertainty.

Even though the risk matrix should not be used as the only tool in assessing cost risk, the type of matrix represented in Table 3.1 is an important factor that should be considered in all quantitative risk assessments. These risks are the ones that a project's technical personnel consider to be important and as such they should be incorporated in any sound risk analysis for resources. Ensuring that a cost or schedule risk estimate includes the potential impact of all technical risks is important.

PROBABILITY DISTRIBUTIONS AND THEIR CHARACTERISTICS

Individual numbers, such as averages, do not provide enough information to model risk. Instead of a number, what is needed is a shape.[30] The shapes we will use are called probability distributions, which are the primary method for the quantitative analysis of risk. Without getting into the technical details of these, we will focus on their properties and how they relate to risk.

The abundance of evidence for historical cost and schedule growth indicates a tremendous amount of resource risk. As the realization of these risks, the characteristics of this data indicate how risk should be modeled. The mean of the historical growth data indicates where risk is centered. The standard deviation and the variance measure the amount of spread around the mean. As we have mentioned, cost and schedule growth data, and hence risk, is skewed to the right, or upside. Risk is not symmetrically distributed. Extreme events tend to occur relatively often. For most types of projects, cost doubles or more once in every six projects. Extreme schedule increases are not uncommon. The likelihood of large cost and schedule overruns is a measure of extreme events. All these factors can be described by probability distributions.

Bernoulli's example that illustrated the adage of not devoting all goods to one ship is a discrete distribution; that is, it considers multiple distinct outcomes. When risk is measured, there is a wide range of outcomes to consider. The score of a football game is a discrete measure, so forecasting it would require a discrete distribution. Modeling the outcome of the weather as cloudy or sunny is discrete since it must be one of these two choices.

On the other hand, the amount I spend at the grocery store on any given trip could range from $2.50 (the cost of my favorite protein bar) to more than $100. While such an outcome is technically discrete since I can't spend less than one cent, using a discrete distribution to model such outcomes would require 100 choices for each dollar range, or 10,000 choices over a $100 range. This is more complicated than necessary. A better way to model this phenomenon is with a continuous distribution. This allows a range of values that encompass all the numbers between the low and the high. If these are all equally likely, then the distribution is called a uniform distribution. This is the simplest type of continuous probability distribution. The only parameters are the lower and upper bounds. The idea of the uniform distribution arose in the eighteenth century from "games of chance," a polite way to say "gambling."[31] An example of a uniform distribution is that you expect your end-of-year bonus at work to be between $1,000 and $5,000, but you have no idea which values are more likely than others.

The Triangular Distribution

A slightly more sophisticated distribution than the uniform would be to combine a fixed range with a most likely value. A continuous distribution that is defined by low, most likely, and maximum values is a triangular distribution. See Figure 3.4 for a graph of the probability density function of a triangular distribution.

The triangular distribution is best used for risks that have hard, absolute bounds. This typically applies to programmatic aspects that have limited amounts of risk, such as number of employees. The number of civil servants typically does not change rapidly over limited time periods, so representing such risk with a triangular distribution may be realistic for modeling that. Two advantages of the distribution are that it is simple, and it is easy to use with expert opinion. It

Figure 3.4   Triangular Distribution

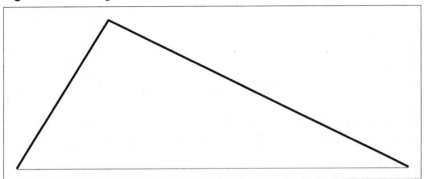

frequently occurs in practice that you need to assess uncertainty for some phenomenon for which you do not have any historical data on which to base your assessment. In such cases, expert advice can be a useful method of last resort. Soliciting an uncertainty distribution can be tricky. With a wide range of values, it can be hard for anyone to accurately assess which values are likelier than others. With a triangular distribution you only need three inputs—a lower bound, an upper bound, and a most likely value. The triangular distribution can be skewed or symmetric. Due to its hard bounds, it has no tails. Unless the bounds are extremely wide, it will only capture limited variation. This is a disadvantage for the triangular distribution as it only applies to situations where what is modeled cannot be lower or higher than a specific amount. Since with this distribution cost or schedule cannot be lower or higher than a specified amount, this distribution should be used with caution in risk analysis, and only where appropriate. In many situations this is not realistic, particularly in the development and production of the major components. For projects already in development, it may make sense that the final cost will not be lower than the contracted amount (although if the contract is canceled, it may well be less than the agreed-upon value). However, as we demonstrated in previous chapters, cost and schedule growth have proven to be endemic phenomena for projects. With few exceptions, the use of triangular distributions will underestimate risk.

The Gaussian Distribution

Another type of continuous distribution that arose from gambling is the most widely used in statistics. Even though it is more complex than the triangular distribution, it was developed two decades earlier than the triangular. This distribution is so commonly used in statistics that it is called the normal distribution. Another name for it is the Gaussian distribution, after the nineteenth-century mathematician Carl Gauss. However, it was first mentioned in a published work in 1733, in the gambler/mathematician Abraham de Moivre's book *The Doctrine of Chances*. Carl Gauss used de Moivre's invention in the study of errors of astronomical observations in the early nineteenth century and developed a formula for it.[32] We will refer to this distribution as the Gaussian rather than the normal because, as we shall see, the normal distribution is anything but normal when it comes to resource risk. The Gaussian distribution is often referred to as a "bell curve" because the graph of its probability density function resembles a bell. See Figure 3.5 for a graphical example of a Gaussian distribution.

Anyone who has taken statistics in college has encountered this distribution. When teachers "grade on a curve," the Gaussian distribution is often used. Contrary to popular opinion, grading on a curve may not always lead to an increase in a grade. If all the grades tend toward the high side, grading on a curve will reduce some of the grades. The idea behind grading on the curve is that the average student is a "C" student. If an "A" is a grade above 90 on a 100-point scale and all the scores in the class are above 90, the scores will be reduced so that the average is a "C."

Figure 3.5   Gaussian Distribution: The Bell Curve

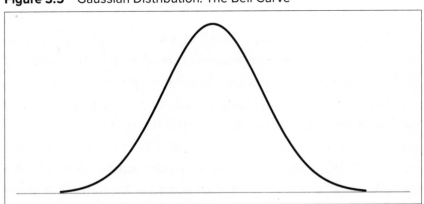

The Gaussian distribution has a wide variety of applications. It represents variations in heights, weights, and life spans of humans; incomes for certain professions, such as dentists and civil servants; damage from car accidents; and IQ. One of the convenient features of the Gaussian distribution is that it has two parameters—a mean and a variance. The Gaussian distribution is symmetric, so the median and mode are both equal to the mean for this distribution. Since it is symmetric, the distribution has no skew. The Gaussian distribution allows for a limited amount of variation—it has thin tails. The Gaussian distribution is a good way to measure random phenomena that have limited fluctuations.

Why Are There No People Who Are Nine Feet Tall?

Height is a good example of narrow variation. Ninety percent of US adults are between 5 feet, 0 inches and 6 feet, 1 inch tall. However, some extremes occur outside these ranges. For example, Verne Troyer, who played Mini-Me in the Austin Powers movies, was 2 feet, 8 inches, and Manute Bol, the tallest NBA basketball player, was 7 feet, 7 inches. These extremes are rare.[33] The tallest person on record is Robert Wadlow, who at his peak height, measured 8 feet, 11.1 inches.[34]

Why are there no nine feet tall people? As height increases, so does girth. Weight is proportional to height times the square of girth. At some point, the stress placed on thigh bones, feet, and so on, requires a significant change in anatomy to accommodate the increase in weight. Wadlow, for example, weighed over 400 pounds despite being thin, wore a size 37 shoe, and had to wear braces when he walked. His feet and legs were largely numb.[35] Animals that are taller or longer than nine feet include whales, elephants, and giraffes. Whales don't have the same stresses as humans because they live in water. Elephants and giraffes support themselves with four legs instead of two. Elephants have extremely thick legs, and giraffes have unique anatomical features that allow them to support their height, including extremely thick and strong ligaments in their legs.[36]

The Normal Distribution Is Not Normal

The problem with the Gaussian distribution is that it has been overused. It has been applied to phenomena that do not fit a Gaussian distribution well. First, the events that follow a Gaussian distribution vary within an order of magnitude, not across several magnitudes. For example, the height for adult humans varies over a small range, from around two feet to approximately nine feet, a factor of less than five. However there many phenomena that exhibit much wider variation.

A second issue is that cost and schedule growth are skewed. This cannot be modeled by a symmetric distribution like the Gaussian, which with its bell shape is symmetric. If cost risk were modeled as a Gaussian and the characteristics were consistent with the cost growth data, there would be a small chance, about 2% for some, that the project cost would be zero or negative. This is impossible.

A third issue with the Gaussian distribution in its application to cost and schedule risk analysis is the limited amount of variation it can model. If cost and schedule risk were modeled as a Gaussian, the chance of cost or schedule increasing by a factor of three would almost never happen. While less common than doubling, the chances of tripling are not negligible—about 5% for cost and 2% for schedule for some types of endeavors. This problem is not limited to cost and schedule risk.

For a Gaussian distribution, any variation greater than k standard deviations from the mean is called a k-standard deviation event. See Table 3.2 for a list of k–standard deviation events and their probabilities for a Gaussian distribution. For a Gaussian, these percentages are the same regardless of the specific values for the means and standard deviations.

Table 3.2   Probability of K–Standard Deviation Events in a Gaussian Distribution

K	Probability
1	1 in 3
2	1 in 20
3	1 in 300
4	1 in 16,000
5	1 in 1.8 million
6	1 in 500 million
7	1 in 400 billion
8	1 in 751 trillion

As can be seen from Table 3.2, a two-standard deviation event has a probability equal to 1 in 20, which is 5%. As the Gaussian is symmetric, the probability of an event that is two standard deviations above the mean is half that, or about 2.5%. The probability of events outside those bounds falls dramatically after that—99.7%

are within three standard deviations. That is, there is a 3 in 1,000 chance of an event more than three standard deviations from the mean. A six–standard deviation event has a probability of less than 1 in 500 million.

The US stock market crash in 1987 was a 22–standard deviation event. For a Gaussian distribution, the chance of occurrence is so low that it should never have occurred—it is on the order of 1 in 10^{50}, which is the number 1 followed by 50 zeroes. The problem to some extent is reflected in the adage "when all you have is a hammer, everything looks like a nail." For a long time, there was no tool kit to move beyond the Gaussian distribution.

There is a parallel here with geometry (pun intended). The foundation of Euclidean geometry is a set of five postulates. Four of these are not controversial, but the fifth one is problematic. This is the parallel postulate, which states that only one line can be drawn through a given point so that the line is parallel to a given line that does not contain that point. For two thousand years mathematicians had wondered about this. It seemed somewhat out of place. Mathematicians tried again and again to derive the parallel postulate from the others. The eventual solution that arose in the nineteenth century was to develop geometries independent of, and that contradicted, the parallel postulate.[37] Similarly, the contemporary mathematician Benoit Mandelbrot, building upon and synthesizing the work of many disparate predecessors, discovered that nature often does not act in accordance with the methods for measuring randomness developed in the eighteenth and nineteenth centuries, like the Gaussian.[38] Just as the Euclidean space model of nature is too simple, Mandelbrot discovered that numerous natural and man-made phenomena are subject to random behavior that does not follow the statistical distributions commonly taught in elementary statistics courses, including the Gaussian distribution.

Benoit Mandelbrot was a true maverick of science. Mandelbrot was much more interested in empirical reality than many mathematicians and scientists, who are devoted to theory. The subject of his PhD dissertation was a pair of related topics that he came up with on his own, without the supervision of an advisor. One of these topics was based on a review of a book by the linguist George Zipf about the distribution of word frequencies.[39] In English, the word *the* is the most commonly encountered word. It accounts for about 7% of the total words in printed text. The second most common word is *of*, which accounts for 3.5% of the total, and third is the word *and*. Zipf's law states that the relative frequency of a word is proportional to the inverse of its rank. The most common word has a ranking of 1. The second-most-common word has a ranking equal to 2, and so it should appear half as often as the top-ranking word. Notice that the 3.5% frequency of the word *of* is half that of the word *the*. Mandelbrot found that this property extended to numerous other phenomena as well. Phenomena that exhibit self-similarity do not follow Gaussian distributions. Instead they follow power laws. Zipf's law of word frequencies is an example of a power law.

The types of phenomena that scale according to self-similar patterns like Zipf's law exhibit much wilder swings around the central tendency than the Gaussian distribution. The scale of these wildly varying distribution vary by multiple orders of magnitude. Nassim Taleb, author of *The Black Swan*, refers to phenomena that follow a Gaussian distribution as belonging to "Mediocristan," which means that these phenomena don't vary much around the average. An alternative to Mediocristan is what Taleb terms "Extremistan," where there is extreme variation around the average. Many phenomena fit in this category. Fluctuations in the stock market are a prime example, as is economic loss due to hurricanes (just think of the damage done by Hurricanes Harvey, Irma, and Maria in 2017). Income and net worth also belong to this category—consider Bill Gates's net worth compared to your own. Book sales per author, populations of cities, and word usage in a vocabulary also belong in this category.[40]

The Pareto Distribution

Phenomena from Extremistan can be modeled with heavy-tailed, or what are sometimes called fat-tailed, distributions. Heavy-tailed distributions can have nonfinite moments. That is, the standard deviation, and possibly the mean, diverge to infinity. An important property of these kinds of distributions is that they often have tail behavior proportional to a power law. A Pareto distribution has a right tail that follows a power law, making it a prominent example of a heavy-tailed distribution. Vilfredo Pareto, a nineteenth-century Italian economist, noticed that 80% of the land in Italy was owned by 20% of the population. The management guru Joseph Juran noticed that this observation was broadly applicable to the world of business. He called it the Pareto principle, which is also known as the 80/20 rule.[41] As a manager, I have noticed time and again that the top 20% of the employees seemed to do 80% of the work, while the bottom 20% of employees caused 80% of the problems.

The Pareto principle is a power-law property. The right tail of a Pareto distribution follows a power law. For example, the contribution of individual cinematic films to overall profitability exhibits a power law. A mere 5% of total films released earn 80% of the profits. More than 75% of films do not break even.[42] Compare how much money a film like *Avatar* has made worldwide compared to the average (mean) film, which loses money. *Avatar*, a 2009 science fiction film directed by James Cameron, has grossed approximately $2.8 billion worldwide, more than any other film in history. The returns from motion pictures follow an infinite-mean and infinite-variance Pareto distribution.

Another example of a scaling phenomenon is the distribution of household wealth data. According to US government data, median household wealth in the US in 2016 was $97,226. Eighty percent of households had wealth equal to $500,000 or less. If a Gaussian distribution is used to model wealth distribution, these two figures imply a standard deviation equal to $478,000. A billionaire would be a 2,100–standard deviation event. This should mean that there would be no billionaires in the United States. While not common, there were 540 US billionaires in 2016, out of a total of more than 126 million households, one in every 233,000.

Instead of providing a graph of a Pareto distribution, we will instead show its tail behavior, which is what distinguishes a Pareto from the other distributions discussed in this chapter. To discuss the Pareto distribution, we first need to discuss the concept of logarithms. Logarithms are an important class of transformations. They replace the scale 1,2,3, . . . with one that adds an increasing number of 0s: 1,10,100, ... A regular linear scale moves up one at a time, while logarithms jump by powers of 10. On a linear scale, the distance between 1 and 2 is the same as the distance between 2 and 3. On a logarithmic scale, the distance between 1 and 10 is the same as the distance between 10 and 100. See Figure 3.6 for a comparison. This transformation provides a means of visualizing data that ranges over several orders of magnitude.

Figure 3.6 Linear vs. Logarithmic Scales

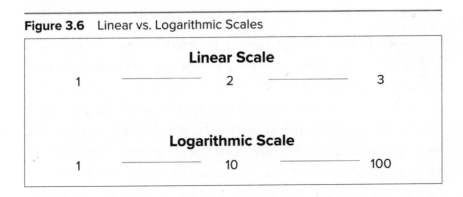

The right tail of a Pareto distribution has the property that when graphed on a logarithmic scale, it appears linear. For example, consider adjusted gross income data in the United States. For 2016, there were more than 150 million tax returns filed in the United States. The data reported by the IRS contains incomes ranging from $0 to $10 million. Two million people report no adjusted gross income at all for that year, while 16,000 people earned more than $10 million. Figure 3.7 plots the percentage of those who exceed a given income.

Figure 3.7 Pareto Distribution Fit to Right Tail of US Income Data

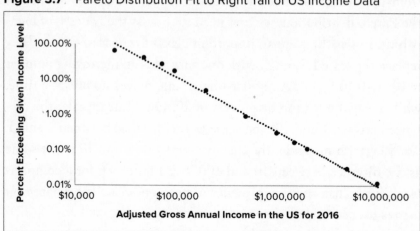

Approximately 17% of returns reported incomes greater than $100,000 in 2016. Only about 0.3% of people reported an income equal to or more than $1 million that year. An even smaller number, 0.01%, reported incomes that exceeded $10 million. That is, one in 10,000 income tax filers had income greater than $10 million. The number decreases significantly as incomes increase to higher levels. However, it does not decline as dramatically in the upper income regions as a Gaussian distribution. The data closely fits a power law, as indicated by the trend line that appears linear when plotted on a logarithmic scale. A Gaussian distribution would indicate that no one would make more than $2 million. The "normal" in this case is clearly not normal.

The Lognormal Distribution

While cost and schedule risk do not fit a Gaussian distribution well, it is often not heavy-tailed enough to model as a Pareto distribution either. Events like hurricanes, which cannot be controlled, exhibit wild variation. While projects can be chaotic, managers can exert control when problems arise, mitigating risk. If necessary, they can cut scope to reduce cost and schedule growth. Their management can cancel a project if things get too out of hand. A compromise between the thin tails of the Gaussian distribution and the heavy tails of the Pareto is the lognormal distribution. Lognormal distributions derive their name from the fact that a random variable follows a lognormal distribution if and only if the logarithm of the random variable is normally distributed. The logarithmic scaling changes the distribution shape. See Figure 3.8 for an example of a graph of the probability density function of a lognormal distribution. The Gaussian distribution is unbounded. The lognormal distribution is bounded below by zero but unbounded above. This quality makes the lognormal appealing for use in cost and schedule analysis. The lognormal distribution is skewed, with a heavier right tail than the Gaussian distribution. However, the right tail of a lognormal distribution is not as heavy as a scale-invariant distribution, such as a Pareto. You can think of a Gaussian as a solid, which has little movement. The Pareto is like a liquid, which can swish around wildly. The lognormal is like Jell-O, relatively solid but with more movement than the Gaussian.

A variety of phenomena have been shown to follow a lognormal distribution. Examples include the length of chess games, the coefficient of friction and wear on mechanical parts, random obstruction of radio signals due to large buildings and hills, and the time to repair a maintainable system. Many natural growth phenomena are driven by the accumulation of small percentage changes. The lognormal distribution arises often in cost estimating. I have found

Figure 3.8   Lognormal Distribution

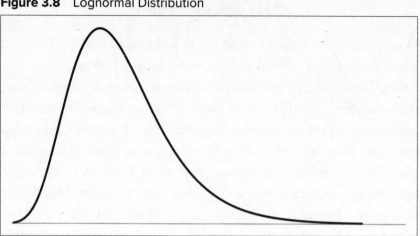

that the lognormal tends to fit most cost and schedule growth data. *The Joint Agency Cost Schedule Risk and Uncertainty Handbook*, which was endorsed by the cost leadership of the Army, Navy, Air Force, Marines, Missile Defense Agency, and NASA, recommends the lognormal as a default. It suggests the use of the lognormal unless you are convinced another choice is better.[43]

THE PROBLEM WITH MOST LIKELY ESTIMATES: AGGREGATING RISK CORRECTLY

We next illustrate the importance of risk analysis by an example. The key idea is that point estimates of cost that do not incorporate risk will show a total cost that is well below the expected value. It will be less than all three measures of centrality we discussed earlier—the mode, median, and mean. Cost estimates are typically the sum of several lower-level cost estimates. Developing an estimate with the most likely inputs will not result in an output that is at the most likely cost. Rather, it will be less than the most likely cost, for two reasons. One is that risks are skewed. More can go wrong than can go right. More risks for cost overruns exist than opportunities for cost savings. In such a case the most likely value, or mode, is less than the median, and the median is less than the mean—the log-normal is an example of a distribution that is always skewed to the right. See Figure 3.9 for an example of a comparison of the mean, median, and mode for a right-skewed distribution. Second, risks are correlated, but ignoring it overlooks this issue altogether.

Figure 3.9   Mode (A), Median (B), and Mean (C) for a Right-Skewed Distribution

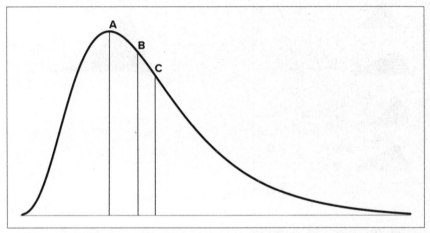

Uncertainty is rarely applied at the system level. Rather, for a project it is often applied to several lower-level elements. These are organized into a product-oriented Work Breakdown Structure (WBS). The cost estimates for these WBS elements are added to obtain a total system cost. Risk is assessed at these lower levels as well, so it must be aggregated to estimate the cost risk for the total system. See Figure 3.10 for a graphical notional example. However, there is no formula for adding probability distributions. The mathematics of combining probability distributions gets extremely complicated quickly as there is no nice, easy formula for accomplishing this task.

Figure 3.10   Total Cost Risk Is the Sum of the Risks for Many
                    Individual Components

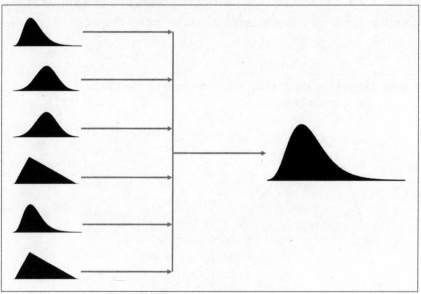

As an example, suppose that we have six cost elements, as in Figure 3.10, with a variety of distributions as in the graph—four lognormal and two triangular distributions. We assume that all these elements are funded at their most likely values, which is the peak of the distribution. Statisticians call this the mode. These six estimates are $90 million, $50 million, $20 million, $40 million, $70 million, and $30 million. The sum of these six numbers is $300 million, which is where the project is funded. How does this total funding compare to the aggregate cost risk for the system? In order to estimate this, we must turn to simulation, which requires the use of a computer.

When People Were Computers: The History of Simulation

For most of human history, calculation was a laborious task. Until recently, a "computer" was someone who worked detailed calculations by hand. Only with the advent of the computing age has complex calculation become efficient. Doing rote calculations was the lowest rung job in science, below that of mathematicians, engineers, and physicists. For many women, especially minority women, it was one of the few technical jobs available to them for much of the twentieth century. The era of modern computing began during World War II with the ENIAC (short for Electronic Numerical Integrator and Computer). When the war began, there were hundreds of women employed as computers. These human computers developed tables to help soldiers in the field to aim artillery. NASA also used human computers in the early days of the space race.

Monte Carlo simulation is a computationally intensive technique that arose during the development of nuclear weapons at the end of World War II. The physics and the mathematics necessary to develop the atomic bomb were extremely complex. Some of the leading minds in physics and mathematics were working on the project. Even these brilliant people found that calculating the formulas for the interaction of subatomic particles was intractable. However, the interactions can be accurately estimated with a simulation. Stanislaw Ulam, a mathematician working on the development of the atomic bomb, developed the idea of simulating these complex interactions using an electronic computer. The notion of sampling had existed before but was difficult to do prior to the advent of modern (nonhuman) computers. Ulam, while recovering from an illness, was thinking about how to calculate the probability of a type of hand in solitaire. He decided it would be easier with statistical sampling. Rather than listing all the possible outcomes of hand types, Ulam had the idea of conducting an experiment that

would generate a series of hands at random. For many random outcomes, the hands that had the desired property could be calculated
as a percentage of the total number of hands generated by repeated
sampling. Ulam then realized that this technique could be applied
to his nuclear weapons work. The Manhattan Project had access to
electronic computers. Their use made random sampling techniques
feasible. This early application of what is now called computer simulation helped the Manhattan Project finish the development of
the first nuclear weapons. The term "Monte Carlo" was inspired by
an uncle of Ulam's who would borrow money from relatives to go
gambling in Monte Carlo, Monaco.

Monte Carlo methods were applied to cost risk analysis as far
back as the 1960s.[44] Simulation techniques like these are necessary
for cost and schedule risk analysis because probability distributions
cannot be added.[45] Even if we know where every single point estimate is located for all elements in the cost estimate, that does not tell
us anything about where the sum of the point estimate lies on the
total, aggregate probability distribution of cost risk. Monte Carlo
simulation for the cost risk analysis example involves a repeated
set of trials. Each trial involves taking a random value from each
probability distribution and then adding the results. This is repeated
several thousand times. The result of these simulations is a type of
empirical probability distribution called a histogram. For the example in Figure 3.10, we ran 5,000 trials of our simulation. The results
of a cost risk analysis are typically presented as an "S-curve," so
named because of the way the graphic typically is displayed. An
example is shown in Figure 3.11. This is a useful format for commu-
nicating the result of cost risk analysis because it is easy to represent
visually. An S-curve matches up two numbers, a probability and a
cost. The vertical axis is the cumulative probability, and the horizontal axis is the cost. For a given cost, the cumulative probability
associated with that is the probability that the actual cost will be
less than or equal to that amount. The points on the curve can be

represented by ordered pairs (x, y), where x is a cost and y is a cumulative probability. The S-curve is not a prediction of an exact cost. Instead, it provides the probability that the cost will be less than or equal to a specified amount. For example, the cost and probability pair ($120 million, 80%) means that there is an 80% chance that the actual cost will be less than or equal to $120 million. If we were to develop this exact same project 100 times, we would expect that 80 of those times, the cost would be less than or equal to $120 million, and 20 of those times, the cost would be more than $120 million.

In cost and schedule estimation, the cumulative probability values on an S-curve are often referred to as "confidence levels." For those readers familiar with probability, this may be confusing because "confidence levels" is not a standard statistical term—they are not the same thing as "confidence intervals." In cost and schedule estimating terminology, an 80% confidence level is the same as the 80th percentile of the probability distribution. We will use the terms "confidence level" and "percentile" interchangeably throughout the book.

Figure 3.11   Risk Depicted as an S-Curve

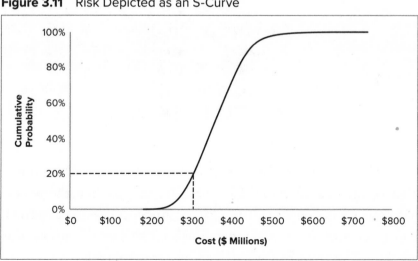

The values along the vertical axis represent probabilities—matching it up to the curve, as with the dotted line in Figure 3.11, this can then be paired with a cost along the horizontal axis. So, for example, as can be seen from the graph, there is slightly less than a 20% chance that the cost will be less than or equal to $300 million. The S-curve shows that less than 20% of the time, the program is sufficiently funded. Actual cost will exceed the initial estimate more than 80% of the time. In the simulation, the most likely cost is $357 million, which is $57 million above the sum of the most likely values. Even funding each element to its most likely cost is no guarantee that the overall program will be funded at its most likely value.[46] Key percentiles included in an S-curve are typically displayed in a table, as in Table 3.3.

Table 3.3   Cumulative Cost Probabilities for Key Percentiles

Cumulative Probability	Cost $ Millions
10%	$285
20%	$309
30%	$327
40%	$344
50%	$360
60%	$375
70%	$394
80%	$416
90%	$448

In Table 3.3, the 80% cumulative probability is $416 million. That is significantly more than the $300 million that the project has received in funding. If the 80% confidence level is exceeded, how much greater can cost grow? The S-curve does not answer this question. This is an issue we will address in Chapter 6.

Aggregation of schedule uncertainty is like the process used for cost, but there is a key difference. Total cost is the sum of the cost of numerous WBS elements. Recall from Figure 3.3 that schedule is more complicated. It typically involves both serial and parallel tasks. The serial tasks can be summed like those in a cost WBS, but the parallel activities cannot. For parallel activities, the total duration is the maximum over the set of durations of each individual activity. If one takes 9 months to complete and the other 10 months, the total duration is 10 months. However, the uncertainty in the schedule network can be simulated using Monte Carlo simulation, as with cost, to calculate total schedule uncertainty.

Simulation Outputs, Cost Growth Data, and Probability Distributions

Although with a variety of inputs and distributions, you might not expect for the results of simulations to closely match a continuous distribution, such as a lognormal or Gaussian distribution. However, I have found that the lognormal is a good fit for the outputs of simulations for cost and schedule risk analysis. For example, see Figure 3.12.

Figure 3.12   Lognormal Fit to a Risk Simulation Output

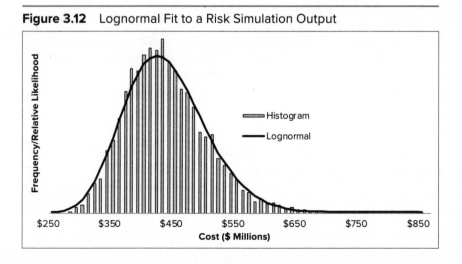

The lognormal provides a close fit to the output of the simulation. I believe this is because cost and schedule growth data fit
a lognormal distribution closely. This is based on my experience
and one of the leading textbooks on the subject of quantitative
uncertainty analysis for projects.[47] Cost and schedule growth data
each closely fit a lognormal distribution. However, the Gaussian
is a poor fit for both cost and schedule growth data. See Figure
3.13 for a comparison of fitting the Gaussian and lognormal to cost
growth data.

Figure 3.13   Lognormal and Gaussian Fit to Historical Cost Growth Data

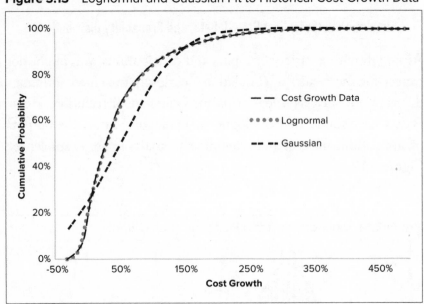

The lognormal provides a similar fit for schedule growth data.
See Figure 3.14 for schedule growth.

Figure 3.14 Lognormal and Gaussian Fit to Historical Schedule Growth Data

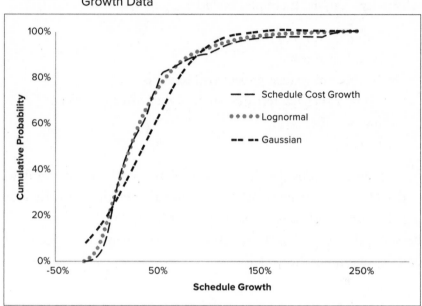

For much of the analysis in the remainder of this book, we will discuss Gaussian, lognormal, and Pareto distributions. We use the lognormal because there is plentiful evidence that the lognormal distribution represents project risk well. In some instances, there is evidence for the Pareto. We discuss the Gaussian as a counterpoint and to point out its many shortcomings in modeling cost and schedule risk.

SENSITIVITY ANALYSIS

An important consideration when conducting risk analysis is to analyze the drivers of risk to see how the effect of the variation in the Work Breakdown Structure cost elements and the schedule activities influence cost and schedule. This can help determine key risk drivers that the project manager can influence. This is called a sensitivity analysis. Examples include:

- Software lines of code
- Number of tests
- Number of years a project will operate
- Technical characteristics, such as the thrust of a motor
- Labor rates
- Inflation

Figure 3.15 provides an example of the influence of the days underway for a marine vessel on the annual operating cost. Reducing the number of days at sea drops cost dramatically down to 240 days and then shows little reduction. This is largely due to the fixed costs of operating the vessel.

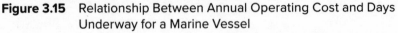

Figure 3.15   Relationship Between Annual Operating Cost and Days Underway for a Marine Vessel

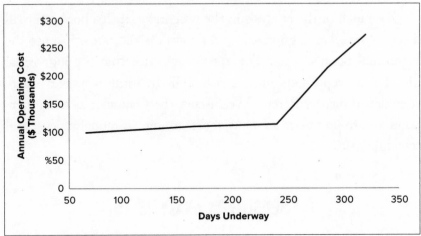

The results of sensitivity analyses can be plotted on a project's S-curve to make risk tangible. For example, suppose that the cost impact of the event that the number of lines of code in a software project doubles is at the 60% confidence level on an S-curve. This gives the project manager a way to think about what could happen to a project that would cause the cost to increase to that level. The amount of resources needed to cover a bad event that a project manager would like to have funds to guard against is important to understand. More of a scenario than a true sensitivity analysis, this might require adjusting multiple inputs and estimating cost and schedule for those inputs. As an example, suppose one scenario that a project manager would like to guard against would be the number of system tests increases from three to six; number of software lines of code doubles; and the development schedule is delayed by two years. This can be plotted on the project's cost S-curve as illustrated in Figure 3.16.

Figure 3.16   Risk Scenario on a Project's S-Curve

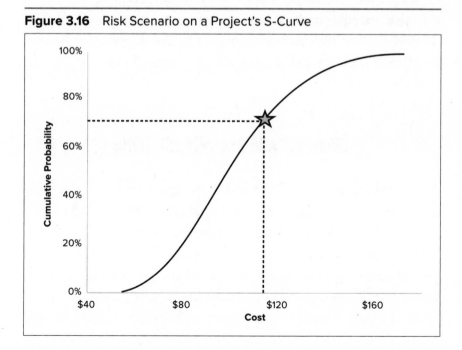

This particular scenario is at the 70% confidence level. This provides a project manager with a tangible sense of what the requirements would be that would result in an estimate that high. It also provides a sense of the level of risk for the project. Even if the project has funds to guard against this scenario, there is still a 30% chance that the project's cost will grow beyond that amount. At a minimum, if a project is not willing or able to conduct a quantitative risk analysis of cost and schedule, it should conduct a scenario analysis: figure out what scenarios it wants to guard against, determine how much more they will cost and how much longer they will take, and provide cost and schedule reserves to those levels.[48]

TECHNICAL REFERENCES

The intent of this book is not to provide detailed methods for calculating cost risk analyses. For more details on how to implement cost risk analysis methods, the reader should seek out *Probability Methods for Cost Uncertainty Analysis: A Systems Engineering Perspective*.[49] For schedule risk analysis, I recommend *Practical Schedule Risk Analysis*.[50]

SUMMARY AND RECOMMENDATIONS

The systematic growth of cost and schedule for all types of projects demonstrates their high degree of risk. This growth is caused by risks that have been realized. Risk is represented by probability distributions. Probability distributions have four characteristics: a measure of central tendency, a measure of the spread around that, the skewness of the distribution, and the heaviness of the tails (chance of occurrence of extreme events). A triangular distribution is a simple type of distribution. The most commonly used probability distribution in statistics is often referred to as the normal distribution. This distribution is good for measuring phenomena that fluctuate over narrow ranges—such as the variation in the heights of human adults. Many other phenomena, such as damages from natural disasters and box office returns for films, exhibit much wilder variation. The normal, it turns out, is not so normal. We instead refer to the normal by an alternative name, Gaussian, after the nineteenth-century mathematician who developed a mathematical equation for this type of distribution. Phenomena that exhibit wilder variation often follow a power law in the right tail. The right tail is where the significant risks occur and are far from the center of the distribution. They are beyond the range where the lowest 80% of the cost lies. Cost and schedule risk tend to fall between the extremes of wild and mild variation. The lognormal is a compromise between the mild variation of the Gaussian and the wild variation of the power law distributions. I have found that the lognormal fits cost and schedule growth data well, indicating it is a reasonable distribution to use in quantifying risk.

Cost and schedule estimators typically estimate at a level below the total system level. The costs of these various elements are summed to yield the total system cost. A schedule network is used to aggregate the individual activities to yield a total schedule. A common practice in the past for cost was to estimate these costs at their most likely value and then sum the most likely values. The belief was that the sum of these most likely values was in fact the most likely value of the total system cost. We provided an example that showed that this is not the case. The sum of the most likely values is typically far below the most likely value of the total system cost. This occurs for a variety of reasons, including that cost risk is typically skewed to the right. More can go wrong than can go right, so risks heavily outweigh opportunities for savings. This shows the probabilities cannot be added—the aggregation of risk often requires the use of computer simulation. The results of cost and schedule risk are often displayed as an S-curve, or cumulative probability distribution. This has a visual representation that is easy to communicate to decision makers. However, as we will see in later chapters, it does not answer critical questions that must be addressed to facilitate risk management.

The examples we provide in the chapter show that cost and schedule risk analysis is an imperative. Risk analysis is not an optional exercise or something that is just nice to have. Riskless point estimates of cost significantly underpredict actual cost. Quantitative risk analysis of resources, both time and money, provides critical information needed for decision makers by providing an assessment of the probability of achieving proposed budgets and schedules. Risk analysis can be used to assess payoffs for implementing risk reduction initiatives, providing both cost and benefit information. In addition to risk analysis, projects should also conduct a sensitivity analysis to determine the impact of assumptions and technical inputs on cost and schedule. When paired with a quantitative risk analysis, the sensitivity values can provide decision makers an idea of what confidence levels represent in terms of tangible impacts to their projects.

CHAPTER 4

Covered with Oil

Incorporating Realism in Cost and Schedule Risk Analysis

Jimmy Buffett's most popular song is "Margaritaville." The easy-listening rock hit has spawned a variety of merchandise, including a restaurant chain. The 1977 song is set in a tropical climate. One of the lines in the song's lyrics refers to beachgoers covered in tanning oil. Jimmy Buffett probably never imagined that this could apply to crude oil instead. However, the 2010 oil spill in the Gulf of Mexico resulted in oily beaches on the US Gulf Coast. Both the cost and environmental impacts were much worse than anyone had predicted. It was the biggest oil spill ever. The leak wasted more than five million barrels of oil and was an environmental disaster.[1] This natural disaster is an example of a black swan event. Not planning for some events such as this one outside of a project's control is reasonable. But project managers have some control over their destiny. They can meet budget, schedule, and scope by cutting content. In the cases of extreme overruns, senior leaders can cancel projects. However, budgets for projects typically include little risk reserves. Most risk analyses do not account for minimal changes in a project's design or relatively mild external forces that should be part of the initial plan.

TYPES OF RISK

Previous chapters discussed two broad categories of cost and schedule growth—internal and external. These are also sources of risk. Another factor is estimating uncertainty, which accounts for two different phenomena. One is that not all program characteristics are known with certainty when estimating. These change significantly from the start of a program to its completion. The other is that even for past data, no model can accurately predict cost or schedule with 100% accuracy. This is true even if program characteristics do not change. Risk analyses typically cover some of these risks. Those typically excluded are black swan events such as the Gulf Oil spill, and good reasons exist to leave out the most extreme events. Risk analysis is intended to provide decision makers with information to help them successfully manage projects. Inclusion of some extreme events with large impacts will not aid decision makers in managing their projects. Thus, exclusion of some risks is advisable. However, over the course of a major development, it is likely that some of these external factors may impact costs across an organization.

Donald Rumsfeld, Secretary of Defense under Presidents Gerald Ford and George W. Bush once stated, "As we know, there are known knowns; there are things we know. We know also there are known unknowns; that is to say, we know there are some things we do not know. But there are also unknown unknowns—the ones we don't know we don't know."[2] The "unknown unknowns" have the biggest impact on projects. They may not be likely to occur, but they have outsized consequences. For a test event, a known known could be a three-day schedule slip. These happen regularly for large test events and are usually incorporated in project plans. A known unknown is a test failure. They are known to happen, but no one knows when they will occur. Cost and schedule reserves are typically not set aside for these events. Numerous project managers have told me that they do not plan for failure, which is a common excuse to avoid planning for or acknowledging risk.[3] I worked on one program that had a test failure that led to a complete re-test. This doubled the total cost of the test event. The impact was an extra $100 million and a one-year delay in the schedule for completing development tests. The unwillingness to plan for risks is also common in infrastructure projects and has even been given a title—the "Everything Goes According to Plan" principle.[4] An unknown unknown could be a hurricane in the Pacific that wipes out the test range infrastructure. This would cause significant cost impacts and long delays in test schedules.

While it is good to exclude some risks, cost and schedule estimates tend to exclude factors that should be incorporated in risk analysis. This includes most estimating uncertainty. For example, the greater uncertainty inherent when estimates are based on small data sets is not considered. The extent to which requirements will change is underestimated. The uncertainty inherent in the degree of heritage from previous, similar programs that can be relied upon is not considered. The amount of technology development that will need to be conducted is taken too lightly. As a result, early project plans sometimes have more in common with science fiction than science fact. For example, one satellite project several years ago maintained that it was developing an apogee kick motor for a project that would be a near carbon copy of a previous one, but the new motor would be twice the size as the close analogy. When looking at the final cost, it was easy to see that a relatively large amount of design cost was required. As mentioned in the discussion on cost and schedule growth, this inherent optimism seems to be common. This optimism reduces the estimate of cost and schedule. Also, it lowers the perceived amount of risk.

Project managers are not the only ones who do not understand risk. As a society, we are risk blind. "There is a blind spot: when we think of tomorrow we do not frame it in terms of what we thought about yesterday on the day before yesterday. Because of this introspective defect we fail to learn about the difference between our past predictions and the subsequent outcomes. When we think of tomorrow, we just project it as another yesterday."[5] Just as the cow who jumped over the moon didn't think about the risks of re-entering the atmosphere, so individuals tend to underestimate risk ranges.

I mentioned Hofstadter's Law in Chapter 1, which was "it always takes longer than you think, even taking into account Hofstadter's Law." As time is money, my cost corollary to Hofstadter's Law is: It always costs more than you think, even taking into account it will cost more than you think. A second, similar corollary regarding risk is: It is always riskier than you think, even taking into account that it is riskier than you think.

THE TRACK RECORD FOR RISK ANALYSIS

One of the ways to get better at something is to measure performance. By doing so, you can assess what you did right and what you did wrong. You can figure out your mistakes and learn from them. You can also see what you did right and learn to do that again. This feedback is critical for improving performance. Projects would have better risk analyses if the profession as a whole had been doing this on a systematic basis for the past 50 years. However, this is rarely done. These actions over the years are like throwing darts but never looking at the dartboard to see how close the darts are to the bull's-eye. Without looking at the results, it is impossible to determine if the methods used hit the bull's-eye or missed the dartboard entirely.

There is a small amount of data on performance of cost risk analysis and even less for schedule risk analysis. Not surprisingly, what is available indicates that risk analyses are far from realistic. For most analyses I have examined, the actual cost is above the 90% confidence level. If done right, a 90% confidence level should be exceeded by only one out of 10 projects. However, I have found the opposite to be true. A severe disconnect exists between risk analysis of cost and schedule and the actual cost and schedule. The statistician George Box famously remarked that "all models are wrong, but some are useful." He went on to further state "the approximate nature of the model must always be borne in mind."[6] As discussed in the previous chapter, single-best estimates are sure to be wrong. That is why risk analysis is needed—to cover the range of variation. The problem is that this variation is consistently underestimated. See Table 4.1 for data on 10 projects for which a quantitative cost risk analysis was conducted.

Table 4.1 Cost Growth and Ratio of Actual Cost to 90% Confidence Level for 10 Historical Projects

Project	Cost Growth	Ratio of Actual Cost to 90% Confidence Level
1	0%	0.6
2	19%	1.1
3	31%	1.0
4	32%	1.1
5	greater than 45%	greater than 1.0
6	52%	1.5
7	84%	1.7
8	93%	1.6
9	121%	2.0
10	280%	2.2

The projects in Table 4.1 are from a variety of applications.[7] I conducted cost and schedule risk analyses for two of the projects in the table, including the one at the top of the table. It was a relatively rare mission that did not experience cost growth. My estimate of the 50% confidence level was within 1% of the actual cost. The project also completed on time, in line with my 50% confidence level for schedule. This kind of outcome is the exception rather than the rule. As can be seen from the table, all the other missions experienced significant cost growth. Even so, 90% confidence levels should have been high enough to capture these variations. However, the actual cost was greater than the 90% confidence level for 8 of the 10. This dismal result is even worse than it appears. Two of the missions listed in the table were cancelled. If they had not been cancelled, the cost growth would have been higher. The fifth project in the table experienced such significant growth from one phase to the next that it exceeded the 90% confidence level well before completion. For 5 of the 10 missions, the actual cost was at least one and a half times the 90% confidence level, and for 2 it was double or more. The term "90% confidence level" for these analyses is grossly erroneous. If it were accurate, for 10 projects, the chance that 2 or fewer would be less than or equal to the 90% confidence level is one in 2.7 million.[8] For the tenth project, the one with the highest cost growth among those listed in the table, a schedule risk analysis was even worse than the cost risk analysis in capturing the actual variation. The actual schedule was 2.8 times greater than the 90% confidence level for the schedule analysis. The ugly truth is that for most projects, the actual cost and schedule will not even be on the S-curve.

Risk is underestimated for several reasons. One is the influence of optimism that we discussed earlier. Just as optimism causes the baseline cost to be too low and the schedule to be too short, it also causes risk ranges to be too tight. The use of distributions that do not have enough variation, such as the triangular and Gaussian distributions we discussed in the last chapter, is a second factor in underestimating risk. A third important cause is neglecting to incorporate correlation.

THE IMPORTANCE OF CORRELATION

The number of shark attacks and ice cream sales at a beach tend to move in tandem with one another. As shark attacks rise, so do ice cream sales. When shark attacks decrease, ice cream sales wane as well. This tendency is called correlation. That does not mean that one causes the other. An increase in ice cream sales does not cause shark attacks. Conversely, an increase in shark attacks does not cause ice cream sales to rise. Correlation is not the same as causation. The two tend to move together because they are driven by a common cause, which is the weather. As temperatures rise in the spring and summer, more people visit beaches. More people at a beach means there are more customers for ice cream and more potential shark attack victims too.

Correlation is a number between –1.0 and +1.0. When two events tend to move in the same direction—when one increases the other increases and when one decreases the other decreases— correlation is positive. When two events tend to move in opposite directions, correlation is negative. Positive correlation is much more common than negative correlation because of the common entropic forces acting on a project during its life cycle. Many of these have a common source, such as an economic downturn that stresses budgets for a multitude of projects, which in turn results in schedule slips as projects have less money in the near term.

Despite its importance, correlation is often ignored in both cost and schedule risk analysis. This is a major cause of underestimation of risk. Recall that probability distributions have a central tendency and a spread around this central tendency. The variation around the central tendency is typically measured with the standard deviation. As the standard deviation of total cost is a function of the standard deviations of the individual elements in the Work Breakdown Structure and the correlation between them, it is impossible to avoid making a choice about correlation. If you ignore it, you are assuming no correlation. Thus, an estimator who disregards correlation is making a choice about correlation—the wrong choice, since assuming no correlation will lead to underestimation of total aggregate risk.

If the elements have a functional relationship between them in a cost estimate, a functional correlation will automatically be incorporated in a simulation. For example, if the cost of project management is estimated as 10% of the total direct cost, the two are functionally correlated. A simulation will account for this. As total direct cost varies, so will project management cost. However, in most estimates at least some of the elements will not capture this. For these elements, correlation must be assigned. The number of correlations grows rapidly as a function of the number of elements. The correlation between an element and itself is 1.0. Correlation is also symmetric, so, for example, in a 100-element Work Breakdown Structure with no functional correlation present, there are $0.5 \times (100^2 -100) = 4{,}950$ correlations to assign. Because of the large number of correlations, a single value is typically used in practice. However, there is no single best value to use.

See Figure 4.1 for a graph that shows how much the total standard deviation will be underestimated when correlation is assumed to be zero between all elements. This graph is for 30 Work Breakdown Structure elements. For example, if the actual correlation is 20%, but it is assumed to be zero between all elements, then the total standard deviation will be underestimated by 60%. The amount of underestimation increases with the size of the Work Breakdown Structure.

Notice in Figure 4.1 that there is an apparent knee in the curve around 20%. Above 20% correlation, the consequence of assuming zero correlation begins to dwindle. This graph is the basis for assuming 20% to 30% for a rule of thumb.[9] However, the graph in Figure 4.2 does not tell us how much the risk is underestimated because correlation is assumed to be 20% but is really 60%. Thus, the widespread use of 20% correlation may not be enough. For example,

Figure 4.1   Impact of Correlation on Cost Risk

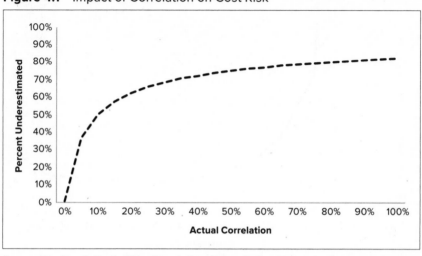

Source: Stephen A. Book, "Why Correlation Matters in Cost Estimating," presented at the 32nd Annual Department of Defense Cost Analysis Symposium, February 1999.

for a 100-element WBS, if the correlation is assumed to be 20% but instead is 60%, it turns out that the total standard deviation is significantly underestimated. The knee-in-the-curve approach still leads to significant underestimation of correlation. A more robust approach to assigning correlations would be to use the value that results in the least amount of error when you are wrong, which is likely to be the case. This approach is robust in the sense that without solid evidence to assign a correlation value, it minimizes the amount by which the total standard deviation is underestimated or overestimated due to the correlation assumption. Using this method, I have derived a recommended value in the absence of other information of 60%, much higher than the 20% knee in the curve.[10] See Figure 4.2.

The impact of correlation on schedule is similar to that for cost, but it is even more critical. Recall from the previous chapter that schedules are more complicated than cost because of parallel activities. Not including correlation for parallel activities underestimates the average completion time as well as the variation in cost. Ignoring correlation for schedule results in a low bias for schedule

Figure 4.2   Average Error for Assumed Correlation Value

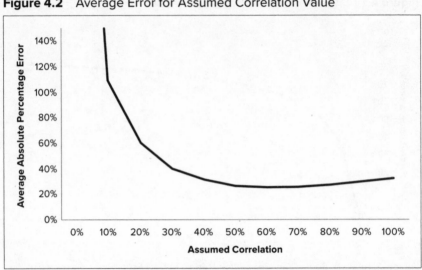

estimates. The guidance on correlation for schedule is like that for cost. All elements should include correlation. As a rule of thumb, without insight into the specific correlation between activities, a value of at least 60% should be used. Since a schedule network has a logical network of activities, there are ways to incorporate these dependencies directly without the assignment of a correlation value. One such method is the risk driver approach, which measures the uncertainty of discrete events that impact multiple schedule activities.[11] For example, in the shark attack and ice cream sales example, it would model the variation in the number of people who visit the beach, which would account for the correlation between these two seemingly disparate events.

Everything Goes Wrong at the Same Time!

Correlation alone is not sufficient to measure dependency among random variables. Correlation is simply a tendency for two elements to move together and is only one measure among many of random dependency. One issue with correlation is that it cannot model some aspects of risk that occur in the real world. Another source of the underestimation of risk is the lack of consideration of tail dependency. At times, the comovement between events may seem small. However, in bad times, the extreme variation seems to occur in tandem—"everything goes wrong at once." This concept is called tail dependency.

The failure to accurately model variation can have significant impacts. Correlation was widely used in the modeling of mortgage default risk in the early 2000s before the financial crisis that occurred in 2008. In a 2009 magazine article, use of correlation to measure dependency was cited as "the equation that killed Wall Street."[12] Financial markets and projects are both inherently risky. The lack of tail dependency in models leads to potential outcomes that do not make sense, such as a program that has a large schedule slip but no cost overrun. We know that, if the completion of a development program is delayed by several years, there will be significant cost growth. However, correlation does not account for this phenomenon. An overreliance on correlation can lead to underestimation of risk.

In the previous chapter, we discussed in detail four different probability distributions. These all modeled variation in one dimension—one project, one element, and so on. When modeling multiple programs or aspects of risk, we can use multivariate versions of these probability distributions. However, the commonly used multivariate distributions that we have discussed up to this point do not account for tail dependency. Methods exist to incorporate any type of dependency structure with any type of marginal distributions. These are called copulas, named after the Italian word for "couple."[13]

Standard practice is to assume that joint cost and schedule variation follows a combination of Gaussian and lognormal distributions, such as a bivariate Gaussian, bivariate lognormal, or bivariate Gaussian-lognormal. The assumption of this model form forces an exclusive reliance on correlation to measure dependency. Developing models that use assumptions that hinder our ability to accurately model risks is to ignore the possibility of extreme risks that happen on a relatively frequent basis. We should attempt to develop models that are as realistic as possible.

As an example, consider a program for which joint cost and schedule risk is modeled with a bivariate lognormal distribution. Suppose the cost mean is $100 million, the cost standard deviation is $25 million, the schedule mean is 72 months, and the schedule standard deviation is 12 months. The correlation between cost and schedule is assumed to be 60%. Figure 4.3 displays the results of 5,000 simulations from this distribution. Some strange pairs pop up, including mismatched pairs, such as one with a cost equal to $180 million and schedule equal to 60 months. This is the cost and schedule labeled B in the figure. At first glance, it appears that the schedule is shorter than average while the cost is higher than average. Indeed, the chance that the schedule does not overrun is 16%. Only about one in six times will the schedule turn out to be that short, while five out of six times it will be longer than that. On the other hand, the cost is significantly higher than average. In this case, the cost is far in the right tail—above the 99% confidence level. This represents a significant cost overrun that has a shorter than average schedule. In this case, there has been an extreme cost growth event but a much better than average schedule. This rarely happens.

As another example, another point on the cloud of simulation outcomes is cost equal to $101 million, while schedule is equal to 114 months. The schedule is much higher than average while the cost is only 1% higher than its average. This is the point labeled A in the figure. An extreme schedule slip has occurred, but the cost is about average. This is also extremely rare. Extreme cost and schedule events should occur together. A significant increase in schedule will increase cost as well, and extreme cost growth is typically accompanied by a big schedule increase. This is the result of the failure to incorporate tail dependency—correlation alone will not account for this.

Figure 4.3   Impact of Not Modeling Tail Dependency

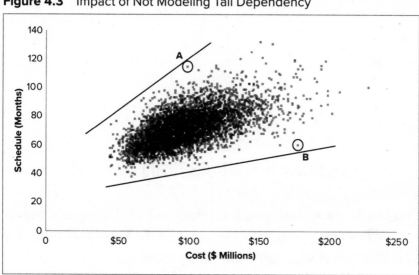

Figure 4.4 displays the results of 5,000 simulations from a joint distribution with the same lognormal distributions as the cost and schedule distributions before but with tail dependency incorporated.

The incorporation of tail dependency fixes the issue. When an extreme cost or schedule event occurs, the other moves in tandem. The copula is a widely used tool in the financial and insurance industries but is rarely discussed in other projects. Wider adoption of this modeling technique and the inclusion of tail dependency will result in more realistic cost and schedule risk analyses.

Figure 4.4   Impact of Modeling Tail Dependency

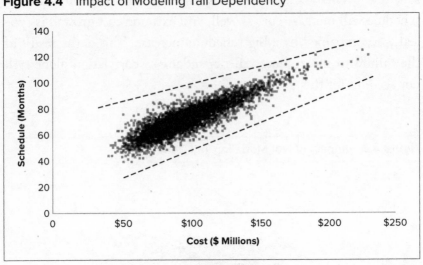

EVOLUTION OF S-CURVES THROUGH PHASES

I was the lead estimator on a team that conducted cost and schedule risk analyses for a large mission. Many of the factors necessary for a credible cost risk analysis—including correlation—were included. We incorporated significant amounts of variation in our models and incorporated the impact of technical risks. Despite this, the final budget for the project was 75% greater than the 50% confidence level developed less than three years prior. See Figure 4.5 for a graph of the S-curve evolution over time compared to the final budget. Over a three-year period, the cost risk analysis was updated several times. With each iteration, the S-curve widened and moved to the right. The cost growth was due to a host of factors, some internal to the project and some external. Internal factors included early overestimation of heritage. Two of the three major elements were supposed to be modifications of existing hardware but turned out to be completely new designs. Another internal factor was underestimation

Figure 4.5   Development S-Curve Evolution for an Actual Project

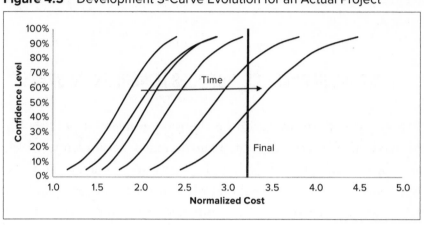

of the technological challenges. External factors included funding delays and two major schedule slips.

Despite incorporating credible methods in our analysis, the final budget was not even on the original S-curve. This is partly due to the estimate reflecting project inputs. This was not an independent estimate but rather a project estimate. As such, it reflected the project's optimistic assumptions. The last S-curve occurred prior to the final design review, called the Critical Design Review. The project was cancelled a year later. Still early in the project, we found that as the design took shape additional risks were uncovered. This led us to widen the S-curve as time progressed, accounting for a greater increase in understanding of the risks involved. Variation in the model inputs increased after receiving additional participation in the risk identification process from project personnel through the implementation of a risk tracking system. While the actual amount of uncertainty may be greater earlier in the project, the way that risk is measured is actually the reverse. Initial optimism eventually gives way to reality.[14] Indeed, an independent cost risk analysis during the middle of this process had a wider range than the one we produced for the project. Its 90% confidence level was greater than the final budget.

IT WORKS IN PRACTICE, BUT DOES IT WORK IN THEORY?

Plato is widely considered to be the most influential philosopher on modern Western thought. Plato founded an academy, which was the precursor to the modern university and is the origin of the word *academic*. Plato believed that what we see in the real world is a reflection of a true ideal.[15] Plato's influence is much deeper than just providing academia its name. His emphasis on abstract ideals in his academy is the model that has shaped modern academic thought in Europe and America. This emphasis on abstractions of real objects led to the triumph of theory over empirical reality.

Milton Friedman was one of the most prominent economists of the twentieth century. Friedman had a significant impact on economics. His theory of positive economics,[16] in which he stated that the assumptions in economics need not make sense, as long as they yield accurate predictions, has been called the "most influential work on economic methodology" of the twentieth century.[17] This would be all well and good if everyone measured the accuracy of their predictions to make sure their simplifying assumptions did not lead their models astray. However, some have used the idea of positivism as a license to make simplifying assumptions that yield elegant mathematical theories, without worrying too much about the business of prediction. William Baumol was a leading economist of the twentieth and early twenty-first centuries who was an exception to the lack of concern for prediction among economics professors. Baumol did some part-time work as a management consultant, where he discovered that the conventional economic theory assumption that firms seek to maximize profits is not true. Rather, firms seek to maximize revenues subject to a minimum profit constraint.[18] Unlike conventional economic theory, this explains the drive in the modern economy to large firms and the relative lack of competition.[19] Baumol was also known for correctly predicting back in the 1960s that the cost of both healthcare and education would rise higher than inflation.[20]

Unlike Friedman, Baumol believed that while "ridiculous premises may sometimes yield correct conclusions," this is the result of "spurious correlations."[21] Correlations like these look good on paper but are worthless in prediction. For example, between 2001 and 2009, the correlation between Brad Pitt's earnings and the average amount of ice cream consumed by Americans was 91.4%. Another example is that, between 2002 and 2010, the correlation between the annual number of tornadoes and the number of shark attacks in the United States was 77.4%.[22] Unlike shark attacks and ice cream sales at the beach, there is unlikely to be even an underlying common cause for these two different pairs of events.

I majored in economics and mathematics in college. I was exposed to Friedman's theory of positive economics by one of my economics professors. This was during the fall semester around the time of the annual football game between the University of Alabama and Auburn University. Known as the Iron Bowl, this game is the biggest annual sporting event in the state of Alabama. One of my neighbors had two tickets to the game that she could not use and was willing to give them away. As she could have easily sold these tickets for a hefty amount, I informed her that her behavior was irrational. The economic assumption of rationality, which states that people choose actions that maximize their self-interest, is a key tenet of economic theory. As this example shows, economic theory often clashes with real-world reality.

The emphasis on theory divorced from reality applies not only to academia but also the current state of practice for risk analysis. The conventional wisdom on cost and schedule risk recognizes that it is not static over time. It evolves as the project matures. Uncertainty shrinks over time. There is a cone of uncertainty that reduces as the project progresses from start to completion. Uncertainty is greatest at the start of a project. This shrinks over time as risks are either encountered or avoided. At the end of development, there is no uncertainty. This is reflected as the cone of uncertainty as illustrated in Figure 4.6.

Figure 4.6   The Cone of Uncertainty

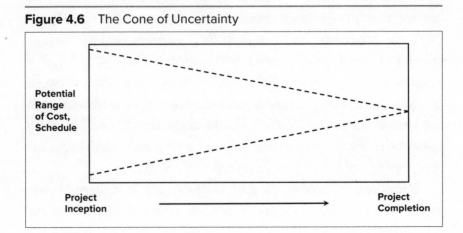

The cone of uncertainty is conceptually correct. However, like many Platonic ideals, it is useless in practice because it ignores how risk is perceived and measured. Rosy optimism prevails early in a project's life cycle, with assumptions of a high degree of heritage and few known risks. While the risk may be greatest at the beginning of the program, the perception is that risk is low. Many risks are assumed away because of inherent optimism. For example, once a project starts, engineers determine that there is a serious technical issue that requires a design fix. The identification of these kinds of risks widens the perception/recognition of risk as they are discovered, leading to an increase in the amount of perceived uncertainty. Eventually, the perceived risk matches the reality; then both narrow close to project completion after most of the risks have been realized or avoided. The way in which risk is measured in practice does not appear to be a cone at all but is more like a diamond. Risk perception starts out narrow, widens to a peak somewhere between the detailed design review and integration, and then eventually narrows as the project approaches completion. See Figure 4.7.

Figure 4.7 Risk Perception vs. Reality

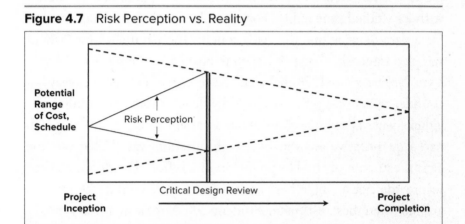

As the physicist Niels Bohr once said, "Prediction is very difficult, especially about the future."[23] Explaining the past is much easier than predicting the future. However, we confuse our ability to explain the past with our capability of predicting the future. This leads to overconfidence in predicting, which results in an underestimation of risk. Nassim Taleb, author of *The Black Swan*, calls this the "narrative fallacy."[24] The need for control leads to ignoring risk and uncertainty. Programs that use cutting-edge technologies are fragile in that the realization of seemingly small risks can have big consequences.[25] In the 1970s, the petroleum engineer Ed Capen recognized that technically trained people such as engineers do not understand uncertainty and that there is a universal tendency to understate risk. Survey studies were conducted to assess people's confidence about their knowledge on a variety of topics. The result found that there was an "almost universal tendency" to underestimate uncertainty because people "overestimate the precision of their own knowledge."[26]

One measure of uncertainty in statistics is called a confidence interval. A statistical procedure, such as sampling, that is used to produce a confidence interval will include the parameter of interest with a specified probability. For example, a 90% confidence interval for a parameter is one that will contain the parameter for 90% of sampled intervals. A paper Capen published in the *Journal of Petroleum Technology* in 1976 included the results of extensive surveys of confidence interval estimates by individuals. More than 1,000 individuals were asked questions about a variety of topics, all of which had a quantitative answer. One such question was "What was the census estimate of the US population in 1900?" People were asked to provide not a single best answer but a 90% confidence interval around their best estimate. Students of American history might provide tighter bounds, while those with less knowledge of the subject might have wider bounds. If people were able to quantify their uncertainty about the answer accurately, 90% of the ranges provided should contain the correct answer. The results indicated that these 90% confidence intervals were more like 40% confidence intervals. People overestimated their knowledge and underestimated their ignorance.[27] The same underestimation of uncertainty holds true today for all projects. (The correct answer to the question about the US population in 1900 is 76 million. Does that seem low to you? I would have estimated it would have been at least 100 million.)

CALIBRATION

One way to correct for early optimism is to calibrate the S-curve to historical cost and schedule growth data. There is a significant amount of risk that no one can predict in advance, especially Donald Rumsfeld's unknown unknowns. We know they will occur for every project, and we can predict their future probability of occurrence in the aggregate based on the historical track record of cost growth. The same notion is used in calculating risks to establish insurance premiums.[28] Calibration is simple. Risk can be calibrated in a variety of ways—it can be done with as few as two inputs. For example, risk can be calibrated to an initial estimate assuming a percentile for the point estimate and a variation about the point estimate.

Applied to the project illustrated in Figure 4.5, an S-curve based solely on the initial estimate and calibrated to empirical cost growth data was much more realistic than the more sophisticated and detailed risk analysis that involved uncertainties on the inputs, uncertainty about the CERs, correlation, and Monte Carlo simulation. See Figure 4.8 for an illustration. The final budget is slightly below the 70th percentile of the empirically calibrated S-curve.

Figure 4.8 Empirical S-Curve Compared to the Final Budget

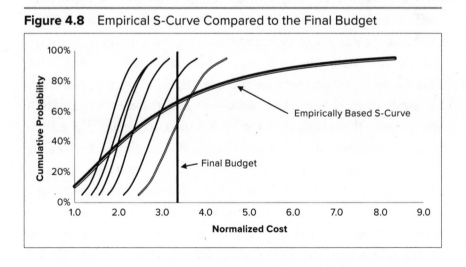

Even with best practices like correlation incorporated, S-curves are still not wide enough to be realistic. Risk is greatly

underestimated in the early stages of a project. Calibrating the risk to historical cost and schedule growth variations is an objective way to overcome this problem. It tempers the inherent optimism in the early phases of a project before most of a program's risks are discovered or admitted. Calibration to empirical cost and schedule growth data is a way to correct for this.[29] Cost and schedule growth is risk in action. By examining historical cost growth, we can develop methods for calibrating risk to make it realistic.

I have witnessed two types of risk analysis in my career. One I call the naive approach. This is a simple analysis that does not incorporate the best practices discussed in this chapter. The naive approach often includes limited risk ranges, does not incorporate correlation, and generally ignores most sources of uncertainty. Even when risk analysis is conducted, the naive analysis is the most common type I have encountered. As an example of the naive approach, I once reviewed a project for schedule risk analysis that had extremely tight, unrealistic risk bounds. For this analysis, the planned schedule was several years long, but the range from the 5% confidence level to the 95% confidence level was only two weeks. That is, 90% of the uncertainty was captured by a two-week period. Any program delay would cause the total schedule to shift by more than that amount. An accident on the shop floor, a loose screw found in test hardware, a funding delay—any of these events by itself would cause the schedule to slip by at least two weeks. The probability of predicting the schedule within a two-week window is zero. The analyst had done a detailed analysis of the schedule, inputting uncertainty on the durations of individual tasks, and then using a Monte Carlo simulation to aggregate the risks. However, the variations were all assumed to be independent. Also, as we mentioned earlier, schedule risk is aggregated differently than cost risk. Cost is broken down into a set of elements. Risk is assessed for those items, and then those values are added. When it comes to schedule, you cannot add everything—there are tasks that occur in parallel. This must be treated differently than addition. The schedule analyst also did not correctly account for this, which further contributed to the narrow range of the schedule prediction.

How Much Risk Is Realistic?

To discuss how much risk is realistic, we need a notion of relative risk, which allows us to compare risk between projects regardless of their sizes. Recall that the amount of cost risk for a project is often characterized by the standard deviation. The mean and median are measures of central tendency for a distribution, and the standard deviation measures the spread around the mean or median. The absolute spread around the center of the distribution varies in accordance with the size of the project. For example, the standard deviation that results from the cost risk analysis of a small project can be measured in millions or tens of millions of dollars, while that derived from a cost risk analysis for a large project will likely be measured in hundreds of millions of dollars, a difference of at least an order of magnitude. A way to compare risk across projects when the absolute magnitude differs greatly is to examine the relative amount of risk. Suppose one project has a standard deviation equal to $100 million, while another has a standard deviation equal to $10 million. The first project has a mean equal to $1 billion, while the other has a mean equal to $10 million. Calculating the ratio of the standard deviation to the mean provides a measure of relative risk. This ratio is called the coefficient of variation. The larger project has a standard deviation that is 10% of the mean, so its coefficient of variation is equal to 10%. The other project has a standard deviation that is equal to the mean, so its coefficient of variation is equal to 100%. Since the standard deviation is in the same units as the mean, the coefficient of variation is a scalar. A scalar is a unitless measure that allows for comparison of the relative risk among projects regardless of dollar value. Although the cheaper project has a lower standard deviation, it is relatively riskier than the more expensive one, as measured by the coefficient of variation.

For a variety of projects, including aerospace, weapons systems, roads, tunnels, chemical processing plants, and information technology, the median coefficient of variation exhibited in cost growth data for a variety of projects is 92%.[30] See Table 4.2 for a list of coefficients of variation implied by cost growth data for 12 different types of projects.

Table 4.2   Comparison of Coefficients of Variation Implied by Cost Growth Data

Project Type	CV
Process Plants	156%
Mining and Metals	153%
Information Technology	111%
Olympics	108%
NASA	94%
High-Speed Rail	93%
Aerospace and Defense	90%
Refineries	81%
Tunnels/Bridges	74%
Urban Rail	67%
Hydropower	56%
Roads	50%
Median	92%

The values in Table 4.2 are much higher than are typically used in cost risk analysis. The values in cost risk analyses often range from 5% at the low end to 30% at the high end. However, the true amount of risk realized in the past as reflected in cost growth data is much higher. The coefficients of variation implied by schedule growth data are just as high as for cost growth, and in many cases even higher.

Comparing Reality with Current States of Practice

The naive approach significantly underestimates risk, as evidenced by historical cost and schedule growth data. The second type of risk analysis, which I refer to as standard, is one I have often produced. Correlation is included and appropriate distributions are used to model risk. However, standard risk analysis often suffers from being anchored to the project manager's optimism. It incorporates as much uncertainty as the project manager is willing to perceive at that point in time.

Figure 4.9 provides a comparison of these two approaches, along with a comparison of a calibrated, realistic risk analysis based on cost and schedule growth data. These are displayed as ranges from the 5% confidence level to the 95% confidence level.

Figure 4.9   Comparison of Realistic vs. Standard and Naive Practice for Cost Risk Analysis

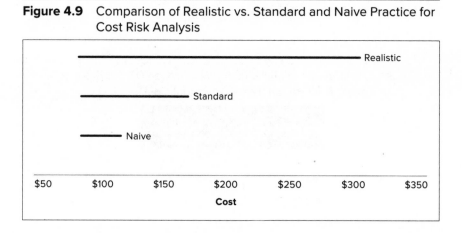

The examples in Figure 4.9 are for a program with a point (risk-less) estimate equal to $100. For the naive estimate, the range is

$87–$118, 13% below the project estimate and 18% above. This is unrealistic. For most programs, a couple of minor events, such as schedule slip and a single integration issue, can lead to more than 30% cost growth. The amount of reserves needed to fund to the 95% confidence level is only 18% more than the point estimate.

For the standard estimate, the range is $87 to $171. The amount of reserves needed to achieve a 95% confidence level is 71% above the point estimate. This is a healthy amount of reserves for a development program and more than I have ever seen a project set aside for contingency. The standard approach is more realistic. It will be conservative for a low-risk program and may be adequate much of the time. However, it is still less than experienced on average by historical development programs.[31] The range for a risk estimate calibrated to real cost growth is $85 to $305. To achieve a 95% confidence level will require 205% reserves.

To convince the skeptical that the coefficient of variation implied by historical cost growth is a realistic approach to risk, we compare it and the other two approaches to see how well they would have done in measuring risk for the 10 historical projects discussed earlier in the chapter. See Table 4.3.

Table 4.3   The Number of Missions for Which the 90% Confidence Levels Are Greater Than the Actual Cost

Approach	Number of Missions for Which 90% Confidence Level Exceeds Actual Cost
Naive	1
Standard	5
Realistic	9

In Table 4.3, we find that the naive approach, much like current practice, produces the opposite of what is expected. For only one of the missions is the actual cost less than the 90% confidence level. The standard approach is better, but still falls short of reality—for only five missions is the actual cost less than the 90% confidence level. This is better than the naive analysis, but the probability of five or fewer projects being less than the 90% confidence level is less than one in 600. One in 600 is still not credible. The realistic case is what is expected. For 9 of the 10, the 90% confidence level is less than the actual cost.[32] Also, the range is not so large that all missions are within the range, which means the bounds are not overly wide.

Figure 4.10 provides a similar comparison based on schedule growth data. Schedule risk is displayed as a range from the 5% confidence level to the 95% confidence level.

Figure 4.10   Comparison of Realistic vs. Standard and Naive Practice for Schedule Risk Analysis

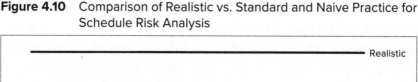

The examples in Figure 4.10 are for a program with a point (riskless) estimate equal to 60 months. For the naive estimate, the 5%–95% confidence level range is 55 to 65 months, 8% below the project estimate and 8% above. This is unrealistic for most projects. Relatively minor changes can delay the schedule by more than six months, more than the 95% confidence level on the S-curves.

The standard schedule risk estimate ranges from 51 months to 98 months. The amount of time needed for a 95% confidence level is 63% higher than the point estimate of the schedule. This is much more realistic than the naive approach, but according to schedule growth history, the 95% confidence as modeled is more like an 80% confidence level. The realistic schedule risk estimate ranges from 54 months to 146 months. The 95% confidence level is 140% more than the baseline schedule.

Unfortunately, in my experience, the naive approach is about as much risk as most managers are willing to bear. The standard approach, even though it is more realistic, is often unpalatable for decision makers. The realistic risk would cause most project managers to choke upon seeing the results and their implications. However, as we will see later, even funding to a 90% confidence level does not consider the big risks that program managers need to prepare for, as setting funding and schedules using confidence levels ignores the risks in the right tail of the uncertainty distribution.

MEDIOCRISTAN VS. EXTREMISTAN: HOW BIG ARE THE TAILS FOR COST RISK?

As discussed in the previous chapter, there are stark differences between phenomena that belong to Mediocristan as compared to those that belong to Extremistan. Recall that Mediocristan is the realm of mild variation. Gaussian distributions belong there. Examples are variations in human height and life span of humans. Phenomena that belong to Extremistan are those that exhibit extreme variation. Examples are losses due to natural disasters and fluctuations in stock market prices.

If cost and schedule for projects belong to Mediocristan, it has significant implications. In a world in which costs have limited variation, they are easy to predict. There is also a pronounced portfolio effect. This makes it easy to reduce the limited risk of a single program even further by combining it with other programs to achieve a portfolio effect. In such a world, we can fund projects to percentiles slightly above the mean and achieve high confidence levels for an entire organization.

One of the rationales for using the Gaussian distribution in cost and schedule estimating is the central limit theorem. This states that if independent, identical distributions are added, the sum will, in the limit, approximate a Gaussian distribution. The only catch is that the variations must not be too extreme. The requirements are that the distributions are independent, none exhibits extreme variation, and the total is the sum of "many individually negligible components."[33] The central limit theorem has been the rationale for modeling many phenomena as Gaussian that are not Gaussian distributed, including cost and schedule. The idea is that even if the lower-level elements are not Gaussian, in aggregate they will be due to the convergence of sums to Gaussian.

As applied to project cost and schedule uncertainty, there are multiple issues with the application of the central limit theorem. One is that it applies at "the limit," which occurs when we add infinitely many random variables together. The real world does not operate "in the limit." In practice, any total will necessarily be the sum of a finite number of random variables. For highly specialized projects, a limited amount of directly applicable data is available. In many cases, less than 10 directly applicable historical data points exist. The central limit theorem requires that everything be independent, but there are a multitude of established interdependencies within and among projects. Earlier in the chapter, we explained why all programs have some positive average correlation and a higher level than is commonly believed. The central limit theorem also requires finite standard deviation. There is some evidence that for cost this may be infinite. Even if the standard deviation is finite, for the central limit theorem to apply, no one project can dominate the total standard deviation. However, it is often the case that there will be a series of programs with small overruns. Then, a project with a huge amount of cost or schedule growth will occur. Thus, when it comes to cost and schedule estimating, all the assumptions required for the central limit theorem to hold are suspect. Not enough elements are summed to be close to the "limit," projects are not independent, and the standard deviation is not well-behaved.

Even if the Gaussian distribution is not representative of cost risk, the lognormal seems to be a good alternative much of the time. However, if the tails of the distribution are even riskier than the lognormal, the analysis is trickier. If this is the case, there are some serious implications for how analysis is done, as many traditional analysis tools, such as regression, are based on limited variation. I have compared fitting the tail of cost growth data to lognormal and Pareto-type distributions. I have found the lognormal distributions fit the tail better in some cases. However, in others, a Pareto-type power law distribution prevails.

The argument for the lognormal is that changes in costs over time are proportional to prior costs. Cost is more likely to increase than decrease over time, as we have discussed. When we talk about cost changes, we almost always mean cost increases. Cost increases often do not result in funding increases in the short term due to funding constraints. Thus, cost increases will result in longer schedules. Longer schedules imply a longer period in which the personnel devoted to a project will charge to that project. Larger projects have more personnel assigned to a project, meaning that increases in cost will result in a proportional increase in cost. This process generates a lognormal distribution.[34] This assumption is not robust. Only a slight change to this generative model is needed to turn the lognormal into a power law. An additional assumption that cost has a lower bound is all that is needed to cause this change.[35] This is reasonable since, once a project begins detailed work, cost decreases are unlikely. Almost any change, apart from cutting scope, will result in cost and schedule increases. The only way to effectively change a project without increasing cost is to cut requirements.

One analysis I conducted for 133 NASA missions indicates that the right tail follows a power law that indicates finite mean but infinite standard deviation.[36] For this data set, a power law (Pareto) distribution for the right tail was a better fit than a lognormal distribution. This evidence puts cost growth in the territory of Extremistan.

Table 4.4   Comparison of Lognormal and Pareto Tails for Modeling Cost Growth

Growth Greater Than:	Lognormal Tail	Pareto Tail
100%	1 in 8	1 in 7
250%	1 in 94	1 in 25
500%	1 in 1,800	1 in 63
1,000%	1 in 100,000	1 in 156
2,000%	1 in 15 million	1 in 393

As is evident from Table 4.4, the chance of extreme cost growth is remote for the lognormal. The probability that a program would experience 1,000% cost growth is practically impossible for a lognormal, while for a Pareto the chance is only a little less than 1%. The Pareto may be conservative, but the lognormal does not provide realistic odds of extreme growth. For example, the James Webb Space Telescope is one program that is not included in the 133 data points. This next-generation space telescope, discussed in the Introduction, is a successor to Hubble and truly cutting-edge technology, as was Hubble when it was launched. Like Hubble, it has also experienced significant cost growth. As of early 2020, the James Webb Space Telescope had grown by more than 500%, more than any program in the database used in the analysis that was used to generate Table 4.3. The lognormal predicts the chance of this amount of cost growth experienced by this project to be 1 in 2,940, while the chance with a Pareto is much higher, 1 in 70. If we were to add this data point to the database, it would be one of 134 data points. So the empirical probability would be between that predicted by the Pareto and lognormal but closer to the Pareto than the lognormal. This kind of extreme growth is not limited to aerospace or defense projects. A notable example of a high-priority project is the Sydney Opera House, which, as discussed in the earlier chapters on cost growth, increased in cost by a factor of 14. To meet an aggressive schedule, funding poured in to support National Missile Defense in the 2000s. The cost to develop the Suez Canal in the 1860s increased 20-fold from the initial plan. The actual cost for the Concorde supersonic airplane was 12 times the initial cost.[37] The cost for the new Scottish Parliament built in the early 2000s was 10 times the initial estimate.[38]

The case for the lognormal is buttressed by the fact that the wild risks of the stock market and natural disasters cannot be easily mitigated, while more traditional projects are more easily controlled. A project manager can cut scope or implement measures to improve project performance. Also, projects that experience extreme cost and/or schedule growth will likely be cancelled. The counterargument is that some of the time a project will be high priority. Even when it experiences extreme cost growth, a high-priority project will not be cancelled. Instead, the schedule will slip and/or funds will be reallocated from other lower priority programs to pay for the program. This occurs for projects that not only double in cost but increase by a greater factor, such as four or more. In some cases, technology is so cutting edge that little can be done to reduce costs. It will cost what it costs. All these are examples of publicly funded projects. (Even though the Concorde was a commercial aircraft, its development was supported with government subsidies.[39]) Private firms would likely go out of business if costs grew by these amounts. For example, FoxMeyer, the pharmaceutical wholesaler mentioned earlier, went bankrupt when its planned implementation of a new enterprise resource planning computer system increased in cost by less than 100%. Also, Airbus's A380 aircraft was a consistent money loser for the company, and its development costs are believed to have doubled from initial plans.

Even though schedules exhibit significant variation in absolute terms, there needs to be extreme variation on a percentage basis to belong to Extremistan. For example, the Sydney Opera House schedule lengthened from 4 to 14 years. In percentage terms, that is a 250% increase. Using Table 4.4 as a comparison, the lognormal models that level of increase as relatively rare (one in 94), while it is four times more likely with a Pareto. A Pareto also estimates 1,000% growth as not uncommon, on the order of one in 156 projects, while for the lognormal it is likely to never occur (one in 100,000). An order of magnitude increase would mean an initial four-year plan would stretch to 40 years or a 10-year schedule would slip to 100 years. These kinds of increases are extremely unlikely. This puts schedule in the realm of Mediocristan. Schedule is not Gaussian, but a lognormal should be sufficient to model time risk, even in the right tail.

Power law distributions have three categories. In one, both the mean and standard deviation are finite. For the second, the standard deviation is infinite, but the mean is finite. In the third, both the mean and standard deviation are infinite. Power law distributions are typically used to model phenomena in which at least one of these first two moments is infinite. See Table 4.5 for a comparison of three Pareto distributions. These have drastically different percentiles, although all three have significant risk. The relative difference between the 70th and 95th percentile for the thinnest-tailed Pareto is a factor of almost four. For the finite mean, infinite standard deviation version, the difference is similar. The relative differences are an order of magnitude greater for the infinite mean, infinite standard deviation Pareto. Also, the 70th percentile is almost an order of magnitude larger for the latter Pareto. The kind of risk exhibited by an infinite mean, infinite standard deviation Pareto is the type of risk seen in box office returns for cinematic films. Most projects do not display this degree of risk. Imagine a large $5 billion nuclear plant or missile development project that suddenly grew to cost $5 trillion.

Table 4.5   Comparison of Percentiles for Three Different Pareto Distributions

Percentile	Finite Mean, Finite Variance	Finite Mean, Infinite Variance	Infinite Mean, Infinite Variance
70th	$300	$600	$5,000
80th	$450	$950	$12,000
90th	$750	$1,800	$50,000
95th	$1,150	$3,200	$200,000
99th	$2,650	$10,500	$5,000,000

If cost growth for most projects indeed follows a Pareto, it is the type with finite mean. This makes predicting the cost of these systems difficult. However, there is still more capability to effectively forecast than cases where the mean is infinite. The answer to the question, "Does cost risk follow a lognormal or a Pareto distribution, at least in the tails?" is, in many cases, "It depends." My hypothesis is that the lognormal applies to most private and public projects. The exception is those projects that have poor planning or execution and that are high enough priority to avoid cancellation once costs spiral out of control. Some of the projects we mentioned with extreme cost growth used advanced technologies, like the James Webb Space Telescope and the Concorde supersonic airplane. The initial planning was poor because it did not adequately account for the difficulty in maturing the critical technologies required. This resulted in extremely optimistic estimates. The issue with the Scottish Parliament building was optimistic initial estimates and design changes during construction. Some of the increase was due to additional security requirements added after the 9/11 terrorist attacks in the United States, but the project was essentially given a blank check, and no one had the discipline to keep requirements from growing.[40] If costs increase by a significant amount, a project that is not high priority will be cancelled. Otherwise, in those instances where a public project is high priority and uses cutting-edge technologies, the right tail for cost risk follows a power law. This issue is partly a matter of incentives. Without some motivation to keep costs low, costs can quickly balloon by a factor of 5 or 10, and still fail to meet objectives. Extreme cost growth for projects is often a matter of a lack of incentives, a subject we will discuss in more detail in Chapter 8.

The one exception of the application of the lognormal in private projects is software and information technology. There is some evidence that these projects have fat tails.[41] The relationship between software cost and size exhibits diseconomies of scale. In percentage terms, the cost of a software project grows more than proportionally to its scale. For example, if the size of the project grows by 50%, the cost will grow 60% or more. Optimistic requirements during the planning process will lead to correcting the initial scale during development. This will lead to large cost increases, possibly tipping the risk into the realm of Extremistan. Approaches to software development have changed over the years to cope with the issues related to complexity. The Agile approach has the promise to potentially reduce cost.[42] The outstanding question is whether it can reduce risk as well.

Evidence of similar extreme variation in financial data arose in the 1960s. Benoit Mandelbrot had applied his analytical framework to financial data and had found that the Gaussian distribution was not a good fit. Instead, it exhibited extreme variation, particularly infinite standard deviation. One of Mandelbrot's early applications of his PhD dissertation topic mentioned in the last chapter was to financial markets in the early 1960s. He found that prices in markets like cotton did not fit a Gaussian distribution but that they had much more variation than would be expected from a Gaussian or even a lognormal. This led to a significant degree of controversy in the academic community for finance, as the foundation of the theory of finance was based on Gaussian and lognormal distributions. The MIT economist Paul Cootner wrote in 1964 that "Mandlebrot, like Prime Minister Churchill before him, promises us not utopia but blood, sweat, and tears. If he is right, almost all of our statistical tools are obsolete . . . almost without exception, past econometric work is meaningless."[43] Mandelbrot's ideas were resisted and eventually rejected for more conventional models. The early 1970s hearkened more financial tools, like the Black-Scholes model of option prices, that rested upon Gaussian and lognormal distributions, pushing Mandelbrot's ideas into the background. While they realized there was evidence for extreme variations, in their view the Gaussian distribution was good enough.[44]

If risk is not lognormal, but fatter tailed, it has significant implications for cost estimating. In the case of extreme risk, point estimates are not useful from a predictive standpoint. Traditional cost estimating practice, including cost risk analysis, uses methods designed for mild variation. Detailed discussion of the implications is beyond the scope of this book. I mention it here to note that for some projects, traditional tools should not be used to estimate cost. This includes standard regression analysis. Fortunately, there are plenty of alternatives, such as basing estimates on absolute deviations rather than squared deviations. There is a plethora of tools available in the burgeoning field of machine learning that do not rely on distributional assumptions.

SUMMARY AND RECOMMENDATIONS

There is a systematic tendency to underestimate risk. Blindness to risk is a human tendency. In Shakespeare's play *Hamlet*, the title character says to his friend Horatio that "there are more things in heaven and earth, Horatio / Than are dreamt of in your philosophy."[45] Projects suffer from Horatio's defect. Numerous sources of risk for cost and schedule estimates exist. If a statistical model is used to predict cost and schedule, there are uncertainties in the inputs to the model. Also, the models themselves only explain a portion of past variation in cost and schedule. If an analogy is used, the similarity of the analogy to the program being estimated is uncertain, as are any adjustments that must be made to the analogy to obtain a program estimate. Programs have internal issues, such as the technologies used for the program. Incorporating new technologies into a program is inherently risky. The integration of existing technologies in new configurations also has substantial risk. The biggest risks are those external to the program. However, as projects do not plan for most of these, risk is underestimated.

The results of past cost and schedule risk analyses are not tracked to measure their accuracy. This has led to no improvement in the accuracy of the application of risk analysis over time. We provided a sample of 10 missions and showed that for 8 of the 10, the actual cost exceeded the 90% confidence level for the cost risk estimate. For the two missions with schedule risk estimates, one of them was 2.8 times greater than the 90% confidence level.

The cause of the underestimation of risk is seen to be the risk perception early in a program's life cycle. Cost and schedule estimates and risk analyses for them are influenced by program office assumptions. Typically, early in a program, the intent is to use existing technologies and leverage existing designs as much as possible. However, as a system design matures, the true risks are revealed (and in some cases admitted). This leads to wider risk ranges that are more realistic. As a result, the ideal "cone of uncertainty" looks more like a diamond than a cone. The amount of risk perceived is tiny at project inception. This increases as risks are discovered or can no longer be ignored. The perceived risk eventually expands until it matches reality. Then both perceived and actual uncertainty narrows as risks are realized, avoided, or mitigated.

The bottom line is that risk is not modeled accurately. The use of sophisticated tools and advanced methods is not sufficient to avoid this problem. The solution to the issue of risk perception is calibration to empirical cost and schedule growth data. This is an objective measure that can avoid the taint of early program optimism. Even if it is not used as the primary risk methodology, it should be used as a cross-check to verify that early risk analysis is realistic. Even with calibration, it is possible that we are missing the boat if we are suffering from another perception issue, which is that we think projects could have mild variation when they could experience extreme variation.

The argument for mild variation is that programs will be cancelled if they experience extreme cost growth. There is a check to ensure things do not get out of hand, unlike with other phenomena that have wild variations, such as natural disasters and stock prices. Also, private firms may go bankrupt once cost growth gets out of hand. Publicly funded projects do not have this constraint. Public projects that are good candidates for extreme cost and schedule growth are those that require technology development and are high priority.

When I was a child, my family had a small, mischievous dog named Tessie. Whenever she did something that caused my mother to reprimand her, she would turn her head away. Tessie was purposely avoiding the reality of my mother's reproach. In a similar manner, project managers often ignore risk. To borrow a phrase from the film *A Few Good Men*, they "can't handle the truth." This needs to change. Project managers must develop a proper appreciation for risk if they want to be successful and to avoid the problems that occur when unplanned for cost and schedule risks are realized. Managers and analysts both need to honestly assess projects to determine if they are candidates for extreme cost and schedule growth.

CHAPTER 5

The Portfolio Effect and the Free Lunch

The Limits of Diversification

Most people know that the Wright brothers invented the motor-operated airplane and that Alexander Graham Bell devised the telephone. However, many people do not know that a more modern innovation that has had a significant impact on people's lives started with a single individual named Harry Markowitz. An investment portfolio is the total of all the investments owned by a single individual or organization. If you invest in the stock market, have a 401(k) at work, or use the services of a financial adviser, you likely have such a portfolio. Your investments are in a portfolio to take advantage of diversification. Before the 1950s, conventional wisdom held this was not a good strategy. Most financial research was focused on identifying the single best stock and investing all your money in that company. The thinking up to that point was encapsulated by Mark Twain in his novel *Pudd'n'head Wilson,* "Behold, the fool saith, 'Put not all thine eggs in the one basket'—which is but a manner of saying, 'Scatter your money and your attention;' but the wise man saith, 'Put all your eggs in one basket and watch that basket!'"[1] The economist John Maynard Keynes considered diversification in a large pool of investments, about which the investor had little direct knowledge, to be a "travesty."[2] Prior to 1950, the leading publication on investing was *The Theory of Investment Value*, a PhD thesis written by John Burr Williams, who had prior practical experience working as a securities analyst. In his dissertation, Williams showed how to estimate the value of a stock by projecting the company's long-run dividend. He recommended finding the single stock with the highest expected return and buying only that particular stock.[3] A best-selling investment book of the first half of the twentieth century, *The Battle for Investment Survival*, stated that "the intelligent and safe way to handle (investment) capital is to concentrate." The author of this book, who worked on Wall Street, wrote that if an investment is "not worth following to the limit, it is not worth following at all." Diversification was described as "undesirable" and "an admission of not knowing what to do and an effort to strike an average."[4]

Markowitz developed portfolio theory in a paper published in 1952.[5] He had noticed that prior research on the selection of stocks and bonds focused solely on expected return. Markowitz realized it was important to consider the spread around the mean return and introduced the consideration of risk. One stock may be growing faster in price than another but, if it is also more volatile, that should be considered as well. For example, a technology stock may have more growth potential than the stock of a company that makes soft drinks or razor blades. However, technology stocks, especially of small, less established companies, are much more volatile and hence riskier. Markowitz noted that the combination of a variety of stocks held in a common portfolio is less risky than the most volatile individual member.[6] This is one of the benefits of diversification. Another is that investing in a broad variety of stocks makes it less likely to miss out on big gains. In investments such as stocks, large gains and losses are possible, depending on the level of risk an investor is willing to take. A stock market investor who is not using leverage can lose no more than he or she invests but has the potential for tremendous gains. For example, during the period 2000-2019, the price of Apple stock shares increased 10,000%. If an investor did not diversify sufficiently to have a stock like this in their portfolio, their overall return was likely significantly lower over this time period. The benefits of diversification led stock pundit Jim Cramer to tout it as the "only free lunch on Wall Street."[7]

THERE AIN'T NO SUCH THING AS A FREE LUNCH

The notion of a free lunch dates to the nineteenth century. American saloons would offer customers a "free lunch" if they purchased an alcoholic drink. The food offered in the free lunch would be over-salted, leading customers to buy multiple drinks. Drink prices at such establishments were also higher than those that did not offer a "free lunch."[8]

The nineteenth-century German philosopher Johann Fichte discussed the evolution of ideas as a debate between opposing forces. In Fichte's view, every thesis would give rise to an opposing antithesis. Ideally these two contradictory ideas would eventually be reconciled into a synthesis.[9] We see an example of the thesis-antithesis-synthesis cycle in our own development as we mature. When we are young, the idea our parents know everything is the thesis. When we rebel against this authority as teenagers and young adults, we think we know everything, which is an antithesis to the original thesis. Eventually our views moderate, and we synthesize these two views, learning to appreciate our parents' advice as well as our own judgment.

British economist John Maynard Keynes became famous during and after the Great Depression for advocating government intervention to stimulate the economy during a downturn. Keynes' ideas have been highly influential in government economic policy in America and Western Europe, and have been primarily associated with big government policies. Libertarian writers and free market economists popularized the phrase "there ain't no such thing as a free lunch" as an antithesis to Keynesian economic policies. The conservative counterpoint to the government's meddling in the economy is that while fiscal stimulus may seem like free money, it must come at some cost. This tension between the ideas of government intervention and free market economics remains in American politics to this day.

Two individuals were key to making "there ain't no such thing as a free lunch" a common phrase. One was best-selling author Robert Heinlein, one of the pre-eminent twentieth-century science fiction writers. Along with Isaac Asimov and Arthur C. Clarke, he was one of the top three early science fiction writers. Several of his books were made into films, including *Starship Troopers*. He coined several phrases that were popular at one point or another, including "pay it forward," the basis for a film of its own in the 1990s. Heinlein was a fiscally conservative libertarian. The phrase "there ain't no such thing as a free lunch" summarizes his economic philosophy. He made it a central concept of his novel *The Moon Is a Harsh Mistress*, about a lunar colony's revolt against rule by planet Earth. Heinlein used it so much in the book that he made it an acronym—"TAN-STAAFL." In this book, he defines it as "anything free costs twice as much in the long run or turns out worthless."[10] The other person to help make the phrase popular was Milton Friedman, a Nobel Prize–winning economist with a knack for explaining abstruse economic concepts in easy-to-understand language. Friedman was a twentieth-century conservative economist and popular speaker and writer on economics. He believed in free markets rather than free

lunches. Friedman was the leading opponent of Keynesian economic policies. Along with Keynes, he was considered one of the
two most influential economists of the twentieth century. Friedman was the leader in developing the antithesis to the Keynesian
thesis. He believed that government economic stimulus would just
lead to inflation and not affect overall employment. As an advisor to
President Ronald Reagan, he had a lasting influence on Republican
policies. Friedman published a collection of magazine columns and
interviews in the 1970s in book form titled *There's No Such Thing as
a Free Lunch*.[11] As we will see, the "no free lunch" principle applies
to diversification as well.

THE PORTFOLIO EFFECT

An important facet of cost risk is that budgets are not typically set
in isolation. Rather, they are established in the context of multiple ongoing and planned projects. This collection of projects can be
considered a portfolio. The risks for these projects are not perfectly
correlated with one another, so overall portfolio risk should be less
than for any single project. The prevailing thesis is that it is possible
to achieve a high level of confidence in the overall budget for an
organization while setting budgets for individual projects at a lower
level.[12] This portfolio effect is relied upon in setting confidence level
policy for programs that consist of multiple projects. Note that this
purported effect applies only to cost, not schedule. Cost is fungible.
An overrun in one element can be offset by another that underruns.
Time is not. An early completion for one project cannot be used to
offset a schedule slip for another.

Markowitz's introduction of the consideration of risk is a
landmark achievement. The application has led to the widespread
appreciation of diversification in investments. However, Markowitz's work has some shortcomings that limit its application to project

risk management. In his research, the benefits of diversification rely upon the ability to measure risk as the standard deviation. There is no accounting for skewness, which, as we have discussed, is a prominent feature of cost risk. It also relies upon mild variation, such as measured by the Gaussian distribution. However, diversification is important in investing because in a limited risk situation, the wild variation in financial prices means that the returns of a portfolio will be dominated by a single investment, such as Apple.[13]

While based on the idea of investment diversification, the notion of the portfolio effect depends on relative risk and reward. For many projects, the situation is the opposite of that faced by the typical stock market investor. For public endeavors, such as roads or satellites, the gain can be valuable, but it is relatively fixed and can be difficult to measure quantitatively. However, there is a large potential downside in that cost can increase dramatically.

The 80% confidence level is commonly used for funding projects when a quantitative cost risk analysis is conducted. The use of S-curves and percentile funding for financial risk management arose in the banking industry in the 1990s.[14] In the banking industry, the use of confidence levels is called Value at Risk. Other types of projects have adapted this approach.

The Department of Energy, the US government agency in charge of nuclear projects, requires confidence levels in the 70% to 90% confidence level. These are separately required for cost and schedule.[15] For infrastructure projects, when funding levels are based on quantitative risk analysis, funding is at the 50% or 80% confidence level.[16] Public projects in Australia,[17] the United Kingdom's rail network division,[18] and US transportation projects[19] are among those organizations that regularly fund to the 80% confidence level. Some projects occasionally fund to higher levels. For example, the Niagara Tunnel megaproject was funded to the 90% confidence level.[20] The 80% confidence level is also commonly used for establishing schedule reserves.[21] NASA policy requires funding at the 50% and 70% confidence levels, depending on the project. This requirement is for a joint cost and schedule confidence level, so a 50% joint confidence level is a 50% chance that neither cost nor schedule will exceed the specified cost and schedule.[22] Two key differences between the use of confidence levels for establishing funding for banks compared with other projects are the horizon, or period over which risk is considered, and the confidence level used. In banking it is a shorter time period, up to one year, and confidence levels equal to 95% or higher.[23]

In 2003, the Office of the Undersecretary of Defense for Acquisition, Technology, and Logisitics published a report that noted high amounts of cost growth for defense programs. It recommended budgeting to the 80th percentile. This was much higher than the mean or median that many defense projects had used as a basis for funding recommendations,[24] so there was naturally a backlash. A year after the release of the report, a presentation at a symposium illustrated the portfolio effect for a set of 10 notional projects. It showed a substantial savings due to diversification.[25] Table 5.1 contains the notional example presented as an antithesis to the recommendation to fund individual projects to the 80th percentile. In Table 5.1, there are 10 mutually independent Gaussian distributions. In this case, an 80% confidence level can be achieved for the full portfolio of 10 missions while budgeting each individual mission at the 61% confidence level. The sum of the 80th percentiles of each individual mission is $16,959. Only $14,720 is required by considering these as a portfolio, approximately a 13% reduction in the total needed to fund to the 80% confidence level for the entire portfolio.

Analysis of the type provided in Table 5.1 was part of the reason the Department of Defense eventually rejected funding to 80% confidence levels. The idea of a portfolio effect did not just take a firm root in military endeavors, it also quickly migrated to NASA and is now firmly established in all types of projects. Bent

Table 5.1   Example of the Portfolio Effect for 10 Mutually Independent
Gaussian Distributions

Project	Mean	Standard Deviation	61% Confidence Level
1	$1,696	$539	$1,846
2	$1,481	$404	$1,594
3	$1,395	$435	$1,516
4	$874	$288	$954
5	$840	$219	$901
6	$1,449	$371	$1,552
7	$1,638	$537	$1,788
8	$1,031	$259	$1,103
9	$1,271	$323	$1,361
10	$1,937	$602	$2,105
Total	$13,612	$1,317	$14,720

80% Confidence
Portfolio Level

*Adapted from Timothy P. Anderson, "The Trouble with Budgeting to the 80th Percentile,"
presented at the 72nd Military Operations Research Society Symposium, Monterey, CA,
June 22–24, 2004*

Flyvbjerg, Oxford professor and expert on risk for large projects, has stated that funding to the 50% confidence level "is often used to forecast projects in a portfolio of projects, because in this manner on average underruns will compensate for overruns and the portfolio will balance overall."[26]

All the aggregation in Table 5.1 can be done with addition because all the distributions are Gaussian. The sum of two Gaussian distributions is also Gaussian. In this example, the analysis is straightforward and there are formulas to do all the calculations. However, this effect is more apparent than real. The analysis in Table 5.1 has at least three issues. One is that cost risk does not typically follow a Gaussian distribution, as we discussed previously. Instead, cost risk is skewed to the right. A second is that projects are rarely independent. The greatest source of risk, Don Rumsfeld's "unknown unknowns" such as budget cuts and funding constraints, affect all projects, which results in some positive level of correlation among most cost elements. A third issue with the analysis in Table 5.1 is that the risk is vastly understated compared to actual experience. The relative riskiness of the notional projects in Table 5.1 is lower than would be expected from cost growth history, although unfortunately it is in line with the way risk is typically assessed, as discussed in Chapter 4.

Adjusting the Assumptions to Match Reality

I was skeptical of the idea of a portfolio effect for public projects as soon as I learned of it. It could be a natural bias on my part. I am the only child of an only child who was also an only grandchild. My son and I are the only lineal descendants of one of my great-grandfathers. I like to say my family tree is more like a family vine. One of the issues I noticed about the analysis in Table 5.1 is that it did not seem realistic. We adjust it in three ways to make it more faithful to the true amount of risk. First, we change the distribution type. We use a lognormal instead of the Gaussian. The lognormal distribution's skew models the fact that more can go wrong than can go right and that extreme events are likelier to occur than with a Gaussian. Second, we add a realistic amount of correlation. Third, we assume relative amounts of risk that are derived from empirical cost growth data, as discussed in the last chapter. When we want to aggregate the risks for 10 lognormal distributions, however, we cannot do this analytically. Unlike Gaussian distributions, lognormal distributions do not add. To sum lognormal distributions, we must use a computational technique known as Monte Carlo simulation, as discussed previously. Simulating these 10 projects with the same means as in Table 5.1, the results are displayed in Table 5.2.

Note that the portfolio effect based on empirical data offers essentially no savings from diversification. To truly fund to the 80th percentile for the portfolio, we must fund each individual project at

Table 5.2   The Portfolio Effect Based on Empirical Data

Project	Mean	Standard Deviation	78% Confidence Level
1	$1,696	$1,476	$2,258
2	$1,481	$1,288	$1,972
3	$1,395	$1,214	$1,857
4	$874	$760	$1,164
5	$840	$731	$1,118
6	$1,449	$1,261	$1,929
7	$1,638	$1,425	$2,181
8	$1,031	$897	$1,373
9	$1,271	$1,106	$1,692
10	$1,937	$1,685	$2,579
Total	$13,612	$6,754	$18,122

80% Confidence at Portfolio Level

the 78th percentile. Thus, the portfolio effect is found to be a myth. There ain't no such thing as a free lunch, and when it comes to confidence level funding, there ain't no such thing as a portfolio effect, either. Reliance by policy makers on this nonexistent safety net will only mean continued issues with cost growth in excess of budgets and reserves.

The standard deviations relative to the mean values in Table 5.2 may appear on the high side for those familiar with cost and schedule risk analysis, but these are in line with historical cost growth data, as discussed in the last chapter. Even if the coefficient of variation were reduced to 50%, near the lower end of the range for the projects discussed in Chapter 4, the effect is still minimal. In that case, every individual project must be funded at the 76% confidence level to achieve an 80% portfolio confidence level.

If we do not assume that all projects have the same coefficient of variation, but different values with the same overall weight average, matters do not get any better. See Table 5.3. The means are the same as before, but the coefficients of variation are different.

Table 5.3   The Portfolio Effect with Empirical Data and Various
Coefficients of Variation

Project	Mean	Standard Deviation	77% Confidence Level
1	$1,696	$339	$2,205
2	$1,481	$1,777	$1,926
3	$1,395	$698	$1,814
4	$874	$760	$1,136
5	$840	$798	$1,092
6	$1,449	$1,449	$1,884
7	$1,638	$1,638	$2,130
8	$1,031	$1,443	$1,341
9	$1,271	$1,525	$1,653
10	$1,937	$1,433	$2,519
Total	$13,612	$6,754	$17,700

80% Confidence at
Portfolio Level

In Table 5.3, the project must be funded at the 77% confidence
level to achieve an 80% confidence level for the portfolio. This is a
trivial difference from the results in Table 5.2.

The promised free lunch of the portfolio effect is illusory.
"Investing" in many kinds of projects is different than buying a
stock. When an investor buys a stock, he or she can lose at most
the amount invested. When the government invests in a public
project, however, the initial investment, or budget, can be exceeded
many times over. Rather than being a stock investor, these organizations are making highly leveraged speculative bets on projects
with multiyear time frames. The use of highly leveraged financial
instruments is known as derivatives. The use of derivatives has
led to some spectacular financial losses and even financial crises.
Derivatives have been the means by which several hedge funds and
banks have lost hundreds of millions and even billions of dollars.
As discussed previously, highly leveraged bets bankrupted Orange
County, California; put out of business a hedge fund run by Nobel

Prize–winning economists in the 1990s; and contributed to the financial crisis of 2008.

Put a Lid on It: Capping Cost Growth

If cost growth could be capped at a specified percentage, say 25%, then the portfolio effect could offer real savings. If each project is initially funded at the mean and cost growth is limited to 25% growth more than the mean, then achieving an 80% confidence level for the portfolio of missions only requires funding each mission at the 69th percentile. Table 5.4 displays the results.

Table 5.4 The Portfolio Effect with Cost Growth Caps

Project	Mean	Standard Deviation	69% Confidence Level
1	$1,696	$1,476	$1,840
2	$1,481	$1,288	$1,607
3	$1,395	$1,214	$1,514
4	$874	$760	$948
5	$840	$731	$911
6	$1,449	$1,261	$1,572
7	$1,638	$1,425	$1,777
8	$1,031	$897	$1,119
9	$1,271	$1,106	$1,379
10	$1,937	$1,685	$2,102
Total	$13,612	$3,976	$14,770

80% Confidence at Portfolio Level

Capping cost growth also significantly reduces the overall 80th percentile. Of course, capping cost growth to 25% will be hard to achieve in practice. Even without optimistic initial budgets, there may be external factors that can add to cost growth, such as funding instability and labor strikes. One possible way to implement a cost growth cap would be to cancel any project as soon as cost growth exceeds 25%. This would provide managers with the incentive to be realistic in setting initial budgets. However, such a policy is draconian and would in many cases punish project managers for externally caused cost growth. It would also mean a lot of wasted time and money on abandoned endeavors.

Another, and perhaps more reasonable, means to implement a cost growth cap would be to purchase cost growth overrun insurance. Such insurance would have a high deductible, such as 100%, but would pay dollar-for-dollar for any cost growth above a set amount. Of course, this insurance is not free. Given the history of project cost growth, it would cost a substantial amount. One common way to price insurance is to use the equivalence principle, which simply states that the amount of the premium should equal the time-discounted expected payout.[27] However, there has historically been no appetite on the part of publicly funded projects to purchase insurance as governmental entities typically do not insure their projects.

THE CURRENT STATE OF PRACTICE AND THE NEGATIVE PORTFOLIO EFFECT

Sadly, the type of portfolio analysis we have provided in this chapter is rarely conducted. I am aware of less than a handful of organizations that have attempted it. While cost estimators often develop risk analyses for individual projects, there is no quantitative portfolio analysis. The estimators conduct a cost risk analysis, document it, and provide it to their project manager. The project manager in turn will consider the risk analysis in his decision-making. If the project manager is optimistically biased and wants to fund the project to a low level, the cost estimator can provide the risk analysis and show him or her that the probability of the actual cost being within the budget is remote.

A negative portfolio effect has two causes. One is funding to a low confidence level on the S-curve when risk follows a Gaussian or log-normal distribution. The other is that risk does not follow a probability distribution like the lognormal. For example, the wild risks of Extremistan reverse the portfolio effect, even for higher confidence levels

How Low Can You Go? The Perils of Funding to Low Percentiles

Instead of performing a portfolio analysis, what typically occurs is that projects blindly fund to a low confidence level, such as the 50th percentile, with the expectation that a hoped-for portfolio effect will ensure that a portfolio of all the projects in the organization is at a high confidence level. I once developed a joint cost and schedule risk analysis for which I assessed the joint confidence level of the baseline schedule and budget as 2%. There was a 98% chance of either a schedule slip or a cost increase from the baseline. Not surprisingly, the project was cancelled a year later. Decision makers often fund at the 50th percentile or below, and the 50% confidence level is commonly used for establishing funding. I have seen it used with military and NASA missions, and we mentioned earlier that it is regularly used in all types of projects when there are multiple projects that are part of a portfolio.

Recall that for a skewed distribution, the 50th percentile is below the mean. The sum of the means is the mean of the overall sums. That is, the overall portfolio mean is equal to the sum of the individual project means. When individual project confidence levels are below their mean, such as the 50% confidence level, the overall portfolio 50% confidence level will be higher than the sum of the project's 50% confidence values. That is, the sum of the 50% confidence levels is less than the overall portfolio 50% confidence level. Any value less than the mean will experience this because summing percentiles below the mean have the property that the percentile of the sums will be lower. Aggregating risk to the portfolio level in such a case increases rather than decreases the overall risk. Funding all projects to the 50th percentile will result in an overall portfolio confidence level of less than the 50th percentile and in many cases well below that level. I calculated the portfolio risk for a selection of major projects for a government agency. All were funded to the 50% confidence level. On aggregating the cost risk, I found that the overall confidence level of the portfolio of those projects was approximately 36%. I term the increase in portfolio risk due to funding at low levels the negative portfolio effect because it does the opposite of what is intended. Funding to the 50% confidence level increases overall portfolio cost risk rather than decreases it.

As a simple example, consider two test events that have identical costs but are statistically independent. Each event will cost $50 million if the test is executed successfully. However, if the test fails, a full retest will be required. The cost of failure is $50 million to repeat the test. The chance that each test will succeed is 80%, and the chance it will fail is 20%. The two test outcomes lead to four possibilities, as illustrated in Table 5.5.

Table 5.5   Possible Outcomes for Two Independent, Identical Tests

	Test 1 Success	Test 1 Failure
Test 2 Success	$100	$150
Test 2 Failure	$150	$200

The chance that both tests succeed is 0.8 × 0.8 = 64%. The chance that one succeeds while the other fails is 0.8 × 0.2 × 2 = 32%. The chance that both fail is 0.2 × .2 = 4%. The 80th percentile for each individual event is $50 million, since there is an 80% chance that each individual test will succeed. The sum of the 80% confidence levels is $100 million. The 80th percentile for the two events considered as a portfolio is $150 million, since there is only a 64% chance that both events succeed. The portfolio 80% confidence level exceeds the sum of the 80% confidence levels for the two tests. The portfolio of these two independent events is riskier than if each one was managed completely independently of the other. This does not make sense. Two events when treated as a portfolio should not be riskier than when considered separately. Common sense would tell you that managing two projects as a portfolio should be no riskier than managing them separately. They should be less risky due to diversification benefits. However, measuring risks with percentiles can lead to the opposite conclusion. This occurs frequently whenever percentile funding is used to measure risk, and the level is below the mean. In the example, the mean test cost is 0.64 × $100 million + 0.32 × $150 million + 0.04 × $200 million = $120 million, more than the sum of the individual 80% confidence levels.

As a comparison with previous continuous distribution examples, consider a portfolio of 10 lognormal distributions, with the same means and standard deviations as in Table 5.2 but with funding of each project set to the 50th percentile. See Table 5.6.

Table 5.6 Negative Portfolio Effect When Funding Is at the 50th Percentile

Project	Mean	Standard Deviation	50% Confidence Level
1	$1,696	$1,476	$1,280
2	$1,481	$1,288	$1,117
3	$1,395	$1,214	$1,052
4	$874	$760	$659
5	$840	$731	$634
6	$1,449	$1,261	$1,093
7	$1,638	$1,425	$1,236
8	$1,031	$897	$778
9	$1,271	$1,106	$959
10	$1,937	$1,685	$1,461
Total	$13,612	$6,754	$10,269

Total Portfolio Funding at 36% Confidence Level

Each individual project is funded at the 50th percentile. The overall funding level, which is the sum of the 50th percentiles for each project, is less than the 50th percentile. The total funding is approximately at the 36th percentile. This illustrates that when we fund individual project below the mean, things only get worse, not better, at the portfolio level. Note that the sum of the 50th percentiles for the 10 projects is $10,269, while the 50th percentile for the portfolio is $12,194. This is about 16% lower than that needed if the goal is for the overall confidence level to be at the 50th percentile.

This example is different than the others we have conducted up to this point. The prior examples all looked at a portfolio target for the confidence level. A confidence level required for each project was then determined. This is how it should be done. However, the example in Table 5.6 is how the process occurs in practice. Each individual project is funded at a set level, and then these funding levels are summed to obtain the overall funds needed for the portfolio. There is a great deal of qualitative analysis and collaborative deliberation by leadership in the budget-setting, but there is no quantitative cost risk analysis conducted at the portfolio level. No one truly knows the total confidence level.

Little upside benefits exist in funding to a percentile above the mean since there are only trivial benefits from a portfolio effect for percentile funding. However, when funding to a percentile below the mean, there is a significant downside in that the odds of overruns for the entire portfolio are worse than the odds of any individual project overrunning. See Table 5.7 for a comparison of the individual project confidence levels and the overall portfolio confidence level for 10 projects. Note that the values in Table 5.7 are based on empirical cost growth data and these values will vary in practice based on the risks for individual projects. The total mean is between the 60th and 70th percentile, so funding individual projects below that amount will result in a negative portfolio effect.

Table 5.7   Comparison of Individual Project Confidence Levels and
Portfolio Confidence Level

Individual Project Confidence Level Funding	Portfolio Confidence Level
10%	4%
20%	12%
30%	21%
40%	32%
50%	44%
60%	56%
70%	70%
80%	81%
90%	92%

We see from Table 5.7 that funding individual projects to the 60th percentile results in an overall confidence level for the portfolio at the 56th percentile. The effect worsens for lower levels. The gap is largest when the individual projects are funded between the 23rd and 24th percentiles (not shown in Table 5.7), in which case the overall portfolio confidence level is 13 percentage points lower. For amounts below these, the effect is not as severe and improves a little. The slight improvement is possible only because the overall portfolio confidence level is greater than zero, despite the sincere and repeated attempts of decision makers. It reminds me of a joke about a student who got a zero on a mathematics test. He asked the professor why he got a zero, and she replied that she gave him a zero only because it was impossible to give him a negative score.

Even when a project conducts a quantitative risk analysis and funds to a value that is at the mean or better, it is still likely below the true mean. This is because, as discussed in Chapter 4, risk is not assessed realistically. The 50th percentile for most risk analyses is closer to the 20% confidence level of actual risk. Underestimating risk sets up a negative portfolio effect.

A Wild Ride: The Negative Portfolio Effect for Extreme Risks

When risk has extreme variation, as exhibited by a power-law distribution such as the Pareto, a negative portfolio effect may be guaranteed regardless of the confidence level used for setting budgets for individual projects. For example, if nine projects follow a lognormal distribution and one follows a Pareto distribution with finite mean but infinite variance, budgeting each endeavor to even the 80% confidence level does not guarantee the portfolio will be funded at the 80% confidence level. See Table 5.8 for an illustration.

Table 5.8   The Negative Consequence of 50% Confidence Level Funding When Risks Are Extreme

Project	Mean	Standard Deviation	80% Confidence Level	
1	$1,696	$1,476	$2,312	
2	$1,481	$1,288	$2,019	
3	$1,395	$1,214	$1,902	
4	$874	$760	$1,191	
5	$840	$731	$1,145	
6	$1,449	$1,261	$1,975	
7	$1,638	$1,475	$2,234	
8	$1,031	$897	$1,406	
9	$1,271	$1,106	$1,733	
10	$4,740	N/A	$3,776	Total Portfolio Funding at 78% Confidence Level
Total	$16,415	$71,189	$19,693	

Note that in Table 5.8, one project does not have a standard deviation listed. This is the one where risk is modeled as a Pareto distribution with finite mean but infinite standard deviation. In Table 5.8, funding projects at the 80% confidence level results in a portfolio confidence level equal to 78%, a negative portfolio effect.

The wild variation and funding to a confidence level that is not in the tail of the distribution are the causes.

Low confidence levels for individual projects is bad, but low confidence levels for a portfolio is worse. If there are reserves held at the portfolio level above the project, at least some individual project overruns can be paid for with these reserves. A low confidence level for the portfolio makes a cost overrun for the entire organization more likely. Once this occurs, there is little recourse. An overrun at the portfolio level will lead to project cancellations, scope cuts, or schedule delays due to funding constraints.

SUMMARY AND RECOMMENDATIONS

You go see your financial advisor. She advises you to invest in diseased sheep. You say you think this is unwise. The sheep will likely all die, and you will lose your entire investment. She replies that would be true if you were only investing in one sheep. However, by investing in a portfolio of diseased sheep, when you aggregate the risk, it suddenly vanishes. Would you buy that argument? While it sounds silly, projects behave this way when aggregating risks to the portfolio level.

The purported notion of a portfolio effect when percentiles are used as the risk measure relies on the idea that each individual program has little risk, and that even this amount of risk dissipates once risks for multiple programs are aggregated to a portfolio level. However, as we have seen from the amounts of cost risk for historical programs, this is not a valid assumption. Many projects are breaking new ground with new technologies or using existing technologies in novel ways. This work is often challenging and has significant inherent technical risk.

We started the chapter with an example that showed a 10% savings in cost due to a portfolio effect. We showed that in practice this does not exist. We then discussed how this is handled in practice, which is that projects are typically funded at low levels and that there is no portfolio level cost risk analysis conducted. This results in a negative portfolio effect of approximately 10%. The bottom line is that all organizations, in addition to conducting risk analysis at the project level, also need to conduct risk analysis at the portfolio level. There is no shortcut provided by an imaginary portfolio effect.

The promised "free lunch" part of the portfolio effect is that projects can experience the benefits from diversification while at the same time ignoring the tails of the distribution. To benefit from diversification, the risk measure must account for the extreme risks. Percentile funding does not account for these. The existence of extreme risk must be recognized. In the next chapter, we will revisit the portfolio effect and show the issue lies largely with the way that risk is measured. With the right risk measures, a true portfolio effect will be shown to exist. This will provide the synthesis between the thesis of a portfolio effect and antithesis that it is as imaginary as a free lunch. However, the portfolio effect will still prove to be no free lunch. As we will discuss, it requires substantial amounts of risk reserves.

CHAPTER 6

Here Be Dragons

Considering the Tails in Risk Management

Ensconced in the Rare Book Division of the New York Public Library is a hollow copper globe of the Earth that measures slightly less than four and a half inches in diameter. Dating to 1504, the Hunt-Lenox globe is one of the three earliest still in existence. The phrase "HIC SVNT DRACONES" is inscribed near the eastern coast of Asia, which translates to "Here Be Dragons." Maps from that era often had monsters, sea serpents, or dragons depicted in uncharted or unexplored areas, signifying uncertainty and risk. See Figure 6.1 for a small portion of the Carta Marina, a map of the Nordic countries drafted in 1539 that depicts a sea serpent. A key problem with current risk management practice is that the way it is currently practiced ignores the risks, or dragons, in the right tail.

Establishing a budget or schedule at any predetermined percentile of a risk S-curve that is near the center of the distribution is planning in the dark, ignoring the risky, bad-day events that projects and portfolios should have funds available to pay for. Setting a

Figure 6.1   A Section of the Carta Marina by Olaus Magnus,
Sixteenth Century

Source: Courtesy of the James Ford Bell Library, University of Minnesota

budget or schedule to a high percentile of an S-curve is not much
better because it still ignores the extreme risk in the right tail. Not
all right tails are created equal. Some distributions, such as the triangular, have no tails whatsoever. The Gaussian has a thin tail. The
lognormal has fatter tails but not as fat as the Pareto. As on old
maps that depicted dragons and other monsters in uncharted territory, who knows what risks lurk beyond the 80th or even 90th
percentile?

PROS OF PERCENTILE FUNDING

Ancient Greece is the cradle of civilization. Attempts by ancient
Greek mathematicians to measure the world led to the development
of geometry. During the Renaissance, Western Europe revived the
study of measuring and mapping the world. These activities spurred
a technological revolution that enabled Europeans to conquer
the world. Similarly, attempts to measure risk more definitively,

realistically, and accurately have the potential to revolutionize project management. Up to this point in the book, the representation of risk has focused solely on S-curves. One of the appealing features of S-curves is that they are easy to explain when presenting cost and schedule estimates to management. However, they have serious shortcomings when they are the only way risk is measured and managed. Risk measurement is important, but it also needs to be meaningful. Unfortunately, the use of S-curves is the extent of risk management for most projects.

Optimal Confidence Levels and Diminishing Returns

Typical risk management practice is to set budgets and schedules to the bulk of the distribution, rather than the tails. Some rationale exists for funding near the middle of the distribution, rather than the tail, if the risk follows a Gaussian distribution. Recall that the Gaussian distribution has a bell shape. In Figure 6.2 the slope is steeper near the peak of the distribution, and the slope is flatter out toward the tails.

Figure 6.2   Upper Inflection Point for a Gaussian Distribution

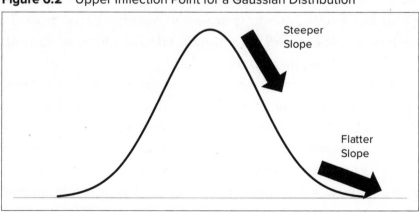

Near the peak, where the slope is steep, the slope is decreasing at an increasing rate. This means for every additional unit of resource, either time or money, added above the mean, it is possible to buy down risk relatively cheaply. At some point, this rate of decrease slows down, and the slope flattens. Mathematicians call this transition between the two different kinds of slopes an inflection point. The inflection point is one at which the slope goes from decreasing rapidly to decreasing slowly. When reducing risk by setting a higher confidence level, the best return is when the slope is steep and negative. Once it slows, it requires increasingly greater amounts of resources to reduce risk.

Consider a Gaussian distribution for cost with mean equal to $100 million and standard deviation equal to $40 million. Recall that for a Gaussian distribution the mean, median, and mode are all equal, so the 50th percentile (median) is equal to $100 million. To set cost to the 60th percentile of this distribution requires an additional $10 million. Another $11 million are required to achieve the 70th percentile. To increase the confidence level from the 70th to the 80th percentile requires an additional $13 million. The inflection point occurs at the 84th percentile. An additional $18 million must be added to the cost to increase the confidence level to the 90th percentile. To go from the 90th to the 99th takes an additional $42 million, and to increase the confidence level from the 99th percentile to the 99.9th percentile takes an additional $31 million. Table 6.1 summarizes these values.

Figure 6.3 shows the rate of change graphically. The required amount increases at an increasing rate above the inflection point. This is a hill that continues to get steeper and steeper. Each additional incremental increase requires more and more time or money to achieve greater confidence levels. I call the inflection point the *pain point* because it is painful to have to spend an increasing amount of resources to achieve only a small increase in the confidence level.

Table 6.1   Diminishing Marginal Returns from Setting Resources to
Extremely High Confidence Levels

Percentile	Cost ($ Million)	Incremental Increase
50th	$100	$0
60th	$110	$10
70th	$121	$11
80th	$134	$13
90th	$151	$17
95th	$166	$15
99th	$193	$27
99.9th	$224	$31

Figure 6.3   Cost and Schedule Needed to Achieve Higher Confidence
Levels Rises Quickly Above the 84th Percentile

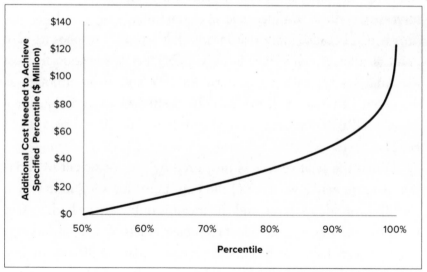

This upward bend makes the cost of using a high percentile to fund a project unpalatable to leadership, as anything beyond the 80th percentile requires large amounts of additional funding to achieve higher confidence levels. However, as mentioned earlier, the "normal" distribution is not so normal when it comes to project risk. Cost risk for projects do not follow a Gaussian distribution. As we discussed in previous chapters, a lognormal distribution better describes fluctuations in project resources. The inflection points for a lognormal are not at fixed confidence levels, and neither is the mean. As the level of risk varies, the equivalent confidence level for the mean and upper inflection point will vary. Recall that the coefficient of variation, the ratio of the standard deviation to the mean, measures the relative risk of a project. A project with a higher coefficient of variation is a riskier one, as this indicates there is more variation around the center of the distribution. As the coefficient of variation increases, the confidence level of the mean increases, and the confidence level of the inflection point decreases. This is bad because more risk means that a project reaches its pain point at a lower confidence level. Coefficients of variation for cost risk analyses typically range between 10% and 50%, although as discussed in Chapter 4, the median coefficient of variation for a variety of different projects at the beginning of detailed development is 92%.

When the relative risk as measured by the coefficient of variation is extremely low, at 10%, the pain point for a lognormal is at the 80% confidence level, and the mean is only slightly higher than the 50% confidence level. Most credible models of risk for development projects have coefficients of variation that are 30% or higher. For a coefficient of variation equal to 30%, the pain point is at the 70% confidence level, and the confidence level of the mean is 55%. When relative risk is 90%, the pain point is a little below the 50% confidence level. At this level of risk, the mean is near the 65% confidence level, past the pain point. As lognormal distributions are better models of cost and schedule risk, this explains why most projects, when they set funding to a confidence level, choose a level that is at or below the 80th percentile. It explains why decision makers, when confronted with funding to 80% confidence levels, have often objected to their use. The real pain point is close to the 50% confidence level and is less than the mean. As we have mentioned most organizations fund to confidence levels between 50% and 80%. However, funding to a percentile below the 90th percentile is funding near the middle of the distribution, rather than the tail. Funding to a percentile at these levels is problematic. It leads to a paradox in that the percentile funding risk measure indicates that the riskier estimate needs less funding than the less risky one.

THE DEVIL IS IN THE TAILS

The tails of a distribution are those values that are far from the mean. They contain outcomes that are unlikely to occur but have big consequences. See Figure 6.4 for a depiction of a Gaussian with the tail areas circled.

Figure 6.4   Gaussian Distribution with Tail Areas Circled

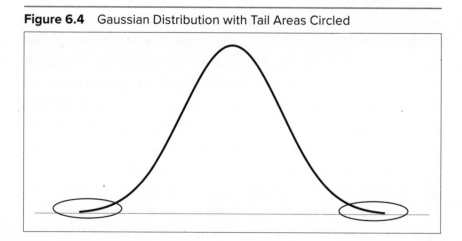

The Gaussian has two tails. One is where outcomes are much lower than average. This is called the left tail. The other is where outcomes are much higher than average. This is called the right tail. For cost and schedule risk, the right tail is the one of concern. This is where the dragons lurk. The Gaussian distribution has the property that about two-thirds of the data points are within one standard deviation of the mean. "Within one" means plus or minus one standard deviation. If the mean for cost risk for a system is $300 million and the standard deviation is $100 million, then the one standard deviation range is $200 on the low side to $400 million on the high side.

Where are the tails of a distribution? The standard for remarkable deviation from the mean is typically two standard deviations. For example, entry into the most popular of the high intelligence quotient (IQ) societies, Mensa, requires an IQ measurement that is at least two standard deviations above mean the IQ. As another example, the mean height for adult males in the United States is 70 inches (5 feet, 10 inches), with a standard deviation equal to 3 inches. I used to work with someone who is 6 feet, 5 inches tall. He is generally considered to be well above average height. One mutual colleague refers to him as "Tall Paul." Tall Paul is definitely in the right tail when it comes to height. He is also more than two standard deviations above the mean height for adult males.

Recall from Chapter 3 that the probability of a two–standard deviation event is 5%. As the Gaussian is symmetric, the probability of an event that is two standard deviations above the mean is half that, or about 2.5%. For a Gaussian, a right tail event has a probability equal to 2.5%. There is a 97.5% probability that right tail events will not occur. For non-Gaussian distributions, defining the right tail is more difficult. As long as the mean and variance are finite, we can use a distribution-free measure to determine the tails. Regardless of the distribution type, the Chebyshev inequality guarantees that at most 12.5% of the distribution is more than two standard deviations above the mean. This puts the two standard deviations mark at the 87.5th percentile. Therefore, regardless of the underlying distribution, as long as the mean and standard deviation are finite, the standard rule for exceptional variation of the mean is beyond the 80th percentile. Exceptional variation, the tail of a distribution, starts near the 90% confidence level.

THE SHORTCOMINGS OF CONFIDENCE LEVELS FOR RISK MANAGEMENT

One of the shortcomings of percentile funding is that projects do not fund to levels that are in the tails of the cost and schedule risk distributions. The confidence level ignores values above it, so confidence levels do not account for extreme events. If a project is funded to a high confidence level, such as the 80th percentile, that is not enough information to make a good judgment. A single confidence level value alone provides no information about what could potentially happen if the value is exceeded. When thinking about risk we focus too much on the likelihood of occurrence and not enough on the consequences. To understand the importance of this, suppose a stranger came up to you and offered you a chance to play a game where you have a greater than 80% chance of winning. Would you play? Chance is much more than just the likelihood of occurrence of a good or bad outcome. The consequence matters just as much as, and often more than, the likelihood, depending on the severity of the consequence. What if the outcome is: When you win you get no reward, but if you lose, you die? I would think no reasonable person would play this game, but many people have. What I have just described are the likelihood of occurrence and outcomes of the potentially deadly game called Russian roulette.

As a second thought experiment, suppose you are shopping for a new car. You mention that safety is your top concern. The salesman says he has a great, safe car available. You ask about airbags. The salesman answers that the airbags work fine 80% of the time. However, 20% of the time, the airbags will fail to deploy. Would you buy such a car? According to hedge fund manager David Einhorn, "Risk management is the airbag that must always work, but only in the multi-[standard deviation] event where you have an accident."[1] This is opposite of percentile budgeting to manage risk. The investment bank Merrill Lynch stated that percentile funding measures "do not convey the magnitude of extreme events."[2] Percentile budgeting does not convey the full picture—it leaves out the part that matters. A leading writer on risk, Nassim Taleb, when asked about percentile funding, stated, "You're worse off relying on misleading information than on not having any information at all. If you give a pilot an altimeter that is sometimes defective, he will crash the plane. Give him nothing at all and he will look out the window."[3] The point is that average, boring events should not be a project's only focus when considering risk. However, that is all the protection provided by setting budgets and schedules to confidence levels.

Unfortunately, another bias I have noticed over time is that there is also a tendency, when an event's likelihood of occurrence is high, to consider that event as an absolute certainty. I have seen cases where any probability that is 80% or above is considered "almost certain." Funding to a specific percentile provides no insight into how much extra money may be needed in reserves. Depending upon the variance of the cost or schedule risk distribution and other statistical characteristics, such as skewness and kurtosis, the amount of extra funding needed can vary significantly. Thus, the right tail (the portion of a probability distribution in the region of the higher percentiles) must be taken into consideration when establishing reserves.

As an illustration of this concept, consider four different distribution types. See Figure 6.5. In this figure, four distributions—a triangular, Gaussian, lognormal, and Pareto—are all displayed. Although each of the distributions has the same 70th percentile, this fact provides no information about the right tails of each distribution. None of them have the same tail behavior, as is evident from the S-curves' right tails, displayed in Figure 6.6.

Figure 6.5   Four Different Distributions with the Same 70th Percentile

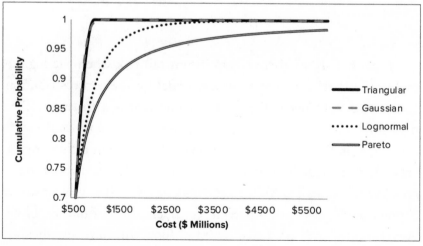

Figure 6.6   The Tail Behavior of Four Different Distributions with the Same 70th Percentile

The triangular distribution has no tail—it is truncated at the maximum value. The Gaussian distribution has a thin tail. There is relatively little risk beyond the 70th percentile. The lognormal has a slightly fatter tail, and the Pareto has an extremely fat tail. The 70th percentile for all four distributions is $600 million. However, to fund to the 80th percentile, an additional:

- $60 million is needed for the Gaussian
- $80 million is required for the triangular
- $163 million is needed for the lognormal
- $220 million more is required for the Pareto

A detailed comparison of the confidence levels of the four distributions beyond the 70th percentile is shown in Table 6.2.

Table 6.2 Comparison of Tail Percentiles for the Four Distributions

Percentile	Triangular	Gaussian	Lognormal	Pareto
70th	$600	$600	$600	$600
80th	$680	$660	$763	$820
90th	$770	$744	$1,064	$1,397
95th	$840	$814	$1,401	$2,381
99th	$930	$944	$2,347	$8,201

Table 6.2 shows there is significant tail risk when the lognormal or the Pareto is an appropriate model for the cost distribution. Indeed the 99th percentile for the lognormal is 4 times the 70th percentile. For the Pareto, the 99th percentile is 13 times the 70th percentile, indicating enormous tail risk. Should four different projects whose cost distributions follow the four different risk profiles seen in this example be funded at the same level? That is what would happen in the case of 70 percent confidence level funding. However, funding each project at $600 million will have significantly

different consequences when the 70 percent confidence level is exceeded.

As discussed earlier, the Pareto distribution in this example models extreme cost-risk behavior, such as that exhibited by a highly complex project that is not subject to cancellation. The lognormal will be the better distribution for most projects. The Pareto is not applicable to schedules at all. The tail risk exhibited by the lognormal will be representative of most project schedules.

PASCAL'S WAGER

The seventeenth-century French mathematician Blaise Pascal was one of the originators of probability theory. After a religious experience, Pascal largely stopped working in mathematics and turned his attention to writing about spiritual matters. His most famous work, *Pensées* ("Thoughts"), was published after Pascal died at age 39. Pascal applied his mathematical skills to the subject of faith. One of the arguments he makes for belief in God is now called Pascal's Wager, which is a good example of the difference between likelihood and consequence. Pascal had noticed that the French nobility would risk wealth and social standing on the rolls of dice, so they should also be willing to wager their souls on the possibility of eternal life. Although many intellectuals at that time thought that belief in God was not rational, Pascal used the logic of mathematics and an analogy to games of chance to argue that it is reasonable to believe in a supreme being. Pascal's Wager considers the risks involved in belief and unbelief. Everyone makes this choice as they actively believe in God or decline active belief. The declination can either be a belief that there is no God (atheism) or an unwillingness to decide (agnosticism). Belief and unbelief can be viewed as two sides of a wager. On one side, suppose someone does not believe in God. The potential long-term consequence if God does exist is eternal damnation. If there is no God, nothing is lost. On the other side, if someone chooses to believe in God, the potential long-term loss if there is no God is nothing. The potential gain in belief in God, if God does exist, however, is eternal life. Pascal cast this as a comparison of expected values.[4] However, the real difference in the outcomes is not the likelihood but the consequences. Even if someone believes that the probability of the existence of a supreme being is low, say 1%, the hidden dragon of potential long-term consequences is lurking in the tail of the distribution. In this case, a 90% confidence level says there is no negative consequence for unbelief and no positive consequence for belief. See Table 6.3 for a graphical illustration of the importance of consequence for Pascal's Wager. Even if the probability of existence is less than 0.0001%, the consequences far outweigh any consideration of probability. The purpose of this example is not to argue the case for religion. Its point is to stress that in assessing risk we need to let go of our intrinsic need to be correct and consider consequences.

Table 6.3 Pascal's Wager: The Importance of Consequence

		Actual	
		Exists	Does Not Exist
Belief	Exists	Good!	No Consequence
	Does Not Exist	Bad!	No Consequence

THE LOGNORMAL PARADOX

Leaving out consideration of the tails of the distribution in risk management leads to logical quandaries. As an example, consider two projects. The schedule estimates for both are best represented by lognormal distributions. The low-risk project has mean equal to 80 months and standard deviation equal to 20 months. The high-risk project has mean equal to 80 months and standard deviation equal to 40 months. The two projects have the same mean, but the high-risk undertaking has a standard deviation that is twice as large as the low-risk one. Although the high-risk project is riskier than the low-risk one, that is not what confidence level funding indicates. Up to the 64th percentile, the high-risk project is less risky than the low-risk one. For example, the 50th percentile for the low-risk project is 78 months, while for the high-risk one it is 72 months. To achieve a 50 percent confidence level for the riskier project, six months less time is required. See Figure 6.7.

Figure 6.7 Scheduling at the 50th Percentile for Two Different Lognormal Distributions

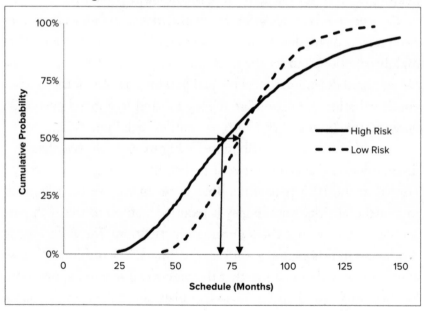

Imagine that you are a schedule estimator working for a project office. You have modeled schedule with a lognormal distribution. As the project matures, a new risk is discovered, and the project

manager wants to know the impact on the initial risk analysis. The schedule was set at the 50th percentile. You are now asked to determine how much extra time will be required to achieve the 50 percent confidence level. Imagine the project manager's surprise when you tell her that she needs less time because of the additional potential hazard. She will likely tell you that you must have made a mistake and tell you to come back once you have found the correct conclusion. However, that is the right answer in this case; it just isn't useful or applicable.

Recall that the lognormal has a fatter right tail than the Gaussian distribution. However for a Gaussian distribution and a lognormal distribution with the same mean and standard deviation, percentile funding will indicate higher risk for the Gaussian distribution from below the 50th percentile to at least the 84th percentile, approximately one standard deviation above the mean.[5] As an example, let two projects be modeled with a Gaussian distribution and a lognormal distribution, and let the mean for each equal $100 million and the standard deviation for each equal $40 million. Then, the Gaussian distribution requires more money to fund to a given percentile between the 22nd and the 90th percentiles. See Figure 6.8.

For the Gaussian distribution in Figure 6.8, we see that this distribution is riskier in terms of percentile funding than the lognormal at the 70th percentile. That is, when we use the Gaussian to model cost risk, more money is required to fund to the 70th percentile than if we use the lognormal distribution. The difference is significant in this example—it is approximately $7 million. We discussed in an earlier chapter that the lognormal is more appropriate for modeling risk than the Gaussian distribution, since it accounts for the wider variations in cost growth that we see in the empirical data. This means that the lognormal models more risk than the Gaussian distribution. However, when we use percentiles of the cost risk distribution as the risk measure, it appears that the Gaussian bears more risk. This is because percentile funding does not consider

Figure 6.8 Funding Required at the 80th Percentile for Gaussian and Lognormal Distributions

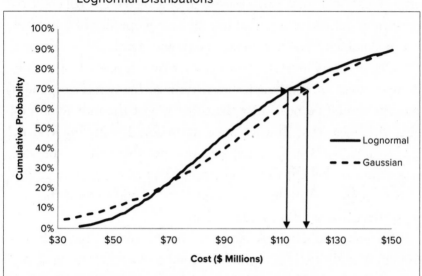

the tail. I term this the Lognormal Paradox—even though the lognormal is used to incorporate more risk than the Gaussian, in the case when confidence levels are used, the lognormal appears to have less risk at confidence levels at or below the 80% confidence level.

THINKING COHERENTLY ABOUT RISK

Funding to percentiles is not a good way to measure risk, nor is it an effective way to manage it, for all the reasons we have mentioned. If percentiles are not a good risk measure, then what should be used to measure cost and schedule risk? A single value that represents the risk for a cost risk distribution is called a *risk measure*. A risk measure quantifies exposure to risk. How do we know which risk measures are "good" and which are not? In other words, what properties should a risk measure have? This issue has been studied for the insurance

industry specifically and for risk measurement in general.[6] Four properties must hold for a risk measure to be coherent. A coherent risk
measure is defined as one that has the four properties of subadditivity, monotonicity, positive homogeneity, and translation invariance.

One property important for a risk measure is that when two random variables are combined, the portfolio of the two corresponding
projects should be no riskier than the sum of the individual projects' risk measures. The technical term for this in financial risk
is *subadditivity*. This property ensures that there should be some
diversification benefit from combining risks from separate projects
into a portfolio. A better-known term for subadditivity is the portfolio effect that we discussed in Chapter 5.

A second property risk measures should have is that, if the cost
of item X is always higher than a second cost Y, then the risk measure of X should be higher than the risk measure for Y. For example,
if for a system the cost of a structural component is higher in every
circumstance than the cost of electronics, then the 80th percentile
of the cost risk distribution should be higher for the structural component than for the electronics. This is the property of monotonicity.

A third property needed for a risk measure is that it should be
invariant with respect to the currency in which the risk is measured
or whether cost is reported in thousands or millions of dollars. It also
includes the characteristic that an equivalent increase or decrease in
exposure to the risk requires an equivalent change in the amount
of capital needed to guard against that risk. This is the property of
positive homogeneity. This property makes sense because risk characteristics should not change based on the unit in which the risk is
measured. For example, the only difference between the measurement of risk reserves in thousands rather than millions of dollars
should be that when measured in thousands of dollars, the risk
reserves should be multiplied by 1,000.

The fourth property—translation invariance—is based on the
recognition that a project may consist of some aspects that are risky

and some that are not. In this case, the project consists of a portion that is subject to risk and another portion that is not. The cost of the portion subject to risk is a random variable, but the cost of the portion not subject to risk is a fixed, constant amount. The total risk reserve should be the sum of an amount determined by the risk of the nondeterministic component and the fixed, deterministic amount. An example of this would be a project that includes a firm fixed-price contract for a single component. The rest of the system will have risk, but from the project's perspective, the contract bears no risk. If the 80th percentile of the risk distribution for the rest of the system is $70 million, and the fixed-price contract for the component is $10 million, then the total 80th percentile is $70 million + $10 million= $80 million.

A simple and popular risk measure is defined as the mean plus a fixed number of standard deviations, which is called the standard deviation principle. As we discussed earlier, the mean, median, and mode are measures of centrality for a random variable, and the standard deviation measures the amount of variation around the central tendency. For a schedule estimate, if the mean is 60 months and the standard deviation is 20 months, then the standard deviation principle using one standard deviation is 80 months. While the standard deviation principle has three of the coherent properties, it is not monotonic. The underlying reason is that standard deviation measures uncertainty rather than risk. Recall from our earlier discussion that uncertainty is the indefiniteness about an outcome, while risk is the chance of loss. Uncertainty includes both the opportunities for reducing cost and schedule, while risk is the chance the cost and schedule will increase. The qualities of a risk measure are focused on risk, so standard deviation and variance should not be used as risk measures.[7]

As a risk measure, confidence level is translation invariant, monotonic, and positive homogeneous. However, if the risk is not Gaussian or lognormal, there is no guarantee of subadditivity.

Indeed, in the last chapter we demonstrated an example of one Pareto and nine lognormal distributions where confidence level funding exhibits a negative portfolio effect. In the case where funding is below the mean, this reverse diversification was shown to occur when modeling cost risk with a lognormal distribution. When funding is at the mean or greater for lognormal distributions, the overall effect is that the sums of the risks are subadditive, so there is a slight diversification benefit. However, when modeled realistically, the benefit is trivially small. This is the reason why the confidence level, when used alone as a risk measure, makes no sense. Up to this point, we have been examining the symptoms, such as the Lognormal Paradox, but lack of logical consistency is the root cause.

EXPECTED SHORTFALL AND THE SEMI-DEVIATION PRINCIPLE

The simplest coherent risk measure is the mean. The mean is a weighted average of all the points in the distribution, so it incorporates the tail. The means add, so the sum of the means is always the mean of the sums. There is no diversification benefit, but there is no negative portfolio effect either. This additivity has its appeal, since it makes this risk measure easier to understand, easy to explain to management, and easy to communicate to budget analysts and accountants. Because of these reasons, the mean is used as a risk measure by some organizations. However, the mean does not provide information about what to do once cost has grown past the expected value. It provides no idea how much more money might be needed. To help with these questions, we look at two other coherent risk measures—expected shortfall and the positive semi-deviation principle.

A risk measure based on confidence levels that is coherent and provides more than just a measure of when things go awry is called expected shortfall.[8] This risk measure is the expected amount of cost or schedule growth conditional on growth reaching a specified percentile. This idea takes the confidence level idea and makes it coherent by incorporating the tail region beyond the percentile.

For example, consider a single project for which schedule risk follows a lognormal distribution with mean equal to 100 months and standard deviation equal to 50 months. The 70th percentile for this distribution is approximately equal to 115 months, and the expected shortfall once the costs exceeds the 70th percentile is 160 months. Therefore, given that the 70th percentile has been reached, the expected amount needed to complete the project will be 160 months, 45 months longer than the 70th percentile schedule. The expected shortfall in this case is 40% longer than the 70 percent confidence level schedule.

Expected shortfall provides a true quantitative risk management approach. It establishes a trigger at a specified confidence level. This is pulled once cost or schedule grows to the percentile at which project funding has been set. It provides risk management by also including an additional amount of reserves set aside once the specified confidence level is exceeded. Expected shortfall provides additional detail about the right tail relevant to a sensible risk management policy, and it is a coherent risk measure.[9] It solves the issue with percentile funding. Because this risk measure takes into account the full right tail of the distribution, it does not suffer from the Lognormal Paradox or any of the other issues associated with percentile funding.

Expected shortfall was introduced in the late 1990s and quickly became the preferred standard for setting liabilities for insurance settings. In Canada, the "actuarial Standards of Practice promulgate the use of [conditional tail expectation] (a risk measure similar to expected shortfalls) whenever stochastic methods are used to set balance sheet liabilities."[10] Expected shortfall forms the basis for the Swiss Solvency Test,[11] which forms a major part of Swiss insurance

policy. The National Association of Insurance Commissioners recommends setting reserves using this method.[12]

See Table 6.4 for a comparison of confidence level funding and
expected shortfall when cost risk is modeled as Gaussian and lognormal distributions. The distribution has mean = $100 million and
standard deviation = $40 million.

Table 6.4   Confidence Level and Expected Shortfall Values for
Lognormal and Gaussian Distributions

		Percentile			
		50%	80%	90%	95%
Percentile Funding	Gaussian	$100	$134	$151	$166
	Lognormal	$93	$128	$152	$175
		50%	80%	90%	95%
Expected Shortfall	Gaussian	$132	$156	$170	$183
	Lognormal	$130	$162	$185	$208

In Table 6.4, for expected shortfall with trigger at the 50th
percentile, an additional 30% is required for both the Gaussian
and lognormal. At the 80th percentile, an additional 56% to 62%
is needed above the mean to fund to the expected shortfall. For
the lognormal at the 95th percentile, more than double the mean
is needed to fund to the expected shortfall. Here there be dragons
indeed!

To see how expected shortfall could be used for risk management, as well as risk measurement, the percentile value gives an
indication that significant risk has been realized. When that happens, the additional expected funding held as a reserve is released
to address the overrun. If risk follows a lognormal as in Table 6.4,
then if we fund to the 80th percentile at $128 million, we would
hold an additional $34 million in reserve. This is a total set of
reserves equal to 62% more than the mean estimate. This seems

like a large contingency, but this model has mild risk. The level of risk is less than implied by historical cost growth—the true risk is likely even greater. While this seems like a significant amount to set aside, keep in mind the alternative. If additional funding is not available when required, project progress is disrupted. If no reserves are available when cost exceeds funded amounts, the project will have to replan, rescope, reschedule, and sometimes issue stop-work orders. As the old saying goes, an army travels on its stomach. Similarly, a project cannot progress without funding. Interruptions in funding, schedule slips, and rescopes introduce inefficiencies in the project. As a result, the product is delivered later, at greater cost, and with less capability.

If expected shortfall requires too much reserves, there is an alternative for quantitative risk management guidance. The positive semi-deviation principle is a coherent risk measure that is like the standard deviation principle. The difference is that the positive semi-deviation principle only considers variations above the mean. Attention is restricted to risk, rather than uncertainty. Because the focus is risk, the positive semi-deviation principle has diversification benefits. This measure also has the other properties of coherence as well, so unlike the standard deviation principle, the positive semi-deviation principle is also monotonic.[13]

To illustrate the difference between standard deviation and positive semi-deviation, consider the following example of two projects that have the same degree of uncertainty but much different risks. Project 1 has an 80% chance that cost will equal $100 million, but there is a 20% chance that the cost of the project can be cut in half, or $50 million. Project 2 has an 80% chance that the cost will be $50 million, with a 20% chance that the cost will double to $100 million. Project 1 is expected to cost $90 million (= $50 million × 0.2 + $100 million × 0.8), while Project 2 has an expected cost equal to $60 million. However, both projects have the same standard deviation, which is equal to $20 million. For Project 1, the standard deviation principle would set the budget at $110 million, or $10 million more than the project will cost in the worst case. For Project 2, the standard deviation principle is more reasonable, since it would set the budget to $60 million + $20 million = $80 million, which is more than the mean, but not more than the project can possibly cost. The positive semi-deviation, by contrast, considers that there is a different skew in the uncertainty in each project and adjusts accordingly. The positive semi-deviation for Project 1 is approximately $9 million, while for Project 2 it is approximately $18 million. See Table 6.5 for a summary of this information.

Table 6.5　Comparing Standard Deviation and Positive Semi-Deviation

	Project 1		Project 2	
	Likelihood of Occurrence	Cost	Likelihood of Occurrence	Cost
	80%	$100	20%	$100
	20%	$50	80%	$50
Mean	$90		$60	
Standard Deviation	$20		$20	
Positive Semi-Deviation	$9		$18	

The semi-standard deviation principle provides not only a risk measurement but also an objective, quantitative metric of how much more should be set aside in case something bad occurs. For example, the trigger could be that the cost grows beyond the mean, setting into place a risk reserve equal to one positive semi-deviation beyond the mean to account for additional cost growth.[14]

For a Gaussian distribution, recall two-thirds of the cost is within one standard deviation of the mean, and 95% is within two standard deviations. With positive semi-deviation, only half of this variation is considered (the risk half of total uncertainty), so two natural values of multiples of positive semi-deviation to consider are 1/2 and 1. The former is the mean plus one-half positive semi-deviation, and the latter is the mean plus one positive semi-deviation. If risk is modeled as a lognormal, with mean equal to $100 million and standard deviation equal to $88 million, the mean plus one-half positive semi-deviation is $139 million. The mean plus one positive semi-deviation is $178 million.

See Tables 6.6 and 6.7 for a comparison of several risk measures, including the mean, percentile funding, positive semi-deviation, and expected shortfall. Table 6.6 compares the risk measures for cost when modeled as a lognormal with mean equal to $100 million and standard deviation equal to $87 million. Table 6.7 compares the risk measures for schedule when modeled as a lognormal with mean equal to 72 months and standard deviation equal to 30 months.

As demonstrated in Tables 6.6 and 6.7, positive semi-deviation does not require the same level of high reserves needed for expected shortfall, at least when the trigger used for expected shortfall uses a high confidence level. For both cost and schedule, setting the expected shortfall trigger at the 80 percent confidence level means setting aside reserves above the 90th percentile. The semi-deviation measures are between the 70th and 90th percentiles.

Table 6.6 Comparison of Risk Measures for a Cost Estimate

Risk Measure	Value	Difference from Mean
50th Percentile	$75	−$25
Mean	$100	$0
70th Percentile	$112	$12
Mean + 1/2 Positive Semi-Deviation	$139	$39
80th Percentile	$142	$42
Mean + 1 Positive Semi-Deviation	$177	$77
Expected Shortfall — 70th Percentile	$197	$97
90th Percentile	$197	$97
Expected Shortfall − 80th Percentile	$232	$132

Table 6.7 Comparison of Risk Measures for a Schedule Estimate

Risk Measure	Value	Difference from Mean
50th Percentile	65	−7
Mean	72	0
70th Percentile	82	10
Mean + 1/2 Positive Semi-Deviation	84	12
80th Percentile	93	21
Mean + 1 Positive Semi-Deviation	96	24
Expected Shortfall — 70th Percentile	108	36
90th Percentile	111	39
Expected Shortfall — 80th Percentile	119	47

THE PORTFOLIO EFFECT REVISITED

Up to this point, the portfolio effect has only been discussed in terms of confidence level funding. We saw earlier that for confidence level funding there is no guarantee of subadditivity. Even when it does occur, the effect is trivially small. However, what about other risk measures? Coherent risk measures are guaranteed to be subadditive. We have considered three: the mean, expected shortfall, and positive semi-deviation principle. As we mentioned earlier, the mean is strictly additive—the sum of the means is always the mean of the sums. There is no portfolio effect when considering the mean. For the other two, we reconsider the portfolio of 10 lognormal distributions with the same means and standard deviations as in Table 5.2 in the previous chapter. See Table 6.8. The expected shortfall for the overall 80th percentile is $27,824. The sum of the expected shortfalls for the 10 projects in the portfolio is $31,565. Looking at Table 6.8, the expected shortfall trigger can be set to the 73rd percentile for each project to achieve an equivalent portfolio level expected shortfall with an 80th percentile trigger. This is a significant portfolio effect, as it is a 12% savings over the sum of the expected shortfalls for the 80th percentile for each of the 10 projects. However, even though there is a significant portfolio effect, the amount of reserves needed is still a staggering sum, more than double the mean. Most decision makers would not be willing to hold anywhere near that much for management reserves.

Table 6.8   Portfolio Effect with Expected Shortfall

Project	Mean	Standard Deviation	ES for 73% Confidence Level
1	$1,696	$1,476	$3,467
2	$1,481	$1,288	$3,027
3	$1,395	$1,214	$2,851
4	$874	$760	$1,787
5	$840	$731	$1,717
6	$1,449	$1,261	$2,962
7	$1,638	$1,425	$3,348
8	$1,031	$897	$2,107
9	$1,271	$1,106	$2,598
10	$1,937	$1,685	$3,959
Total	$13,612	$9,161	$27,824

Expected Shortfall for 80% Confidence at Portfolio Level

Compared to expected shortfall, the positive semi-deviation principle does not typically require as much reserves. However, the positive semi-deviation principle has a significant portfolio effect. Each project can be funded at the mean plus three-quarters of one positive semi-deviation and still achieve the mean plus one positive semi-deviation at the overall portfolio level. See Table 6.9 for an example.

Table 6.9 Portfolio Effect with the Positive Semi-Deviation Principle

Project	Mean	Standard Deviation	Mean + 0.75 × Positive Semi–Deviation
1	$1,696	$1,476	$2,667
2	$1,481	$1,288	$2,329
3	$1,395	$1,214	$2,194
4	$874	$760	$1,375
5	$840	$731	$1,321
6	$1,449	$1,261	$2,279
7	$1,638	$1,425	$2,576
8	$1,031	$897	$1,622
9	$1,271	$1,106	$1,999
10	$1,937	$1,685	$3,047
Total	$13,612	$9,161	$21,409

Mean + One Positive Semi-Deviation at Portfolio Level

For the 10 projects in Table 6.9, the sum of the means plus each project's positive semi-deviation is $24,063. The portfolio positive semi-deviation value equal to $21,409 is an 11% savings. There is still a significant amount of reserves needed above the mean for the positive semi-deviation principle but not nearly as much as the reserves needed for the expected shortfall as in Table 6.8.

A portfolio effect can be achieved. The catch is that a coherent risk measure must be used, such as expected shortfall or the positive semi-deviation principle. The portfolio effect is still not a free lunch. The cost of achieving it requires holding high levels of reserves.

SUMMARY AND RECOMMENDATIONS

The use of confidence levels as the sole quantitative measure for risk management is not logically consistent. The underlying reason is that this approach ignores the tails of the distribution, where the true risks/dragons lurk. Also, using confidence levels to set budgets and establish schedules only reports that risks have been realized. As a risk management strategy, it fails to provide any advice on reserves needed in case significant risks are realized. Funding to low percentiles on an S-curve magnifies the problem. This is illustrated by the Lognormal Paradox—when funding to confidence levels below the 85th percentile, riskier programs require less funding, not more.

Better risk measures that also provide risk management reserves exist. Expected shortfall is like confidence level funding but also looks at the expected overrun of a set confidence level when it is breached. The positive semi-deviation principle is like the standard deviation principle but only considers risk above the mean, rather than the spread around it. These measures provide a significant portfolio effect. They do this because they consider the full right tail of the cost and schedule risk distributions. This is the synthesis of the portfolio effect thesis and the antithesis that the portfolio effect is as fictional as a free lunch, which is that a portfolio effect exists when the right tail of the cost risk distribution is considered. A portfolio effect can be achieved, but it's not free. Hefty reserves are required with these coherent methods. After all, "there ain't no such thing as a free lunch"! Confidence levels provide useful information but should not be used on their own. All projects should use coherent risk measures to provide effective quantitative risk management.

CHAPTER 7

Trying to Do Too Much with Too Little

The Importance of Portfolio Planning

Anyone who has driven during rush hour in a big city knows that traffic can be a nightmare. The problem is worse when weather conditions are less than optimal. A rainy day can slow already congested traffic to a crawl. I almost missed a flight home from Ronald Reagan Washington National Airport once because I did not consider the impact of rain on traffic. I am someone who tries to get to the airport at least two hours beforehand to make sure I make my flight, but even taking this into account was not enough. The only reason I did not miss my flight was because the rain had also delayed flights into and out of the airport.

A primary cause of the problem with traffic in big cities is more cars than a road system can handle. A variety of things can and have been done in some cities to optimize traffic signals, add mass transit, add new roads, and other measures. Optimization of traffic signals only helps so much. Even when cities expand roadways, they

195

have trouble keeping up with the growth in demand. A primary problem continues to be too many cars on roads. In some cities where there is a lot of pedestrian traffic, the number of people on foot also has an impact of traffic flow. Likewise, when an organization tries to execute too many programs relative to its budget, the result is congestion. Without enough money to spread across the many programs, funding constraints lead to schedule delays and cost overruns. This is a common problem in organizations that conduct multiple projects at the same time. A root cause of this problem is a lack of risk analysis at the portfolio level. An absence of understanding of the portfolio risk contributes to the tendency to try to accomplish too much with the available resources.

The genesis of new projects is often the search to spend idle funds. An organization's leadership may discover that it has a relatively small amount of money that can be used to research a new technology or to begin initial development of a new project. New ideas abound to improve systems or to develop better ones. To convince leadership, project managers tend to provide success-oriented, optimistic projections. Projects take several years to complete, but often only the initial year is considered when starting these endeavors. The initial year, which only requires some seed money, is only the tip of the iceberg and does not consider the significant full cost of development, production, operations, and sustainment. As a result, projects often begin small, but there are insufficient funds to adequately execute these projects as they mature. This strains the other projects in the portfolio. To keep from cancelling projects in which a great deal of time and money have already been invested, all the schedules are stretched. This results in cost overruns throughout the portfolio. These cost increases further lead to hitting funding constraints of the portfolio in future years, leading to still more schedule slips. This is a vicious downward spiral that results in producing less by trying to do too much.

Cost and schedule are highly correlated and closely linked. An increase in schedule results in a fixed labor cost charging to the project for a longer period of time, which results in an increase in cost. On the other hand, a decrease in schedule may also require additional labor due to a suboptimal allocation of resources. For example, some tasks may have to be performed in parallel that work better when performed sequentially. Also, immature technologies are often incorporated in a design before they are fully developed, leading to implementation problems. Thus, changes in schedule have a significant impact on cost. In addition, changes in cost affect schedule. A funding ceiling or cap can increase overall program cost and lengthen schedule by causing a nonoptimal allocation of resources.

COST PHASING

Three connected areas of a project are cost, schedule, and phasing of cost over the schedule duration. For a given cost and a given schedule, cost must be phased throughout a project. Cost phasing is done on a consistent periodic basis, such as a monthly, quarterly, or annual spread. The format is a percent spread of cost compared to the percent completed for the schedule. For a project with a five-year duration with a total cost equal to $100 million, suppose that the annual costs are phased: 5% in the first year; 30% in the second year; 40% in the third year; 20% in the fourth year; and 5% in the fifth and final year. This phasing is displayed graphically in Figure 7.1.

Development projects tend to be front-loaded, and empirical evidence suggests that approximately 60% or more of the cost being spent at the schedule midpoint is appropriate for phasing the cost of such projects.[1] See Figure 7.2 for a notional comparison of front-loaded, back-loaded, and evenly loaded cost profiles.

Figure 7.1   Cost Phasing Example

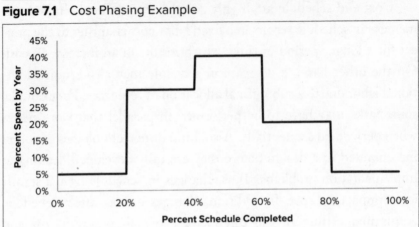

Figure 7.2   Comparison of Cost Profiles

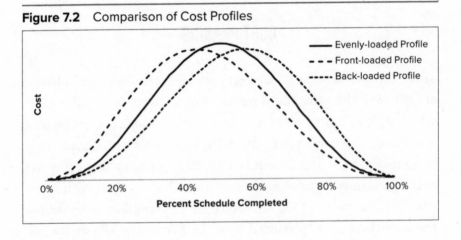

ZUGZWANG: ANY CHANGE IN SCHEDULE INCREASES COST

We saw in Chapter 2 that when cost, schedule, and technical performance are not aligned, problems arise. In the game of chess, the German word *zugzwang* is used to refer to a position in which a player cannot move without weakening his or her chances of winning. Any change to a schedule is like that—any move—will increase cost. Unlike chess players, projects can avoid making a change to the schedule, although that is not always subject to the project's control. The abundance of external factors on projects is a major source of risk. Most external risks, such as funding constraints, cause the schedule to lengthen. When a schedule lengthens, cost increases. Part of the reason for the increase is that projects have a significant fixed cost. If this fixed cost occurs over a longer period, the total amount increases. The other factor is that depending on when the slip occurs, the cost that varies over the schedule also charges to the project longer, increasing cost. This can be represented as a stretching of the funding profile to the right. Since the area under the funding profile is equal to the total cost, the extra area created by the schedule increase represents the amount of cost growth. See Figure 7.3 for an illustration of this concept. In the graph, Added Cost is the cost growth due to the schedule slip.

Figure 7.3   The Impact of a Schedule Increase on the Cost Profile

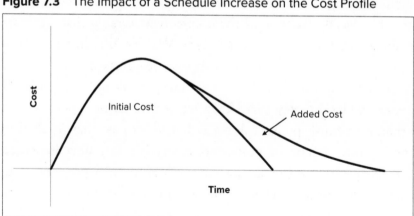

The effect of changes in cost depends upon three factors: the shape of the phasing profile, the amount of schedule growth, and the point at which the schedule increase occurs. The shape of the

phasing profile includes the degree to which it is front-loaded or back-loaded and how high the peak funding is relative to the rest of the phasing. Schedule increases have a bigger impact on cost when profiles are back-loaded or when the schedule growth occurs near the peak of the funding profile.[2]

Optimistic project managers often claim that proposed schedules have significant slack. In a few instances, projects have been able to cut cost and save time by optimizing the schedule. In the most dramatic instance, the Delta 180 project cut both cost and schedule by more than 50% from the initial plan. This 1980s missile defense experiment was able to achieve significant savings by reducing project oversight, establishing a small set of requirements, and keeping requirements steady throughout development.[3] However, this project is the exception rather than the rule. The history of schedule growth for most programs indicates that, if anything, planned schedules are optimistic. Schedules that are already optimistic are compressed to a lesser or larger degree during the planning stages. Attempting to do too much in too short a time frame typically has one of three outcomes. One is that steps are skipped, leading to technical failure. We saw this in the case of Knight Capital in Chapter 2. This once leading financial services firm put test software into operations, resulting in significant losses and bankruptcy. NASA's faster-better-cheaper policy was an attempt to finish projects faster and at lower cost that resulted in more project failures. Another possibility is that money is poured into the project. In the rare instance of high-priority projects where money is no object, overtime work and multiple shifts can get more work accomplished in a shorter time period. If some serial schedule activities can be rearranged to be conducted in parallel, this can also reduce the expected time to complete the schedule. However, as we saw in the aircraft refurbishment example in Chapter 3, activities conducted in parallel often result in additional risk. Any delay in one set of parallel activities results in a delay of the next set of activities that follow. A third possibility is that, like a compressed spring on which pressure is not maintained, the schedule recoils and lengthens significantly, which leads to cost growth. Corners can be cut to save time and money, but this comes at a high risk of technical failure. One such corner commonly cut in projects is the attempt to develop and build the project at the same time.

As an example of the negative effects of trying to compress schedule, the United Kingdom's National Health Service embarked on an information technology project in the early 2000s. The goal was to integrate all healthcare records into one system. Initial planned cost was 6.4 billion pounds.[4] The project encountered significant problems from the outset due to multiple poor decisions. Contracts were awarded to multiple lead contractors, which as we mentioned in the discussion on cost and schedule growth, typically leads to significant cost increases. The project leaders set short timelines for contractor schedules, setting them up for failure. One of the contractors eventually walked away from multiple billions of pounds. Project management also tried to shorten the schedule by not taking time to thoroughly establish requirements up front. As a result, work scope was not clear, which led to rework.[5] Nine years into the endeavor, with technical issues unresolved and with cost up to 11.4 billion pounds, the project was cancelled.[6]

An optimal schedule will help avoid cost growth. Any change from that, either an increase or a decrease, will increase cost.[7] See Figure 7.4 for the relationship between cost and schedule growth based on research I have conducted, which is similar to other studies I have seen.[8]

Figure 7.4 demonstrates that schedule compression, if it can be achieved, is more costly than schedule expansion. This relationship assumes the technical performance is maintained. If schedule compression does not result in more cost, the project will likely fail.

Figure 7.4   The Impact of Schedule Changes on Cost Growth

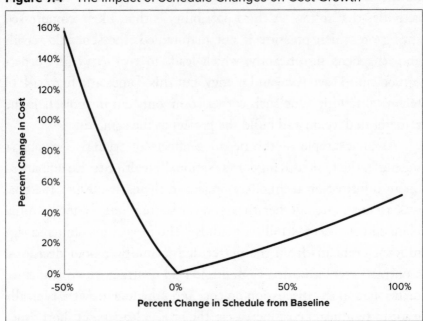

Percent Change in Cost / Percent Change in Schedule from Baseline

HITTING THE CEILING: FUNDING CONSTRAINTS

For each project, there is an ideal funding profile, one that ramps up as the design work gets underway and then ramps down as fabrication and assembly nears completion and testing ensues. For large, complex projects, the ideal funding peak may exceed the budget for the entire organization. This will require project funding caps that constrain expenditures in some time periods. If this constraint flattens the funding profile it will necessarily lead to delays in activities, leading to schedule and cost growth. Tests may be delayed, which may lead to expensive redesigns later. Funding constraints may result in design work becoming fragmented. This limits communication across design groups, which results in integration problems that require additional time and money to fix late in the development schedule. The funding profile peak may move to the right, shifting the profile from front-loaded to back-loaded, which increases risk. If the constraint is severe enough, there may only be enough funding for the program to avoid laying off staff, keeping critical people on board performing nonessential activities that do little to aid forward progress. This latter state is akin to making the interest payments on debt without paying down any principal.

Funding constraints may result from changes external to an organization. Even in the absence of that, organizations have funding limits. Failure to adequately plan for project inclusion leads to too many projects competing for the total amount of money available for allocation. A domino effect occurs once the funding ceiling is reached. The impact of slipping schedules in one year directly affects the next. The slips that occur the next year in turn have a direct effect on the following year, and so on. See Figure 7.5 for an example of a change in the funding profile due to an annual funding constraint.

Figure 7.5 Funding Profiles Before and After Cap Is Applied

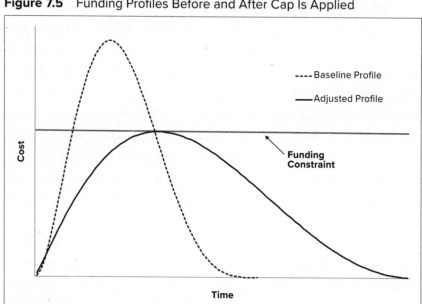

Portfolio optimization requires consideration of cost, schedule, and the phasing of cost over the schedule. Beginning new projects in order to spend all available funds involves only looking one year ahead, leading to suboptimal results. The first year of a project is the least expensive. The ensuing years, when funding ramps up, can result in funding constraints. This in turn leads to cuts to other projects in the portfolio and significant schedule delays. The stretching of schedules in turn results in cost overruns. This process of looking only a single year ahead is an example of a greedy algorithm for optimization. A greedy algorithm is one that follows a problem-solving heuristic of making the locally optimal choice at each stage with the hope of finding a global optimum. This type of approach when applied to coordinating a set of projects in a portfolio leads directly to trying to do too much (too many programs ongoing at the same time) with too few resources. A greedy strategy is not guaranteed to produce an optimal solution. In some cases, it may yield locally optimal solutions that approximate a global optimal solution. However, most of the time a greedy algorithm does not. This approach is often characterized as being shortsighted or myopic.

As discussed earlier, the cost of the development phases is often small compared to the costs of producing, operating, and disposing the system. The beginning of a program is just the small tip of a big iceberg. Unless organization leaders recognize this, they risk crashing their projects into an iceberg of funding constraints, much like the *Titanic*. In portfolio management this occurs when budget wedges are established. A wedge is a small amount of funding provided to a project for a year or two to get it started. However, when this is done, little to no consideration is given to the full cost impact on the overall portfolio.

As an example, consider a series of projects, each of which costs $500 million. Schedule delays can impact budgets due to inflation. Plans typically take inflation into account, but a shift in schedule will increase cost in futures years due to the general increase in price levels. Also, commonly used inflation indices tend to underestimate inflation, which is another source of cost growth from the plan to the actual cost. For the sake of simplicity, we will ignore the effects of inflation in this example. Assume that the annual budget for the entire portfolio is $1 billion. Further assume that the cost phasing is a front-loaded one such that 60% of the cost is planned to be spent at the schedule midpoint. The spread for five years is: 11.00% in the first year; 31.30% in the second year; 33.70% in the third year; 20.04% in the fourth year; and 3.96% in the fifth and final year. The cost planned for the first year is $500 million × .11 = $55.0 million. Table 7.1 displays the cost for a $500 million program that is spread according to this phasing. In this example, we assume project scope is constant—any funding constraints result in temporary cuts that delay work that will be completed at a later time.

Table 7.1   Yearly Planned Phasing Example

Year	Cost ($ Millions)
1	$55.00
2	$156.50
3	$168.50
4	$100.20
5	$19.80

Consider how to optimally plan the entire portfolio of programs to maximize the number of projects. Assume for simplicity that no other types of projects exist. Recall that the total annual portfolio budget is a flat, fixed $1 billion. A naive approach would be to start 18 programs in the first year, since that is what can be afforded in the first year. However, this leads to disaster in year two, as the total budget will not increase and the annual planned cost will have to be cut by two-thirds for each program in year two. Under such a scenario, it is likely that none of these endeavors would be achievable. Assume instead that the portfolio manager more prudently decides to take both years one and two into consideration and only begins six projects in year one, since they realize that in year two, $156.5 million × 6 = $939.0 million will be required. The entire portfolio is affordable in year one, and in year two there is $1,000 million − $939 million = $61 million left over. Since only $55 million is needed for the first year of a new project, management decides to begin a seventh project. In year three, however, there is a budget constraint. Six projects need $168.5 million, and the seventh project requires $156.5 million. The total bill amounts to 6 × $168.5 million + $156.5 million = $1,167.5 million, which is $167.5 million more than is available in the total annual budget. Thus, temporary funding cuts are now required in year three. Assuming that the funding constraints are spread equally among all seven projects, this results in an approximately $24 million cut for each project in year three. The funding constraint results in a nonoptimal allocation of resources, leading to schedule delays for all projects. The cut results in a one-year schedule slip for all projects. Applying a model that I developed to determine the impact of this kind of schedule slip,[9] this leads to 18% cost growth for each project. The total cost for each of the seven programs is now $591 million. After adjusting the phasing to accommodate the additional cost, the extra year, and the annual budget cap, the phasing of the seven projects at the end of year three is displayed in Table 7.2.

The phasing of an individual project, after accounting for the schedule slips, is compared to the original phasing in Figure 7.6. In year four, there is not enough money to fully fund the seventh project. A funding cut of $17.5 million is applied, leading to another year of schedule delay, and a total cost of $699.1 million for the seventh project. In year four, no new projects are started. In year five, the total cost of the seven projects is only $644 million, meaning that there is $1,000 million − $644 million = $356 million available

Table 7.2 Phasing for Seven Projects Impacted by Funding Constraints

Year	1	2	3	4	5	6	7	8
Project 1	$55.0	$156.5	$144.5	$145.5	$76.5	$13.0		
Project 2	$55.0	$156.5	$144.5	$145.5	$76.5	$13.0		
Project 3	$55.0	$156.5	$144.5	$145.5	$76.5	$13.0		
Project 4	$55.0	$156.5	$144.5	$145.5	$76.5	$13.0		
Project 5	$55.0	$156.5	$144.5	$145.5	$76.5	$13.0		
Project 6	$55.0	$156.5	$144.5	$145.5	$76.5	$13.0		
Project 7		$55.0	$133.0	$127.0	$185.0	$127.0	$61.4	$10.7

Figure 7.6 Planned Annual Phasing of Cost Before and After a One-Year Schedule Slip

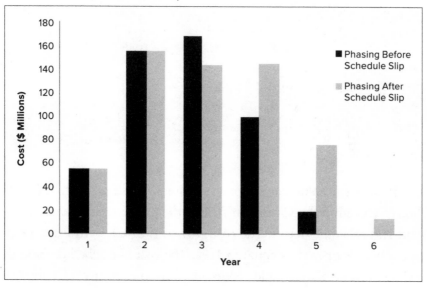

to start new projects. Noting that $356/$54.9 is approximately 6.5, six new projects can be funded and are started under the myopic policy. This creates no problems that year, but the planned funding in year six is $144 million over budget. Assuming that only the six new projects receive a funding constraint, this means a $24 million funding budget cut in the second year of these six projects, leading to a one-year schedule delay, and a total cost equal to $591 million for these six projects. These problems continue to occur in wave after wave of funding constraints, schedule increases, and cost growth. After 20 years, 26 projects are completed. The total cost is $15.394 billion. The initial cost of these 26 projects was $13 billion total. See Table 7.3 for the phasing of the costs for the first 10 projects.

Table 7.3 Phasing of the First 10 Projects in the Portfolio

Year	1	2	3	4	5	6	7	8	9	10	11
Project 1	$55.0	$156.5	$144.5	$145.5	$76.5	$13.0					
Project 2	$55.0	$156.5	$144.5	$145.5	$76.5	$13.0					
Project 3	$55.0	$156.5	$144.5	$145.5	$76.5	$13.0					
Project 4	$55.0	$156.5	$144.5	$145.5	$76.5	$13.0					
Project 5	$55.0	$156.5	$144.5	$145.5	$76.5	$13.0					
Project 6	$55.0	$156.5	$144.5	$145.5	$76.5	$13.0					
Project 7		$55.0	$133.0	$127.0	$185.0	$127.0	$61.4	$10.7			
Project 8					$55.0	$132.5	$156.3	$164.8	$124.9	$58.4	$7.9
Project 9					$55.0	$132.5	$156.3	$164.8	$124.9	$58.4	$7.9
Project 10					$55.0	$132.5	$156.3	$164.8	$124.9	$58.4	$7.9

Poor portfolio management was responsible for more than $2 billion in cost growth. More than 70% of the projects experienced both cost and schedule delays. The cost growth is equal to 18% and average schedule growth is equal to 19%. The cost and schedule growth exhibited for this example represents only one source of cost and schedule growth and demonstrates that poor portfolio management may be a significant unrecognized cause of cost and schedule growth. In some respects, projects are their own worst enemy. This is something entirely within leadership's control. Leadership sabotages their own success due to a lack of thoughtful planning.

A counterpoint in support of the greedy algorithm is that, while it may result in cost growth and schedule delays, it could lead to more projects being completed than with other strategies. However, consider the strategy of starting two new projects each year. This will not make full use of the $1 billion annual budget until year five. However, at years five and after, the entire budget is used, and no schedules are delayed. The result is that there is no cost growth due to portfolio management issues. Under this strategy, 32 projects are completed, 6 more than with the myopic strategy. This is 23% more than with the greedy approach to portfolio management. This is a significant inefficiency for the greedy algorithm. This example also shows that cost growth and schedule delays are not just problems for individual projects but a larger problem—these issues lead to accomplishing less overall. The moral is that trying to do too much with too little results in less being achieved in the long run. Investing time, energy, and even dedicated staff, whose sole purpose is portfolio management, will save a significant amount of both time and money.

PRODUCING MORE, BUT GETTING LESS: THE IMPACT OF FUNDING CONSTRAINTS ON PRODUCTION

What we have discussed up to this point is largely development projects. This problem of trying to achieve too much with too little also affects the production phase, when a project produces multiple quantities. We discussed this as a reason for cost growth in Chapter 2 and provided several examples. Fixed cost is a major issue in most manufacturing projects, as there tends to be excess production capacity. In manufacturing, there are two types of costs—fixed and variable. The fixed costs are amortized across the number of units produced. The more units produced in a given time frame, the less each unit costs on average because the fixed cost is divided among more units. For example, if a project has a fixed cost equal to $100 million each year and variable costs equal to $10 million for each unit, then the average cost of 10 units is ($100 million + 10 ×

$10 million)/10 = $20 million. However, if 100 units are produced each year the average cost is ($100 million + 10 × $100 million)/100= $11 million, almost half the cost per unit at the lower quantity. Figure 7.7 shows that as the number of units produced increases the average cost of the units produced declines.

Figure 7.7   Inverse Ratio Between Number of Units Produced and Average Cost

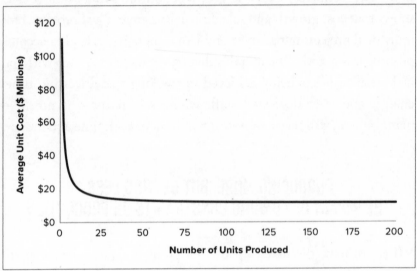

Extending this to a portfolio, suppose two production projects each have fixed cost equal to $100 million and variable cost equal to $10 million. Suppose the total production budget is equal to $1 billion. Then 80 units total can be produced each year. This is because the total cost of 80 units is $100 million + $100 million + 80 × $10 million = $1,000 million = $1 billion. If this is expanded to five such projects, all with the same fixed and variable costs, the total production drops to 50 units, since 5 × $100 million + 50 × $10 million = $1,000 million = $1 billion. If this is expanded to 10 systems, no units can be produced since the fixed costs consume the entire production budget. See Figure 7.8.

Figure 7.8   Inverse Ratio Between Number of Systems and Total Units Produced

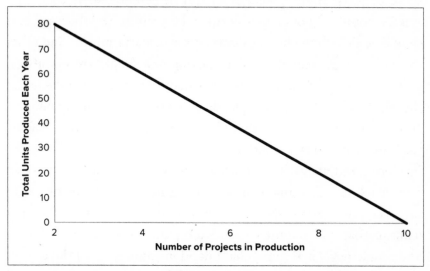

Norm Augustine analyzed defense projects from the 1960s and 1970s, and he found that most were at the edge of producing just enough units to stay economical, which he considered to be the output produced by a one-shift, five-day-a-week basis. Anything less resulted in idle labor. When he updated his original book, Augustine found that Department of Defense budget cuts in the 1990s led to production rates for many projects falling into the uneconomical region. For example, the B-2A stealth bomber had a production run of only 15 aircraft with an average variable production cost equal to $907 million. Augustine noted this tendency to produce at a minimally efficient rate to be so strong that he named it the "Law of Marginal Survival," which he defined as, "The more one produces, the less one gets."[10]

SUMMARY AND RECOMMENDATIONS

A lack of sensible portfolio planning pervades project management. The way to fix this issue is to develop quantitative risk analysis of life-cycle cost and schedule estimates before allocating funds for these projects. Budget wedges should be prohibited. If there is a small amount of money that needs to be spent in the short term, it should be used for technology development, staff training, and other short-term expenses rather than starting new long-term initiatives. I have witnessed firsthand the poor planning that is conducted at the portfolio level. For example, during a time of declining budgets and cost overruns for multiple development efforts, senior leadership planned to start multiple new projects, some of which were significant initiatives. The situation was like a household that does a terrible job of managing its money. Imagine a couple, one of whom was recently unemployed. There has been a minor flood, causing damage that will require expensive repairs to the couple's home. The couple neglected to purchase flood insurance, so all the repairs will have to be paid for by the couple. Taking these two factors into account, it would make sense for the couple to cut back on expenses for a while to adjust to less income and to set aside money for the needed house repairs. Instead, they plan an elaborate vacation.

Portfolio planning is hindered by the lack of quantitative risk management at the organization level. Even when quantitative risk analysis is conducted, it is typically done on a project-by-project basis. We have seen in this chapter and in Chapter 5 the negative impact of not conducting risk analysis at the portfolio level. Analyzing projects in isolation without looking at the ramifications at the full portfolio level is like the blind men who studied an elephant. Using their sense of touch to try to determine the characteristics of an elephant, one touched a leg, a second the tail, the third the trunk, the fourth the ear, and the fifth the tusk. The blind man who felt a leg says the elephant is like a pillar; the one who felt the tail says the elephant is like a rope; the one who felt the trunk says the elephant is like a tree branch; the one who felt the ear says the elephant is like a hand fan; and the one who felt the tusk says the elephant is like a solid pipe. Each is partially correct, but none of them truly understands that these are different features of a single animal. In the same way, if we do not analyze cost and risk at the portfolio level, we are blind to the consequences of the impact of project decisions on the entire portfolio.

To ensure success, organizations should analyze the impact of new potential projects on the entire portfolio before embarking on them. While it may seem paradoxical, organizations will only be able to achieve more by attempting to do less. Focus on fewer projects and do them right, providing sufficient funds and time for them to be successful. Trying to do too much with too few resources only causes what is achieved to cost more and take longer.

CHAPTER 8

Thinking Strategically

Managing Risk, Establishing Reserves, and Setting Incentives

I n AD 228, the military leader Kong Ming and a few of his body-guards had retreated after defeat in battle to the city of Yangping, China. Fleeing an army of 50,000 soldiers, Ming opened the gates to the city, made all the guards hide, and removed all battle flags from the city walls. He then placidly sat in one of the towers, in unobstructed view of the approaching army, playing a lute. Suspecting a trap, the large army quickly departed. The moral of the story is that a little strategic thinking can deliver big results.[1] Like Kong Ming, organizations can benefit tremendously from strategic thinking when it comes to managing risk, establishing reserves, and setting incentives.

The study of these kinds of conflicts emerged in the twentieth century as game theory, an important field of economics. Game theory was applied to the strategic concept of mutually assured destruction where both the Soviet Union and the United States were (and may still be) willing to threaten the ultimate destruction of the other if attacked. The intent of such a strategy is to dissuade the other side from launching a nuclear strike. This strategy proved to be effective in preventing the Cold War from turning into a thermonuclear hot one.

GUARDING THE COOKIE JAR:
QUANTITATIVE COST RISK MANAGEMENT

To implement the ideas discussed in previous chapters requires careful consideration. For example, a simple approach to combatting cost growth would be to fund projects to higher confidence levels. However, critics of funding to a high level say that signing a contract for a given amount will cause the contractor to plan for that. As a result, a project funded to a 50% confidence level will spend at least that much. Likewise, a project funded to an 80% confidence level will also spend at least that amount. The other factors that contribute to cost growth, such as the constant change in requirements and external factors, will then add cost growth beyond the baseline. In an earlier chapter we mentioned MAIMS, "money allocated is money spent," which is the observation that, once project managers know how much they have been allocated, they will spend at least that amount, if not more. Likewise, if projects are allocated more time, managers will find a way to fill it, in keeping with Parkinson's Law. The proverbial cookie jar needs to be guarded to keep projects from accessing it easily.

The answer for cost involves holding reserves at various levels. For example, in a public project, if managers want to include reserves, they can sign a contract for a lower amount and hold the excess at the portfolio level. Organizations can likewise hold reserves outside of individual projects to incentivize project managers to keep costs low. If a project does not have additional funds within its control, the project manager will have incentives to control cost growth. If the contractor is aware that additional funds will not be forthcoming, then it too would have incentives to keep costs from increasing. However, reserves are still necessary, as whenever a need for more money due to cost growth arises, it creates a chain reaction. If additional funds are not available when required, schedules may slip, work can stop until additional funding can be obtained, requirements may have to be scaled back, or contracts may have to be renegotiated.

Reserves are needed at the portfolio level outside of the control of individual projects. Allocating all the reserves to individual projects and then reallocating based on the needs of individual projects can be hazardous. The movement of funds from one project to another may identify the project from which money is being moved as having too much money. This can make it a target for funding cuts. Also, the movement of funds from one project to another can be seen by other projects in an organization as a potential source of additional funds. As one of my former bosses, a chief financial officer with a government agency, used to say, "Money in motion is money at risk."

Improving the State of Practice

Even when quantitative risk assessment is conducted, confidence levels are typically used for portfolio management. This is a poor fit and like trying to shove a square peg into a round hole. Although confidence levels provide no information on extreme risks, when quantitative portfolio management is used for projects, the current practice is to use two or three different levels for the establishment of reserves. For example, a project may set a low target goal, which in the case of a publicly funded project may be a competitively awarded contract. This value is lower than the 50% confidence level. The project manager is provided funding near the middle of the distribution, such as at the 50% confidence level. These both provide incentives to keep cost as low as possible. The organization then holds a second set of reserves not immediately available to the project manager. This will be at a conservative value, such as the 70% or 80% confidence level.[2] See Figure 8.1 for an illustration of the different funding levels on a cost S-curve.

Figure 8.1   Risk Management Using Confidence Levels

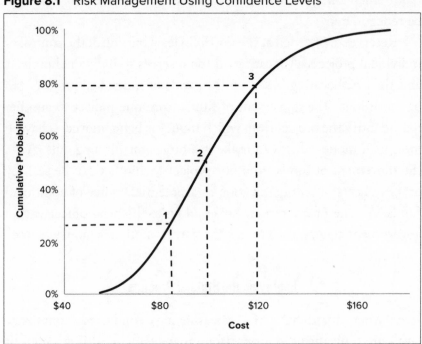

In Figure 8.1, the cost target is labeled as "1." The individual project funding is labeled as "2," and the organization level funding for the project is labeled as "3."

However, the use of multiple confidence levels in this manner is still not effective risk management because it ignores the right tail of the cost risk distribution. For example, consider a set of 10 projects whose cost risk follows lognormal distributions, such as considered in Table 5.6 in Chapter 5. See Table 8.1.

Table 8.1   Example of Portfolio Risk Management with
Confidence Levels

Project	Mean	Standard Deviation	50% Confidence Level	80% Confidence Level	Portfolio Reserve
1	$1,696	$1,476	$1,280	$2,407	$1,127
2	$1,481	$1,288	$1,117	$2,102	$985
3	$1,395	$1,214	$1,052	$1,980	$928
4	$874	$760	$659	$1,240	$581
5	$840	$731	$634	$1,192	$558
6	$1,449	$1,261	$1,093	$2,056	$963
7	$1,638	$1,425	$1,236	$2,324	$1,088
8	$1,031	$897	$778	$1,463	$685
9	$1,271	$1,106	$959	$1,804	$845
10	$1,937	$1,685	$1,461	$2,749	$1,288
Total	$13,612	$9,161	$10,269	$19,317	$9,048

The organization funds to the 80% confidence level, and there
is a minimal portfolio effect. The sum of the 80% confidence levels for the 10 projects in Table 8.1 is $19,317, which is at the 81%
confidence level. This value is a little higher than the portfolio level
80% confidence level of $18,883. However, even with setting indi-
vidual projects to high confidence levels, the total portfolio level
will be exceeded with a 19% probability. The expected shortfall if
this level is breached is 45% greater than the portfolio funding level.
Funding to high confidence levels, even if it is a smart way to avoid
projects from overspending, is not effective risk management. As
we have established, the real risks are beyond the 80th and even the
90th percentile. A project that does not have extreme risks, such as
one that is using mature technologies, should not have as many risk
reserves as one that is riskier, but the confidence level approach is
one-size-fits-all.

A better alternative is to aggregate the project level risk analyses into a portfolio-level analysis. The risk management strategy

is determined at the portfolio level. Funding is allocated into organization-held reserves for each project in case an overrun level is triggered. For example, if the goal is to fund individual projects to their 50% confidence levels, an expected shortfall above this level can be established for setting portfolio level reserves. This total level can then be set aside for individual projects based on their marginal contribution to the total risk.[3] Individual projects are funded to their 50% confidence level allocation. See Table 8.2.

Table 8.2 Example of Portfolio Risk Management with Expected Shortfall

Project	Mean	Standard Deviation	50% Allocation	Expected Shortfall Allocation	Portfolio Reserve
1	$1,696	$1,476	$1,422	$2,472	$1,050
2	$1,481	$1,288	$1,241	$2,153	$912
3	$1,395	$1,214	$1,168	$2,026	$857
4	$874	$760	$732	$1,258	$526
5	$840	$731	$704	$1,212	$508
6	$1,449	$1,261	$1,214	$2,114	$900
7	$1,638	$1,425	$1,373	$2,387	$1,015
8	$1,031	$897	$864	$1,493	$629
9	$1,271	$1,106	$1,065	$1,843	$778
10	$1,937	$1,685	$1,623	$2,829	$1,206
Total	$13,612	$9,161	$11,405	$19,786	$8,381

In Table 8.2, organization level portfolio reserves are established with expected shortfall with a trigger at the portfolio 50% confidence level. This value is $19,786. The total portfolio reserve is $8,381, approximately 5% higher than the 80% portfolio confidence level. Reserves for individual projects are held at the organization level. These values are established using a gradient allocation method that assigns reserves based on projects' contributions to the overall risk.[4] This is a coherent way to measure and manage risk at the portfolio level that incorporates the possibility of extreme risk.

The mean is a better trigger value than the 50% confidence level. The mean cost risk is greater than the 50% confidence level for projects, so there is less likelihood that project managers will need to access reserves if they are funded to the mean. The positive semi-deviation risk measure can be used to establish portfolio level reserves. This can be allocated to projects using the principle of gradient allocation, as with the expected shortfall example. See Table 8.3 for an example. We use one-half semi-deviation to offset the conservatism provided by funding projects to their mean values.

Table 8.3 Example of Portfolio Risk Management with Positive Semi-Deviation

Project	Mean	Standard Deviation	Mean + 1/2 Semi-Deviation Allocation	Portfolio Reserve
1	$1,696	$1,476	$2,158	$462
2	$1,481	$1,288	$1,783	$302
3	$1,395	$1,214	$1,759	$364
4	$874	$760	$1,483	$609
5	$840	$731	$1,335	$495
6	$1,449	$1,261	$1,890	$441
7	$1,638	$1,425	$2,005	$367
8	$1,031	$897	$1,263	$232
9	$1,271	$1,106	$1,502	$231
10	$1,937	$1,685	$2,333	$396
Total	$13,612	$9,161	$17,511	$3,899

Cost Risk Reserve Phasing

Once reserves are established, they must be phased. Risks do not occur uniformly during a development project. To provide reserves at the right time requires considering the relationship among cost, schedule, and risk. For a development project, the bulk of the risk is in the latter stages of development, after the detailed design is approved and production begins. Risk reserves are needed later in the development of a project, while relatively little is needed until a project reaches peak funding. The timing of risks should be established by considering when the project believes the big risks will occur and by historical trends, which indicate that cost and schedule growth most often occurs late in the development process. The relationship is illustrated in Figure 8.2 for a $1 billion project with 30% risk reserves. Figure 8.2 is notional. Actual reserves will be established on a yearly basis and will not have the smooth phasing shown in the illustration.

Figure 8.2   Relationship Between Cost and Reserve Phasing

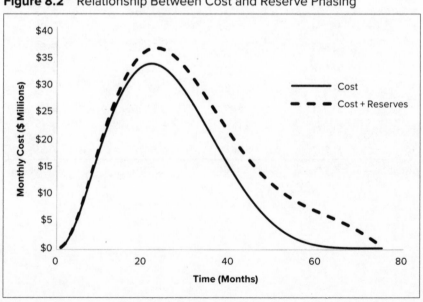

QUANTITATIVE SCHEDULE RISK MANAGEMENT

Because time is not fungible, the reserve setting process cannot be as automatic as for cost. Just as organizations should not provide all the cost reserves to the project level and projects should not provide all theirs to contractors, schedule reserves need to be carefully planned as well. Contingency should not be added directly to pad schedules, as this will lead to additional cost that can be avoided if the schedule can be executed efficiently. Careful thinking about the critical path, which is a path through the schedule network in which any slip will lengthen the entire schedule, should be considered. Discrete schedule risks should be examined to determine which activities are most likely to slip and should be a prime area for setting reserves. Plans should be in place to handle schedule slips when they arise, as they likely will. Schedule reserves should be explicitly included in the schedule. Any contracts should include both penalties for schedule slips and positive incentives to finish early if the work included in these contracts is on the critical path or a risky part of the schedule.

ANALYZING COST AND SCHEDULE RISK JOINTLY

Quantitative risk analysis of cost and schedule is typically conducted separately. Schedule is an important consideration for project risk and should be analyzed jointly with cost due to their strong link. Joint cost and schedule risk analysis has been used in a variety of projects around the world. The oil industry, financial institutions, the intelligence community, NASA, and a variety of other government organizations use this in planning for large projects. NASA incorporated this in official policy and as of 2019 required its use in all projects whose planned cost is at least $1 billion.[5]

Measurement of joint confidence levels for cost and schedule is more stringent than measuring them separately. This is because it is possible for one to zig (meet the criteria) when the other zags (does not meet the criteria). Achieving joint confidence levels requires more time and money than separately achieving the same cost confidence level and the same schedule confidence level. Figure 8.3 provides a comparison.

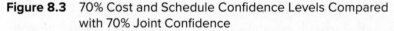

Figure 8.3 70% Cost and Schedule Confidence Levels Compared with 70% Joint Confidence

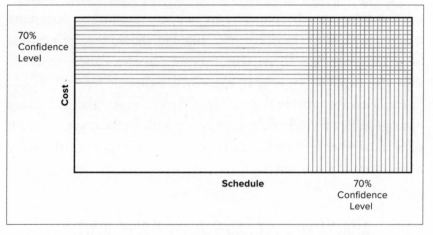

The area shaded with the horizontal lines represents the costs that are at or above the 70% confidence level for cost. The area shaded with vertical lines represents those schedules that are at or above the 70% confidence level for schedule. The cross-hatched area shows the cost and schedule pairs that meet both criteria. That is, they are values such that both cost and schedule meet the 70% criteria. As is evident from the graph, there are pairs of cost and schedule for which cost is at or above the 70% confidence level but for which schedule is below the 70% confidence level, and vice versa.

The S-curve for a joint cost and schedule risk is a three-dimensional curve. Because cost and schedule are highly correlated, but not 100% correlated, a confidence level is not a single pair of cost and schedule values. To visualize the confidence levels, two-dimensional iso-confidence level plots are used to illustrate the cost and schedule pairs with a specified confidence level. See Figure 8.4.

Figure 8.4   Iso-Confidence Level Curves for a Joint Cost and Schedule Risk Analysis

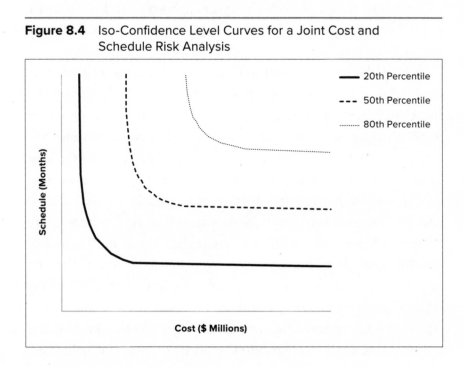

Figure 8.4 depicts 20%, 50%, and 80% confidence levels. Cost and schedule pairs on these curves all have the same confidence level. These iso-curves also represent frontiers. Any pair of cost and schedule values that are to the right and above a given iso-curve have a joint confidence level equal to or greater than the confidence level for the pairs on the iso-curve. The graphs have been simplified for this illustration. In practice, not all values on the iso-curve may

be likely to occur or even attainable, particularly the values at the ends of each iso-curve (recall the discussion on tail dependency in Chapter 4).

The current state of practice for joint cost and schedule risk analysis suffers from the same shortcomings as traditional risk analysis in its exclusive reliance on the use of confidence levels to measure risk. While confidence levels provide useful information, coherent risk measures such as expected shortfall and the positive semi-deviation principle should be used in joint cost and schedule risk analysis as well.

I have developed several joint cost and schedule risk analyses for NASA. After I left a position supporting NASA to work for the Department of Defense, my boss at the time told me not to mention using joint cost and schedule risk analysis because the extra time and money required to achieve joint confidence level made them unaffordable. However, I think the practice of joint cost and schedule analysis should be more widely adopted. People who analyze risk say that a single estimate is always wrong, but I have estimated one $500 million project using joint cost and schedule analysis whose actual cost and schedule were within 1% of my 50% confidence level estimates. Of course, not all of my other estimates were as accurate as this one, but the story presents anecdotal evidence that providing projects with joint cost and schedule risk analysis contributes information that can help them succeed.

RISK MANAGEMENT FRAMEWORK

An integrated risk management framework puts together all the elements we have discussed throughout the book, including the establishment of reserves. First, the context and scope of risk management should be identified. Context involves the relationship between risk and reward. Private businesses, particularly those that can make massive profits from one product, such as a pharmaceutical company or a technology company, have different risk and reward profiles than public projects.

The scope of risk management should exclude certain extreme external events outside of a project's control, such as black swans. But to realistically assess risk, the scope should not be too limited. This step is key in setting the foundation for a credible risk analysis. Next is quantification of individual risks, which includes discrete internal and external risks as well as statistical uncertainty in cost and schedule models. These risks are then aggregated to determine the overall risk. As we have discussed, this is not a simple addition but typically involves a computer simulation. Once total risk is measured, it should be allocated to individual projects based on their contribution to the overall portfolio risk.

After measurement comes the management of risks. There are two parts to this activity—mitigation and reserve setting. A project should mitigate the likelihood and consequence of adverse events over which it can exert control. A project has a variety of options available. It can work to reduce a risk, such as switching from the use of an advanced technology to one that has already been proven to work in practice. Firms may purchase insurance to offset some risk. This includes traditional insurance, such as property protection from fire and floods, as well as less traditional insurance, such as launch vehicle risk for commercial satellites. Reserves that are allocated need to be managed in a strategic way to keep these funds from being used unless necessary. The total process is iterative and needs to be updated regularly throughout a project's life cycle. The monitoring and review of risks is a continual process from the beginning to the end of a project. See Figure 8.5 for a flowchart of this process.

Figure 8.5   Integrated Risk Management Framework[6]

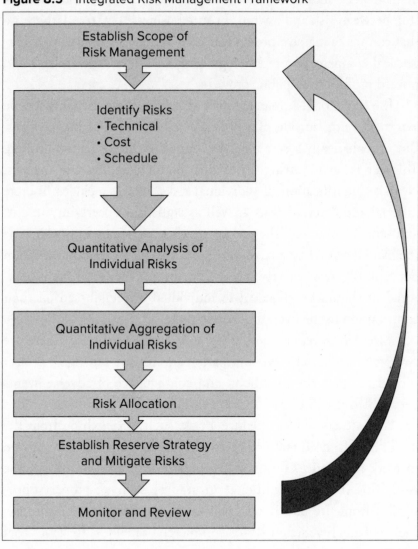

This process applies both to individual projects and to organizations that manage multiple projects simultaneously. Quantitative portfolio management is critical for both individual projects and the organizations that manage them. The integration of risk throughout an organization is called enterprise risk management, which began

in the 1990s with systematic attempts to measure risk quantitatively. Many private corporations have established chief risk officer
positions as a corporate suite level executive position.[7]

Enterprise risk management can help ensure company success.
A good example of risk management in practice has been the success of the Merck Corporation, one of the largest pharmaceutical
companies in the world. Judy Lewent, the company's chief financial
officer in the 1990s, was instrumental in introducing quantitative
risk management to the company. The pharmaceutical business is
a risky one. On average, the time required to bring a drug to market is 10 years, and the cost is more than $300 million. While the
risk is high, so is the reward. A successful drug can be extremely
profitable. By considering both the risks and the potential rewards,
Lewent realized that to be successful, the company needed to take
the risk of pursuing the development of more drugs.[8]

INCENTIVES AND INFORMATION

In the ancient Greek city-state of Ephesus, public projects required
the submittal of a cost estimate. The city would pay up to 25% cost
growth without penalty, but anything beyond that was taken from
the contractor's personal property.[9] If such a policy were followed
today, that would definitely be an incentive for contractors to not
bid low and for them to keep costs in line. However, there is little such discipline in practice. Even though oversight tries to act
tough, once an organization blinks and accedes to the contractor's
bills for more time and money, the game of chicken is lost. Why? In
public projects, the contractors have a higher incentive to win this
game. Their incentive is they make a large profit resulting in larger
bonuses. The financial rewards for the government are much more
limited. Also, canceling a project and switching to a competitor is a
long and costly process. To avoid losing progress already made, the

government needs access to the blueprints for the design that the original contractor has developed. The government must negotiate this up front. The cost of this is high, so in my experience, to save money, the government typically does not pay for the data rights up front. This inaction holds the government hostage for not only the duration of the design but also the full production and operations cycle. Also, contractors typically require a termination liability clause in their agreements so that if the government cancels, they are paid a large sum of money. For a contract in the billion-dollar range, this can be $100 million or more.

We discussed contract types in the chapters on cost growth. As a reminder, these can be divided into cost-plus and fixed-price contracts. Cost-plus is most often used for development efforts, where there is the most uncertainty. Cost-plus contracts are attractive for contractors because they place the risk of overruns on the government. However, they provide no incentive for contractors to control costs. The government has limited insight into whether contractors are trying to keep costs low. If a contractor were responsible for all overruns, it would work hard to keep down costs. The fact that there are no incentives to a contractor to expend effort on controlling costs means that the contractor will not try to do so. In insurance, this situation is called moral hazard. For example, a homeowner who does not have insurance may be more likely to install a security system to prevent burglaries and do more home maintenance to prevent costly repairs such as water damage from a roof leak than a homeowner who has insurance. In contracting, a cost-plus contract is a moral hazard because there is no incentive for the contractor to control cost. The fee is the profit the contractor makes on the work. Because the fee is typically a percentage of the cost, the higher the cost, the higher the fee. A 10% fee on a $100 million program is a $10 million profit, while a 10% fee on a $200 million program is a $20 million profit. Basic economics teaches that firms seek to maximize profits. Cost-plus contracts create an incentive to overrun. We saw in Chapter 4 that unless this tendency is kept in check, the result can be a wildly risky project, one that can grow by a factor of five or more.

In theory, the government bears all the risk of cost overruns in a cost-plus contract. In fixed-price contracts, in theory the contractor bears all cost risk. I use the phrase "in theory" because even with fixed-price contracts, the government often pays part or all of the overrun. In some cases, the government changes the scope or schedule, so it is only fair that there is an increase in the amount paid to the contractor. However, in my experience, there have been plenty of times that a contractor has signed a fixed-price contract only to sue the government to pay its overrun costs or threaten to walk away from the project.

Evidence suggests that the cost growth risk to the government is much lower for fixed-price contracts. Based on data I have seen, the average fixed-price contract grows on average by an amount that is in the 5% to 10% range, significantly less than the 50% average for all projects.[10] If that is the case, why not make all contracts fixed price? The problem is that, because of the risks involved, contractors are not willing to sign up for a fixed-price contract for a development project. With this type of arrangement, contractors bear the bulk of the cost risk, so they price that into their fixed-price bids. Profit rates for fixed-price contracts are thus typically higher than their cost-plus counterparts. The trade-off for less risk to the government is a greater profit for contractors. Contractors are more likely to participate in a fixed-price contract when they are confident they can make a large profit on a contract, more than with a cost-plus contract. Contractors can do this because they have better insight into their costs than the government does. Participating in fixed-price contracts seems like a good idea from the government's perspective. Contractors will have an incentive to control costs—in this case, the lower the cost, the higher the profit. Also, the government bears minimal risk of cost overruns. However, all the profit and risk are loaded into the price of a fixed-price contract, and the government has limited insight into whether it is getting a good deal or is overpaying. In insurance this is called adverse selection. An example of adverse selection is the market for used cars. Potential sellers of used cars know more about the cars' condition than potential buyers do. Because of this uncertainty, used car buyers will demand a steep discount compared to new cars. People who own high-quality used cars will not be willing to sell the cars they own for these discounts, leading to a high quantity of poor-quality used cars, which are often referred to as lemons. The equivalent of a lemon in a fixed-price contract is an overpriced project, one that would likely have cost less under a cost-plus arrangement.

Many contracts are a blend of both cost-plus and fixed price. Cost-sharing contracts offer incentives for contractors to keep their costs low without paying the risk premium of a fixed-price contract. Incentives in contracts for public works projects have been shown to work well in practice. A good example is a road construction project completed in Huntsville, Alabama, in 2018 that was originally planned for four years. By using incentives for finishing early as well as a penalty for finishing late, the project was completed 11 months ahead of schedule. The contract included a $30,000 fine to the contractor for every day the project went past its planned completion date.[11] These kinds of incentives should be used more often.

Engineering the Process: Achieving Better Values in Production

Game theory can be used to achieve better value using incentives. As we have discussed, game theory is not the study of chess or poker but rather models of conflict and cooperation among decision makers. The way to develop better acquisition outcomes in public projects is to design games to achieve desired outcomes. This approach is called mechanism design.[12] In project terms, this is a method for engineering the acquisition process to achieve goals. It has been successfully used to auction the radio spectrum and oil drilling rights. The creators of mechanism design were awarded the Nobel Prize in Economics in 2007.[13] A similar field of study is market design, which has been successfully used to match kidney donors and recipients. The creators of market design were awarded the Nobel Prize in Economics in 2012.[14] The government already applies such mechanisms to a limited extent. An example of such a mechanism is the multiyear contract, in which the government gives up the ability to manipulate quantities purchased every year in exchange for lower prices.

Consider the problem of obtaining better outcomes when multiple units are purchased from a contractor that is effectively a monopolist. As we have mentioned, this is a common situation in defense and aerospace. We assume that the demand curve is known to both the firm and the regulator and that the government does not know the firm's costs exactly. Even though data reporting requirements are written into contracts, in my experience, the government does not always have clear insight into a contractor's costs. Many challenges exist in obtaining useful cost information from contractors. Contractors have no incentive to provide high-quality cost data, as it provides the government with leverage for negotiating contracts. Rather, they have an incentive to conceal their true costs. If the government knew the contractor's cost, it could make a take-it-or-leave-it offer to cover the contractor's fixed and variable costs, leaving the contractor with no profit. Even if the government had to offer some profit to get the contractor to deliver the product, it could greatly reduce the contractor's profits.

Government project managers have no interest in having the cost reports, as it does not benefit their current project, even though it will benefit their successors. There can be some negative incentive if cost reporting requirements are an award fee criterion, but, in my experience, rarely is a contractor penalized for not providing high-quality cost reports. Even when the cost reports provided are technically correct, they can still be misleading. One project I am familiar with reported the bulk of the cost in the correct account, but overages were reported in a different one. A deep dive into the contractor's cost information was required to discover this discrepancy. For another project, the initial cost report requirements were removed from the contract after the contractor told the project manager that he would save millions of dollars if it were removed. After reports were later added to follow-on work, the contractor could not provide accurate values for the unit costs of the system. It was only after a yearlong effort to dig into the prime contractor and major subcontractors' data and multiple face-to-face meetings that the project office had accurate details on the unit cost of the system. The government needs detailed insight into the fixed and variable costs for a project to know the true production costs, particularly how production costs change as a function of the total quantities and the rate at which they are produced. In my experience, when government project managers take the time to collect detailed information on cost, they are in a much better position to negotiate favorable cost terms on contracts.

If the government knew the contractor's costs, it could simply tax some portion of its profits. However, this is inefficient in the sense that the government pays the contractor and then gets some of its own payment back in the form of taxes. A better way to handle the issue is for the government to employ a mechanism for achieving a better value up front. A variety of mechanisms have been designed to deal with limited competition. The two mechanisms we will consider require the contractor to report its true costs.[15]

An example of a monopoly producer is displayed in Figure 8.6. Basic economics teaches that private companies seek to maximize profits. This happens at the point where marginal revenue equals marginal cost. The monopolist produces 10 units and charges the price associated with 10 units on the demand curve, which is $30. The contractor cost is the area below the marginal cost (MC) line,

Figure 8.6   Contractor Profit, Cost, and Government Surplus

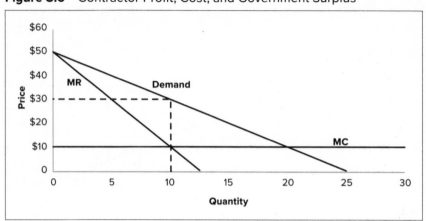

up to the quantity produced. The contractor profit is the area above the marginal cost line and below the price charged to the government, which in this example is $200. The government's surplus is the area above the contractor's profit. The total value to the government is the total area under the demand curve up to the quantity produced. The surplus is the difference of the value it derives as provided by the demand curve minus what it pays to the contractor. A simple mechanism developed by Loeb and Magat for achieving higher output would be to pay the contractor its reported cost plus all the government's surplus.[16] See Figure 8.7.

Under this mechanism, the contractor reports its cost. The government then buys the quantity on the demand curve that intersects the contractor's marginal cost curve, which is 20 units at $10 each. Note that the contractor will maximize its profits under this agreement only by reporting its true costs. If it were to report a higher cost, the government would buy less. Thus, the contractor would leave money on the table. For example, if the contractor said its cost is $20 for each unit, the government would reduce the quantity it purchases to 15 units, and the contractor

Figure 8.7   Achieving Higher Output by Sacrificing Surplus

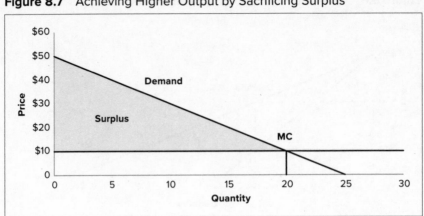

would miss out on the profits it would receive for units 16–20. Since it receives all money under the demand curve, the contractor does not gain by selling for a higher price. If the contractor underreported its cost, the government would buy more than 20 units at a value less than the contractor's cost. Up to a quantity of 20 there is a surplus, so the contractor would cover its cost. For quantities greater than 20, there is no surplus, so the contractor would lose money on every unit above 20 units. This outcome is the market solution. However, in this case the government provides the contractor its entire surplus. The contractor's profits are the entire area under the demand curve that is greater than the cost. The surplus is now the contractor's profit, which is $400. Note that the contractor profit under the standard monopoly situation without the mechanism, as in Figure 8.6, is $200. The average unit cost to the government in the standard monopoly situation is $30. Under the mechanism, the average unit price is ($400 + $200)/20 = $30. This only accounts for the marginal costs. Once fixed costs are added in, this mechanism will result in a lower average unit price. By implementing the mechanism, the government can buy greater quantities. Procuring greater quantities for the same unit

price is a significant benefit if this is a weapons system that is critical for the defense of the nation. The Loeb-Magat mechanism
results in increased output with little change in the unit price to the
government.

We now consider a different mechanism, one that will result in
less quantity produced than with the Loeb-Magat mechanism but
at a lower price.[17] We assume that the government knows the fixed
cost but is uncertain about the marginal cost and that the contractor
knows the marginal cost. (While it seems like this should always
be the case, after looking at contractor cost reports for many years,
I have doubts.) We further assume that the government has some
idea about the marginal cost and can bound the cost and form a distribution around it. In this example, the government knows that the
contractor's marginal cost is between $6 and $12 a unit and models
the uncertainty about the contractor cost as a uniform distribution.
The government provides a payment structure that incentivizes the
contractor to reveal its actual cost. This payment structure changes
the effective demand curve from the average revenue curve to the
kinked demand curve shown in Figure 8.8.

Figure 8.8   The Baron-Myerson Mechanism

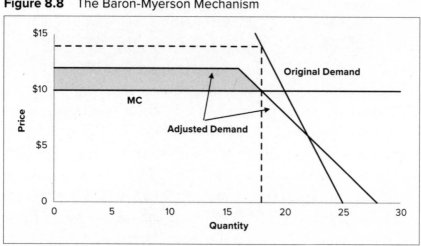

Under this payment structure, the government gives all the surplus to the producer under the new demand curve. This effectively reduces the monopolist's profits. The contractor's actual marginal cost is \$10, the government pays the contractor 2 × \$10 − \$6 = \$14 for each unit. At this price, the demand curve indicates that the government wants 18 units. It will purchase 18 units at \$14 each. Without the subsidy, the profit for each unit would be \$4 for each unit. However, the government takes back a significant amount of this profit and provides the contractor with the profit marked by the shaded area in Figure 8.8. The total profit for the contractor is cut to \$33. Thus, the net average marginal unit price is equal to 33/18, which is approximately \$1.83. The value of the hidden cost information is equal to the profit, in this case \$33.[18]

See Table 8.4 for a comparison of no mechanism with the Loeb-Magat and Baron-Myerson mechanisms. Loeb-Magat results in higher quantity but does nothing to shrink monopoly profits, while Baron-Myerson increases quantity while cutting profit substantially.

Table 8.4 Comparison of Profits

Mechanism	Quantity	Profit	Profit/Unit
None	10	\$200.00	\$20.00
Loeb-Magat	20	\$400.00	\$20.00
Baron-Myerson	18	\$33.00	\$1.83

Incentives such as those provided by cleverly designed mechanisms can be used to achieve better outcomes. This kind of market intervention is in keeping with free market principles. Friedrich Hayek wrote in *The Road to Serfdom* in 1944, "There is, in particular, all the difference between deliberately creating a system within which competition will work as beneficially as possible and passively accepting institutions as they are."[19] Hayek, who was awarded the Nobel Prize in economics in 1974, was a fierce defender of free market capitalism.

SUMMARY AND RECOMMENDATIONS

The final piece of the risk management puzzle is a quantitative portfolio level analysis, which results in the setting of cost and schedule reserves at both the total project and the portfolio levels. This requires some strategic thinking to provide incentives to not take too much time or spend too much money. Implementing risk analysis requires that reserves be fenced off from other competing programs. This should be done quantitatively for cost. A common practice is to use two different percentiles to establish reserves. This still ignores the dragons lurking in the right tail of the cost risk distribution. Quantitative cost risk management requires setting reserves using a coherent approach. As time is not fungible, the process for schedule reserves requires careful deliberation. The reserves can be set in a variety of ways, such as providing more time for events that are sensitive to significant schedule risks.

Two additional considerations involving the integration of cost and schedule risk were discussed. One is that the phasing of reserves is distinct from the phasing of the baseline estimate. This needs to be considered when phasing reserves. Cost and schedule are closely linked and should be considered jointly. The best quantitative analysis of cost and schedule is one that analyzes them jointly.

A risk management framework that integrates all the puzzle pieces together into a complete picture was presented. This provide a full prescriptive approach to analyzing and managing risk. Risk management is not something that is conducted at the beginning of a project and then ignored. It requires continual monitoring and updating to achieve its full potential in ensuring project success.

Incentives can be a powerful means to achieve better value. They are important in setting reserves to avoid the potential pitfalls of Parkinson's Law and MAIMS ("money allocated is money spent"). Incentives can also be used to achieve better outcomes in a variety of situations, including public projects that use contractors. We discussed an example of achieving this in the production phase of a project.

CHAPTER 9

Summary and Conclusion

Reaping the Rewards of Risk Management

Satirical cartoonist Walt Kelly was best known for his syndicated comic strip *Pogo*, which ran from the early 1940s until the early 1970s. The title character was Pogo Possum. A poster for the first Earth Day in 1970 features Pogo and his friend Porky Pine walking in a forest, the floor of which is covered with litter. This situation leads Pogo to proclaim, "We have met the enemy and he is us!" Like Pogo, projects are their own worst enemy when it comes to risk management.

When everything is going well, people ignore risk. Only after a significant bad event do people regain a fleeting appreciation for it. Between 2000 and 2020, a major event that reminds us of the dragons lurking in the tails of risk has occurred three times: the terrorist attack on September 11, 2001; the financial crisis of 2008; and the pandemic in 2020. All renewed a temporary interest in risk analysis. Enterprise risk management, which we mentioned in the last chapter, was a hot topic in the early 2000s. It gained some traction after the financial crisis of 2008. However, as of early 2020, the enthusiasm and appreciation for risk management had cooled again. Despite a growing emphasis on risk, in surveys between 2007 and 2017, only 20% to 25% of respondents said they conducted quantitative risk analysis on a regular basis.[1]

THE TWIN PROBLEMS OF COST AND SCHEDULE GROWTH

While extreme risks like black swans occur infrequently, projects regularly experience cost and schedule growth from the realization of risks. More than 70% of all types of projects, large and small, experience cost and schedule growth. Few projects spend less or take less time than planned. The average cost growth for most types of development projects exceeds 50%. More important, the severity of the increases is large. Approximately one in six projects experiences cost growth in excess of 100%. This problem has been around a long time and shows no signs of abating. The frequency of projects that more than double in cost is the biggest factor in project risk. It makes comprehending the magnitude of risk more difficult and makes traditional methods less meaningful in modeling risk.

Technical failures occur occasionally, but resource risks are more common. All the factors that impact technical performance also affect cost and schedule, but not all resource risks have an impact on technical performance. Much more can go wrong than can go right, so the risk of an event occurring that increases cost or schedule is much more likely than seizing an opportunity to reduce cost or schedule. A variety of sources of cost and schedule risk exist, both internal and external. A major internal reason is optimism. As a profession, project management tends to plan for the best-case scenario, which sets up cost and schedule growth from the outset. Significant mistakes are made during planning and execution.

One planning issue is the use of immature technologies, which is a major driver of cost and schedule growth. Also, not every project manager or team is better than average. Errors are often made during execution, including unnecessary requirements changes. Mistakes are often made in the estimation of cost and schedule. These errors typically underestimate, leading to increases during execution.

The alignment of cost, schedule, and technical requirements is critical. Project decision makers do not always take the time to understand these relationships, but any misalignment among them leads to problems. Either cost and schedule will increase or the project will likely fail. An important source of external cost and schedule growth is the constantly changing world in which we live. This change is accelerating, as the rate of growth in technology is exponential. Projects take years to develop. Due to the rapid pace of change, leaders often face the issue of either updating the design multiple times during development or delivering a product that is already obsolete at completion. When projects produce multiple units, less production means higher cost per unit. Projects also have external dependencies. Any issues with these delay schedule and increase cost. These include the black swans we have mentioned, a recurring problem that we cannot predict and for which we cannot plan. Most projects experience the realization of multiple sources of risk. The problems of cost and schedule growth are even worse than they appear, as they do not account for technical failures, cancelled projects, or cuts in scope, features, or performance.

The frequency and severity of project cost and schedule growth provide compelling evidence of the need for better risk management. By ignoring the potential for large increases in cost and schedule, projects are unprepared to deal with these problems when they arise. Paradoxically, the attempt to achieve lower cost and shorter schedules leads to higher cost and longer schedules.

RISK BLIND: THE NEED TO APPRECIATE UNCERTAINTY

The first step in risk management is gaining an appreciation for uncertainty and risk. As a society, we tend to fixate on averages and not the variation around them. We are blind to risk. There is much more to the variation in the cost and schedule of projects than can be captured by an average. The use of averages results in a significant underestimation of risk. A lack of appreciation of risk led Nobel Prize–winning economists to drive a successful hedge fund into bankruptcy; bankrupted Orange County, California; and contributed to the 2008 financial crisis.

Risk and uncertainty should be assessed using rigorous quantitative methods. The use of qualitative methods and simple risk matrices is prevalent. However, they do not provide credible cost and schedule risk estimation. Fortunately, methods for analyzing risk the correct way are straightforward and can be implemented on any computer. Uncertainty is not a number but a shape. These shapes are called probability distributions. We have looked at four that are commonly used to model risk. The triangular distribution is a simple distribution that requires three inputs—a low value, a most likely value, and a high value. Triangle distributions are easy to use, especially when risk ranges are estimated with expert opinion. However, their practical use is limited due to their inability to model events outside the low and high bounds. The Gaussian, or normal, distribution is the most commonly encountered probability distribution. However, its use in modeling project risk is limited due to its lack of skew and its inability to model extreme variations in cost and schedule. The Pareto distribution can be used to model the wild risks exhibited in financial markets, motion picture profits, and natural disasters. Most projects will not experience these wild variations, as project managers can exert some control over an endeavor. Decision makers can develop and implement mitigation plans, cut scope, or even cancel an effort if things get too out of hand. A compromise between the mild variation of the Gaussian and the extreme swings of the Pareto is the lognormal distribution, which will be a good choice for modeling project risk in most situations.

Once risk is measured, it must be aggregated. This aggregation requires more than simple addition. Risks cannot be summed deterministically. A computer simulation, often called Monte Carlo simulation, is typically used to aggregate risk for both cost and schedule.

ISSUES IN RISK ANALYSIS

Even when risk is analyzed quantitatively, several issues with current practice hinder its effectiveness. One is that risk is significantly underestimated. This has several negative consequences. The belief is that, when an organization conducts multiple projects concurrently, low confidence levels can be aggregated to achieve a high confidence level for a portfolio. This is a myth. Current practice in risk analysis relies almost exclusively on the use of confidence levels to measure risk. Confidence levels provide useful information, but sole reliance upon them leads to logical inconsistencies in modeling risk because it ignores the right tail of cost and schedule risk distributions. Better risk measures should be used. Project managers do not conduct portfolio level risk analysis, which leads to the problem of trying to achieve too much with too few resources. Decision makers need to conduct portfolio level risk analysis, which provides guidance on setting cost reserves. Setting schedule reserves is not an automatic process and requires considering the timelines of activities for each specific endeavor.

Underestimation of Risk

The analysis of risk is adversely affected by optimism. The use of risk matrices also significantly underestimates cost and schedule risk.

We saw that project cost risk analyses significantly underestimate risk. More recent trends, such as consideration of correlation and inclusion of model uncertainty in addition to the standard inclusion of variation in cost and schedule drivers, have helped make more recent analyses more credible. However, these estimates still have tended to under account for risk relative to the amount of cost and schedule growth experienced. Simply including correlation and model uncertainty is not a sure means of developing credible risk estimates. Incorporating tail dependency is an improvement that will help. More important, empirical cost growth data provides a means for understanding how much risk projects have experienced and can provide a means for comparing the amount of risk a project can expect to see versus what is predicted from project cost and schedule risk models. The empirical cost growth data has been shown to exhibit fat tails, although these tails are not as fat as found in some other industries, such as stock market prices and financial losses due to hurricanes. This is expected, based on differences between government projects and the denizens of Extremistan, such as stock markets and the whims of Mother Nature. For projects, leadership can have a significant influence in ameliorating cost and schedule growth through remedial measures, project rescoping, or outright cancellation. Schedule risk is not subject to fat tails, but as more can go wrong than go right, it should be modeled with an appropriate distribution, such as a lognormal.

We demonstrated the use of empirical cost growth data in calibrating project cost risk analyses to history. We compared this to a small sample measuring the performance of risk analyses. Empirical calibration measures historical growth well, unlike standard practice. This highlights that project risk often ignores major sources of uncertainty. Excluding some uncertainties from risk analysis is warranted, but decision makers need to realistically assess risk as well. Even if they don't always have the budget to protect against some risks, they may be able to plan potential alternate courses of action, such as cutting scope. Understanding such risks may also help to enforce discipline and stress the impact of changing requirements or deviating from project plans.

The Mythical Portfolio Effect

When organizations conduct multiple projects, they tend to underfund individual projects in the hopes that the benefits of diversification will raise the confidence level of their entire organization to a high level. This is not realistic. Just as there is no such thing as a free lunch, there is also no such thing as a portfolio effect when funding to confidence levels. We also showed that the government funds to such low levels that the overall confidence level is lower than for individual programs. Organizations set themselves up for cost and schedule growth in such cases. The result is not only that lunch is not free, it is more expensive than the price quoted on the menu!

Confidence Level Funding Ignores the Dragons in the Tails

Current practice in quantitative risk management consists largely of setting reserves at fixed percentiles. This policy has much in common with the banking industry. However, it ignores the tails of the risk distributions, which is dangerous to the financial viability of the project. Funding to a percentile does not even provide a cushion for bad times. Exceeding a percentile funding level simply tells you that things are indeed bad. Confidence level funding will not cure the problem of cost and schedule growth. Empirical evidence suggests that an 80% confidence level funding policy will result, on average, in a significant amount of cost growth. Funding resources to percentiles is not a risk management policy but rather reflects a lack of thought in not implementing sophisticated and meaningful risk measures. Worst of all, percentile funding can result in a reverse portfolio effect, which means that funding an agency as a whole could be riskier than funding any single project! A better policy would be to use a risk measure such as expected shortfall, since it takes into account the right tail of the distribution. Such a policy will offer both a signal of a bad event (a specified confidence level is exceeded), as well as a cushion for the expected amount of money to guard against this event. Expected shortfall is a simple measure, represented by a single number just like percentile funding. It too can be easily explained to senior management and project managers, since it is simply the additional amount of money required to fund a project in case a specified confidence level is breached. It need not be significantly more expensive for the agency than current confidence level funding policies. Since it considers the full right tail of the distribution, a lower-level threshold such as the 50% confidence level could be chosen for the trigger. A reserves strategy should not consist of solely using confidence levels. Without a change in budgeting policy, projects will continue to incur cost increases and schedule delays.

Using Mountains to Produce Molehills

Portfolio management is critical to containing cost growth. A lack of planning in the portfolio management process leads to schedule delays and cost growth. Properly introducing new projects in a timely fashion can lead to getting more done in the long run. Other issues at the portfolio management level are a lack of risk analysis at the portfolio level and under accounting for risk at the project level. Relying upon a chimerical portfolio effect is not a substitute for calculating risk at the portfolio level. Accurately estimating risk is critical for project realism. Addressing these issues will go a long way toward addressing endemic cost growth in government projects and programs, which will result in accomplishing more.

Cost, schedule, and the phasing of cost over schedule are intrinsically linked. Changes in schedule for an established program result in cost growth. Reduction in annual funding also leads to schedule growth, which in turn leads to cost growth. Indeed, there is ample empirical evidence that schedule delays and funding constraints are strongly correlated with cost overruns.

Quantitative Risk Management: Guarding the Cookie Jar

Organizations that control multiple projects need to do quantitative portfolio management. This involves aggregating project cost risks to the portfolio level. Reserves need to be set. This must be carefully done to avoid running into the "money allocated is money spent" problem. A smart way to do this involves holding reserves at a variety of levels and providing incentives to keep costs down and schedules short. Schedule reserve setting requires careful deliberation to avoid Parkinson's Law. This involves looking at the riskiest schedule activities and providing more time to those events likely to delay the entire schedule, such as those on the critical path.

Risk management is not just a set of individual activities. Rather, effective management of risk is a process. The steps we have described work in series. It begins with setting the scope and context. Risks are then identified and measured. Once risks are measured, they need to be aggregated to the project level. If the project is part of a larger portfolio, the risk of all projects must be combined to the portfolio level. Once aggregated, the risks need to be allocated to individual projects. Management of risks is both active and passive. The active part involves mitigating and eliminating critical risks a project manager can efficiently act on. The passive part involves setting reserves to guard against the risks the project either chooses to accept or cannot control. The process is iterative and must be repeated multiple times as a project progresses toward completion. The process encapsulates the discipline of enterprise risk management, which began in the 1990s and has been adopted to a greater or lesser degree in a variety of companies. However, surveys find that a small minority of companies conduct quantitative risk analysis. The discipline of risk management is relatively new with a significant amount of room for improvement.

Incentives can and should be used to achieve better outcomes. They have been successfully used in a variety of projects. Their widespread adoption will help projects achieve better value.

RECOMMENDATIONS AND LAST THOUGHTS

In summary, mature processes for quantitative risk measurement and risk management are sorely lacking. We have discussed several issues and ways these can be addressed. Optimism should be avoided. This can be accomplished with independent estimates or cross-checks. Also, quantitative risk analysis should be a standard practice and needs to be done well. Developing a cost or schedule risk analysis that vastly understates the amount of risk in a project is all too common. Care must be taken to avoid underestimating risk, particularly in the early stages of a project. Calibration of risk estimates to historical cost and schedule growth data should be done to ensure they are realistic.

S-curves provide useful information but are not good risk measures when used alone. Coherent measures of risk should be used, ones that take the full tail risk into account. These include expected shortfall and positive semi-deviation. Both are easy to calculate from Monte Carlo simulations.

Portfolio level risk analysis needs to be conducted, at least on an annual basis, before budgets are submitted. No shortcuts, such as the purported portfolio effect, can be used to circumvent a full-fledged quantitative portfolio risk analysis. Risk analysis also needs to be updated before a decision is made to start new projects, which can begin small but can soon take up a large amount of total budget at the peak of development.

A great deal of care needs to be taken to implement coherent risk measures and quantitative risk management. Careful setting of reserves for both cost and schedule must be done to ensure neither time nor money is wasted. Risk management should follow a consistent, iterative process that takes all necessary steps.

My purpose in writing this book is not just to be a critic. The flaws are evident, and pointing out the many shortcomings is the easy part. The harder task is to provide fixes. My intent is to provide helpful advice to enhance the odds of success. If decision makers want to perform better, spend less, and take less time, they need to pay more attention to risk management. Ignoring the possibility that something bad will occur ensures that projects are not prepared when these adverse events occur, and they will. Not all risks can be controlled. The impacts of these should be mitigated by setting aside reserves.

Two adages spring to mind. One is, "If you always do what you've always done, you'll always get what you've always got." Another is that the definition of insanity is doing the same thing over and over but expecting different results. The psychologist Daniel Kahneman discusses two primary systems of thought. One is intuitive and makes judgments quickly. The other is more thoughtful and deliberate. The intuitive system is good at some tasks, but it does a poor job at others, such as those that require careful planning.[2] As a whole, project results indicate that the planning process uses the more intuitive system of thought. However, what is needed is the more deliberate one. Project managers need to stop the insanity and be serious about planning for risks in an intelligent way. The project management profession needs to incorporate the lessons in this book into their projects. Otherwise, the dismal track record with regard to risk will not improve. In the words of the philosopher George Santayana, "Those who cannot remember the past are condemned to repeat it."[3]

We have mentioned that risk and opportunity are the two different faces of uncertainty. However, there is opportunity in risk. If you want to set yourself apart from the competition and provide exceptional support and leadership to projects, start incorporating proper risk management. Even small steps can help set you apart, as illustrated by the story of the two hikers in the woods who spot a brown bear headed their way. One frantically digs out a pair of running shoes from her pack. The other hiker tells her that she cannot outrun a bear. She responds that she does not have to outrun the bear, she only must outrun her hiking partner. Similarly, to succeed, you only have to be better than the competition. Risk management can make that difference.

This book has been written for a general project management audience. For readers interested in more technical details behind these concepts, visit https://www.iceaaonline.com/solvingprm for a collection of my technical conference papers and presentations. For interactive examples that provide a hands-on exploration of quantitative risk, visit my website https://christianbsmart.com.

NOTES

Introduction

1. Lee Billings, "Space Science: The Telescope That Ate Astronomy," *Nature* 467 (October 2010): 1028–30, doi:10.1038/4671028a.

2. Andy Prince and Christian B. Smart, "Being Certain About Uncertainty: Part 2," Paper presented at the International Cost Estimating and Analysis Association Professional Development and Training Workshop, Phoenix, AZ, June 12–15, 2018, https://www.iceaaonline.com/phx18papers/.

3. Niki Doyle, "Madison County Jail Cost Approaches $80 Million as Sheriff Asks for More Fixes," al.com (blog), June 11, 2009, http://blog.al.com/breaking/2009/06/madison_county_jail_cost_appro.html.

4. Steve Doyle, "8-Year-Old Madison County Jail Construction Lawsuit Finally Set for Trial," al.com (blog), September 5, 2014, http://www.al.com/news/huntsville/index.ssf/2014/09/8-year-old_madison_county_jail.html.

5. Myron Tribus and Edward C. McIrvine, "Energy and Information," *Scientific American* 224, no. 3 (September 1971): 179–90.

6. David Graham, "Continuous Cost Risk Management at NASA," in *Space Systems Cost Risk Handbook: Applying the Best Practices in Cost Risk Analysis to Space System Cost Estimates*, eds. Timothy Anderson and Raymond Covert (Hampton, VA: Space Systems Cost Analysis Group, 2005), 35–51.

7. Walter B. Wriston, *Risk & Other Four-Letter Words* (New York: Harper & Row, 1986), 219.

8. This is not the definition provided by its inventor, but is how it is commonly used and comes directly from the subtitle of the book—Nassim N. Taleb, *The Black Swan: The Impact of the Highly Improbable* (New York: Random House, 2007).

9. James Griffith, "Taiwan's Coronavirus Response Is Among the Best Globally," CNN, April 5, 2020, https://www.cnn.com/2020/04/04/asia/taiwan-coronavirus-response-who-intl-hnk/index.html.

10. https://www.worldometers.info/coronavirus/, as of May 8, 2020.

Chapter 1

1. Gottfried Leibniz, *Discourse on Metaphysics and Other Essays*, trans. Daniel Garber and Roger Ariew (Indianapolis: Hackett Publishing Company, 1991), 53–55.
2. Alfred O. Aldridge, *Voltaire and the Century of Light* (Princeton: Princeton University Press, 1975).
3. Matthew S. Goldberg and Charles A. Weber, "Evaluation of the Risk Analysis and Cost Management (RACM) Model," Institute for Defense Analysis, IDA Paper P-3388, August 1998.
4. Dan Grazier, "Why Do Air Force Planes Need $10,000 Toilet Seat Covers?" *The American Conservative*, June 14, 2018.
5. Bent Flyvbjerg, Nils Bruzelius, and Werner Rothengatter, *Megaprojects and Risk: An Anatomy of Ambition* (Cambridge: Cambridge University Press, 2003).
6. Andy Prince and Christian B. Smart, "Being Certain About Uncertainty: Part 2," paper presented at the International Cost Estimating and Analysis Association Professional Development and Training Workshop, Phoenix, AZ, June 12–15, 2018, https://www.iceaaonline.com/phx18papers/.
7. Norman R. Augustine, *Augustine's Laws* (Reston, VA: American Institute of Aeronautics and Astronautics, 1983), 253.
8. Augustine, *Augustine's Laws*, 152–153.
9. Douglas R. Hofstadter, *Godel, Escher, Bach: An Eternal Golden Braid* (New York: Basic Books, 1979), 152.
10. Nate Silver, *The Signal and the Noise: Why So Many Predictions Fail—but Some Don't* (New York: Penguin Books, 2012), 268.
11. C. Northcote Parkinson, *Parkinson's Law and Other Studies in Administration* (Boston: Houghton Mifflin Company, 1957), 2.
12. Christian B. Smart, "Covered with Oil: Incorporating Realism in Cost Risk Analysis," *Journal of Cost Analysis and Parametrics* 8, no. 3 (December 2015): 186–205, doi:0.1080/1941658X.2015.1096220.
13. Smart, "Covered with Oil."
14. Karen W. Tyson, Bruce R. Harmon, and Daniel M. Utech, "Understanding Cost and Schedule Growth in Acquisition Programs," Institute for Defense Analysis research paper, July 1994, IDA paper P-2967.
15. Jeffrey A. Drezner and Giles K. Smith, *An Analysis of Weapon Systems Acquisition Schedules* (RAND Corporation: Santa Monica, December 1990), RAND Report R-3937-ACQ, 32.

16. Bent Flyvbjerg, Nils Bruzelius, and Werner Rothengatter, *Megaprojects and Risk: An Anatomy of Ambition* (Cambridge: Cambridge University Press, 2003) 11–21.

17. Capers Jones, *Quantifying Software: Global and Industry Perspectives* (New York: CRC Press, 2018), 198.

18. Michael Popp, "Calibrating Software Code Growth," paper presented at the 39th Department of Defense Cost Analysis Symposium, Williamsburg, VA, February 14–17, 2006.

19. Daniel Strickland, *Software Cost Estimating and Analysis Handbook* (Huntsville, AL: Missile Defense Agency, 2016), 49.

20. The Standish Group, *CHAOS Manifesto: The Laws of CHAOS and the CHAOS 100 Best PM Practices* (Standish Group: Boston, MA, 2010), 10–13.

21. Reuters, "Cost Overruns Common on Oil Projects—Schlumberger," June 2, 2011, https://www.reuters.com/article/schlumberger-clientcosts-idAFN0211573620110602.

22. Edward W. Merrow and Ralph F. Shangraw Jr., "Understanding the Costs and Schedules of World Bank Supported Hydroelectric Projects," The World Bank Industry and Energy Department Working Paper Energy Series Paper No. 31, July 1990; Atif Ansar, Bent Flyvbjerg, Alexander Budzier, and Daniel Lunn, "Big Is Fragile: An Attempt at Theorizing Scale," in Bent Flyvbjerg, ed., *The Oxford Handbook of Megaproject Management* (Oxford University Press: Oxford 2017), 60–95.

23. Bent Flyvbjerg, Allison Stewart, and Alexander Budzier, "The Oxford Olympics Study 2016: Cost and Cost Overrun at the Games," University of Oxford's Said Business School Research Paper, July, 2016.

24. Some of the studies do not provide this information; in those cases, I have estimate it using information about the mean and the standard deviation, taking into account the skewness of the data.

25. Bent Flyvbjerg, Nils Bruzelius, and Werner Rothengatter, *Megaprojects and Risk: An Anatomy of Ambition* (Cambridge: Cambridge University Press, 2003), 3.

26. Christian B. Smart, "The Portfolio Effect and the Free Lunch," paper presented at The International Society of Parametric Analysts and The Society of Cost Estimating and Analysis Professional Development and Training Workshop, St. Louis, MO, June 2–5, 2009.

27. Government Accountability Office, "Cost, Schedule, and Performance of NASA's Ulysses Mission to the Sun," GAO Report No. 88059, May 1988.

28. Jared Sichel, "Cost of California's High-Speed Train Just Skyrocketed . . . AGAIN!," The Daily Wire, January 17, 2018, https://www.dailywire.com/news/cost-californias-high-speed-choo-choo-train-just-jared-sichel.
29. Tony Bizjack, Tim Sheehan, and Rory Appleton, "No, Gov. Gavin Newsom Didn't Kill High-Speed Rail. What's His Plan B?" *Sacramento Bee*, February 18, 2019.
30. Phil Wilson and Taryn Luna, "Gov. Gavin Newsom Pledges to Scale Back High-Speed Rail and Tunnel Project in State-of-the-State Speech," *Los Angeles Times*, February 12, 2019.
31. ABS News, "California High-Speed Rail Project Costs Could Increase by $1.8 Billion, Bringing Total to $12.4 Billion," May16, 2019, https://abc7.com/5280622/.
32. Richard H. Thaler, *Misbehaving: The Making of Behavioral Economics* (New York: W.W. Norton & Company, 1986), 65.
33. Edward T. Chen, "Enterprise Resource Planning System: Issues and Implementation," in *Emerging Topics and Technologies in Information Systems*, eds. Miltiadis D. Lytras and Patricia Ordonez de Pablos (Hershey, PA: Information Science Reference, 2009), 102–14.
34. Judy E. Scott, "The FoxMeyer's Drugs Bankruptcy: Was It a Failure of ERP?," *Proceedings of the 5th Americas Conference on Information Systems*, Milwaukee, WI, May 13, 1999, 223–25.

Chapter 2
1. Daniel Kahneman, *Thinking Fast and Slow* (New York: Macmillan, 2011), 249–50.
2. Lawrence N. Goeller, "Military Satellite Communications: Why So Many, Why So Hard?," paper presented at the 42nd Department of Defense Cost Analysis Symposium, Williamsburg, VA, February 16–19, 2009.
3. Claude Freaner et al., "An Assessment of the Inherent Optimism in Early Conceptual Designs and Its Effect on Cost and Schedule Growth," paper presented to the Planetary Science Subcommittee, NASA Goddard Space Flight Center, MD, June 23, 2008.
4. Eric M. Lofgren, "A History of Thought in Defense Acquisition," paper presented at the International Cost Estimating and Analysis Professional Development and Training Workshop, Portland, OR, June 6–9, 2017, http://www.iceaaonline.com/ready/wp-content/uploads/2017/07/PS09-Paper-Lofgren-History-of-Thought-in-Defense-Acquisitions.pdf.

5. Norman R. Augustine, *Augustine's Laws* (Reston, VA: American Institute of Aeronautics and Astronautics, 1983), 52.

6. Eric M. Lofgren, "A History of Thought in Defense Acquisition," paper presented at the International Cost Estimating and Analysis Professional Development and Training Workshop, Portland, OR, June 6–9, 2017.

7. Greg Mankiw, "Ranking Economics Papers," blog post, August 30, 2006, http://gregmankiw.blogspot.com/2006/08/ranking-economics -papers.html.

8. Richard H. Thaler, *Misbehaving: The Making of Behavioral Economics* (New York: W.W. Norton & Company, 1986) 25–34.

9. Erik L. Burgess and Hany S. Gobreial, "Integrating Spacecraft Design and Cost-Risk Analysis Using NASA Technology Readiness Levels," paper presented at the 29th Annual Department of Defense Cost Analysis Symposium, February 1996.

10. James W. Bilbro, "Systematic Assessment of the Project/Program Impacts of Technological Advancement and Insertion," in William L. Nolte, *Did I Ever Tell You About the Whale? Or Measuring Technology Maturity* (Charlotte, NC: Information Age Publishing, 2008), 151–86.

11. Cristina Garcia-Ochoa Martin, "The Sydney Opera House Construction: A Case of Project Management Failure," blog post, January 14, 2012, https://www.eoi.es/blogs/cristinagarcia-ochoa/2012/01/14/the-sidney -opera-house-construction-a-case-of-project-management-failure/.

12. This is commonly attributed to John Glenn, but in my research, I cannot find a definitive source.

13. Jonathan Tepper and Denise Hearn, *The Myth of Capitalism: Monopolies and the Death of Competition* (Hoboken: John Wiley & Sons, 2019).

14. Jake Widman, "IT's Biggest Project Failures—and What We Can Learn from Them," *Computerworld*, October 9, 2008, https://www .computerworld.com/article/2533563/it-s-biggest-project-failures—and -what-we-can-learn-from-them.html.

15. Terry Roberts, "Muskrat Falls: A Story of Unchecked Oilmen and Their Boondoggle Hydro Project," Canadian Broadcasting Corporation News, April 19, 2019, https://www.cbc.ca/news/canada/newfoundland -labrador/muskrat-boondoggle-reasons-1.5088786; "COVID-19 Situation Forcing Nalcor to Curb Operations at Muskrat Falls Facility," *The Telegram*, March 18, 2020.

16. Christian Davenport, "Under Trump, the F-35's Costs, More Than $1 Trillion over 60 Years, Continue to Draw Scrutiny," *Washington Post*, December 8, 2017.

17. United States Government Accountability Office, Defense Acquisitions: Assessments of Selected Weapons Programs, March 2017, GAO-17-333SP, https://www.gao.gov/assets/690/683838.pdf.

18. International Monetary Fund (IMF), "World Economic Outlook Database," April 2018, available online at https://www.imf.org.

19. United States Government Accountability Office, *Defense Acquisitions: Assessments of Selected Weapons Programs*, GAO Report, March 2017, GAO-17-333SP, https://www.gao.gov/assets/690/683838.pdf.

20. United States Government Accountability Office, *Defense Acquisitions: Assessments of Selected Weapons Programs*, GAO Report, March 2017, GAO-17-333SP, https://www.gao.gov/assets/690/683838.pdf.

21. Joseph W. Hamaker, "But What Will It Cost? The History of NASA Cost Estimating," in *Issues in NASA Program and Project Management*, ed. Francis T. Hoban (Huntsville, AL: NASA Marshall Space Flight Center, 1993), 1–12, NASA SP-6101, https://ntrs.nasa.gov/archive/nasa/casi.ntrs.nasa.gov/19940017026.pdf.

22. Michael A. Dornheim, "Aerospace Corp. Study Shows Limits of Faster-Better-Cheaper," *Aviation Week & Space Technology*, June 12, 2000, 47–49.

23. Christian B. Smart, "Exploring the Limits of Faster-Better-Cheaper with the Mission Cost Risk Assessment Model," presented to the Office of Management and Budget, Washington, DC, January 4, 2001.

24. Dominic Gates, "Boeing's 737 MAX 'Design Failures' and FAA's 'Grossly Insufficient' Review Slammed," *Seattle Times*, March 6, 2020.

25. Chris Isidore, "The Cost of the Boeing 737 MAX Crisis: $18.7 Billion and Counting," CNN Business, March 10, 2020, https://www.cnn.com/2020/03/10/business/boeing-737-max-cost/index.html.

26. Paul Huggins, "Schools, Motorists Celebrate Reopening of Key Bridge," *Huntsville Times*, November 26, 2014.

27. Norman R. Augustine, *Augustine's Laws* (Reston, VA: American Institute of Aeronautics and Astronautics, 1983), 158.

28. Casey Dreier, "Reconstructing the Cost of the One Giant Leap: How Much Did Apollo Cost?," *The Planetary Society* (blog), June 16, 2019, https://www.planetary.org/blogs/casey-dreier/2019/reconstructing-the-price-of-apollo.html.

29. Government Accountability Office, "Weapon Systems: Concurrency in the Acquisition Process," Statement of Frank C. Conohan, Assistant Comptroller General National Security and International Affairs Division Before the Committee on Armed Services, United State Senate, May 17, 1990, GAO/T-NSIAD-90-43.

30. Government Accountability Office, *Defense Acquisitions: Assessment of Selection Program*, GAO Report GAO16-329SP, March 2016, http://www.gao.gov/assets/680/676281.pdf.

31. Matthew Heuser, "Software Testing Lessons Learned from Knight Capital Fiasco," *CIO*, August 14, 2012, https://www.cio.com/article/2393212/software-testing-lessons-learned-from-knight-capital-fiasco.html.

32. Nathaniel Popper, "Knight Capital Says Trading Glitch Cost It $440 Million," *Dealbook*, August 2, 2012, https://dealbook.nytimes.com/2012/08/02/knight-capital-says-trading-mishap-cost-it-440-million/.

33. Dealbook, "Knight Capital and Getco to Merge," December 19, 2012, https://dealbook.nytimes.com/2012/12/19/knight-capital-and-getco-to-merge/.

34. Calleam Consulting, Ltd., "Case Study—Denver International Airport Baggage Handling System—An Illustration of Ineffectual Decision Making," undated, http://calleam.com/WTPF/wp-content/uploads/articles/DIABaggage.pdf.

35. Personal correspondence with former NASA Cost Director Thomas Coonce.

36. Norman R. Augustine, *Augustine's Laws* (Reston, VA: American Institute of Aeronautics and Astronautics, 1983), 168; Congressional Research Service, "Continuing Resolutions: Overview of Components and Practices," April 19, 2019, Report 42647, https://fas.org/sgp/crs/misc/R42647.pdf; Committee for a Responsible Federal Budget, "Appropriations Watch: FY2020," blog post, December 24, 2019, http://www.crfb.org/blogs/appropriations-watch-fy-2020.

37. Tom Murse, "All 21 Government Shutdowns in U.S. History," Thought.Co, January 29, 2020, https://www.thoughtco.com/government-shutdown-history-3368274.

38. Norman R. Augustine, *Augustine's Laws* (Reston, VA: American Institute of Aeronautics and Astronautics, 1983) 103.

39. Henry Apgar, "The Legacy of Parametric Estimating," paper presented at the International Cost Estimating and Analysis Association Professional Development and Training Workshop, Tampa, FL, May 14–17, 2019, http://www.iceaaonline.com/ready/wp-content/uploads/2019/06/CV01-Paper-The-Legacy-of-Parametric-Estimating-Apgar.pdf.

40. My colleague Doug Howarth is a pioneer in this arena. His website is https://www.meevaluators.com/.

41. Riccardo Bastianello and Crispian Balmer, "Venice Still Waiting for Moses to Hold Back the Seas," Reuters, November 13, 2019.

42. Claudio Lavanga, "As Sea Levels Rise, Venice Fights to Stay Above the Waterline," *NBC News*, February 14, 2020, http://www.nbcnews.com /news/amp/ncna1135661.

43. Shane Reiner-Roth, "Venice's (Failed) Plan to Protect Itself from Flooding Is over 15 Years in the Making," *The Architect's Newspaper*, December 3, 2019, https://archpaper.com/2019/12/venice-failed-plan-to-protect -itself-from-flooding/.

44. M. Mitchell Waldrop, "The Chips Are Down for Moore's Law," *Nature* 530 (February 9, 2016): 144–47, doi:10.1038/530144a.

45. Intel, "Intel's 10 nm Technology: Delivering the Highest Logic Transistor Density in the Industry Through the Use of Hyper Scaling," 2017, https://newsroom.intel.com/newsroom/wp-content/uploads/sites/11 /2017/09/10-nm-icf-fact-sheet.pdf.

46. David Rotman, "We're Not Prepared for the End of Moore's Law," *MIT Technology Review*, February 24, 2020, https://www.technologyreview .com/s/615226/were-not-prepared-for-the-end-of-moores-law/.

47. Wilmer Alvarado, Daniel Barkmeyer, and Erik Burgess, "Commercial-Like Acquisitions: Practices and Costs," *Journal of Cost Analysis and Parametrics* 3, no. 1 (2010): 41–58, doi:10.1080/1941658X .2010.10462227.

48. Steve Keen, *Debunking Economics: The Naked Emperor Dethroned?* (New York and London: Zed Books Limited, 2011), 113–14.

49. Mark Hirschey, *Fundamentals of Managerial Economics*, 9th ed. (Mason, OH: South-Western Cengage Learning, 2009), 310.

50. David Axe, "It's Official: The U.S. Navy's Littoral Combat Ship Is a Complete Failure," *The National Interest*, May 22, 2019.

51. Mandy Smithberger and Pierre Sprey, "Overhaul of Littoral Combat Ship Program Likely to Increase Risks and Costs," *POGO*, December 13, 2016, https://www.pogo.org/investigation/2016/12/overhaul-of -littoral-combat-ship-program-likely-to-increase-risks-and-costs/.

52. James Holmes, "The U.S. Navy's Littoral Combat Ship: A Beautiful Disaster?" Real Clear Defense, February 18, 2020, https://www .realcleardefense.com/articles/2020/02/18/the_us_navys_littoral _combat_ship_a_beautiful_disaster_115049.html.

53. United States Government Accountability Office, Defense Acquisitions: Assessments of Selected Weapons Programs, March 2017, GAO-17-333SP, https://www.gao.gov/assets/690/683838.pdf.

54. Anand Krishnamoorthy, "A Humiliating End to the Superjumbo Era," February 14, 2019, bloomber.com, https://www.bloomberg.com/news /features/2019-02-14/airbus-a380-superjumbo-how-it-happened -and-what-went-wrong; https://www.airbus.com/aircraft/market/orders -deliveries.html.

55. Karl West, "Airbus's Flagship Plane May Be Too Big to Be Profitable," *The Guardian*, December 28, 2014.

56. Dan Reed, "The Plane That Never Should Have Been Built: The A380 Was Designed for Failure," February 15, 2019, forbes.com, https://www .forbes.com/sites/danielreed/2019/02/15/the-plane-that-never-should -have-been-built-the-a380-was-designed-for-marketplace-failure/ #a7c4ce73c59d.

57. Andy Prince and Christian B. Smart, "Being Certain About Uncertainty: Part 2," paper presented at the International Cost Estimating and Analysis Association Professional Development and Training Workshop, Phoenix, AZ, June 12–15, 2018, https://www.iceaaonline .com/phx18papers/; and Joseph N. Tatarewicz, "The Hubble Space Telescope Servicing Mission," in *From Engineering Science to Big Science*, ed. Pamela E. Mack (NASA: Washington, DC, 1998), 365–96.

58. Nassim N. Taleb, *The Black Swan: The Impact of the Highly Improbable* (New York: Random House, 2007).

Chapter 3

1. British Broadcasting Corporation, "O Fortuna is 'most listened to classical piece,'" December 28, 2009, http://news.bbc.co.uk/2/hi /entertainment/8432499.stm.

2. Kenneth J. Arrow, "'I know a hawk from a handsaw,'" in *Eminent Economists: Their Life Philosophies*, ed. Michael Szenberg (Cambridge: Cambridge University Press, 1992), 46.

3. Andy Prince, "Being Certain About Uncertainty: Part 1," paper presented at the International Cost Estimating and Analysis Association Professional Development and Training Workshop, Portland, OR, June 6–9, 2017.

4. Ian Hacking, *The Emergence of Probability: A Philosophical Study of Early Ideas About Probability Induction and Statistical Inference* (Cambridge: Cambridge University Press, 2006), 8.

5. Hacking, *The Emergence of Probability*, 102–10.

6. David Mumford, "The Dawning of the Age of Stochasticity," paper presented at the Mathematics Towards the Third Millennium Conference, Accademia Nazionale dei Lincei, May 27–29, 1999, Rome.

7. Mumford, "The Dawning of the Age of Stochasticity."

8. Bent Flyvbjerg, Nils Bruzelius, and Werner Rothengatter, *Megaprojects and Risk: An Anatomy of Ambition* (Cambridge: Cambridge University Press, 2003), 5.

9. Paul R. Garvey, *Probability Methods for Cost Uncertainty Analysis: A Systems Engineering Perspective* (New York: CRC Press, 2000), 24–25.

10. Charles A. Murray and Richard Herrnstein, *The Bell Curve: Intelligence and Class Structure in American Life* (New York: Simon and Schuster, 1994).

11. Stephen Jay Gould, *The Mismeasure of Man*, revised and expanded edition (New York: W.W. Norton & Company, 2006), 176–263.

12. Stephen Jay Gould, *Full House: The Spread of Excellence from Plato to Darwin* (New York: Harmony Books, 1996), 118.

13. Gould, *Full House*, 118–19.

14. Christina Gough, "Major League Baseball Average Player Salary 2003–2019," statista.com, https://www.statista.com/statistics/236213/mean-salaray-of-players-in-majpr-league-baseball/.

15. Sam L. Savage, *The Flaw of Averages: Why We Underestimate Risk in the Face of Uncertainty* (Hoboken: John Wiley & Sons, 2009), 11.

16. Savage, *The Flaw of Averages*, 18–19.

17. Stephen Jay Gould, "The Median Isn't the Message," *Discover* magazine, June 1985.

18. Gould, *Full House*, 44.

19. Carol Kaesuk Yoon, "Stephen Jay Gould, 60, Is Dead; Enlivened Evolutionary Theory," *New York Times*, May 21, 2002.

20. Christian B. Smart, "The Signal and The Noise in Cost Estimating," paper presented at the ICEAA International Training Symposium, Bristol, UK, October 17–20, 2016, http://www.iceaaonline.com/ready/wp-content/uploads/2016/10/MM01-paper-Smart-Signal-Noise.pdf.

21. Compton Construction, "7 Things You Need to Know About Contingency Budgets," blog post, April 2, 2015, http:www.comptonllc.com/contingency-budgets/.

22. Margaret M. Phillips, *The Adages of Erasmus* (Cambridge: Cambridge University Press, 1964).

23. Riccardo Rebonato, *Plight of the Fortune Tellers: Why We Need to Manage Financial Risk Differently* (Princeton: Princeton University Press, 2007) 22–25.

24. Stephen A. Book, "The Morass of Software Costing," presentation to the Maxwell Air Force Base, November 14, 2001.

25. This example is adapted from Philip Fahringer et al., "The Flaw of Averages in Project Management," PMI Virtual Library, September 16, 2011, https://www.projectmanagement.com/articles/283939/The-Flaw -of-Averages-in-Project-Management.

26. Phillipe Jorion, *Big Bets Gone Bad: The Largest Municipal Failure in U.S. History* (Bingley, UK: Emerald Group Publishing Limited, 1995).

27. Jorion, *Big Bets Gone Bad*, 91.

28. Roger Lowenstein, *When Genius Failed: The Rise and Fall of Long-Term Capital Management* (New York: Random House, 2000), 234.

29. Michael Lewis, *The Big Short: Inside the Doomsday Machine* (New York: W.W. Norton and Company, 2010).

30. The idea of considering a probability distribution as a shape is from Savage, *The Flaw of Averages*, 56.

31. Stephen M. Stigler, *The History of Statistics: The Measurement of Uncertainty before 1900* (Cambridge: Harvard University Press, 1986), 92.

32. Stigler, *The History of Statistics*, 73–76 and 141–43.

33. Nassim N. Taleb, *The Black Swan: The Impact of the Highly Improbable* (New York: Random House, 2007), 231–32.

34. Rachel Swatman, "Tallest Man Ever," February 22, 2019, Guinness World Records website, https://www.guinnessworldrecords.com/news /2018/2/on-this-day-in-1918-the-tallest-man-in-the-world-is-born -515815.

35. Swatman, "Tallest Man Ever."

36. Kelly Dickerson, "How Giraffes Stand on Their Spindly Legs," Live Science, July 10, 2014, https://www.livescience.com/46746-how-giraffe -legs-support-weight.html.

37. Jeremy J. Gray, *Janos Bolyai, Non-Euclidean Geometry, and the Nature of Space* (Cambridge, MA: Burndy Library Publications, 2004).

38. Benoit B. Mandlebrot, *The Fractal Geometry of Nature* (New York: W.H. Freeman and Company, 1983); and Benoit B. Mandlebrot, *Fractals and Scaling in Finance: Discontinuity, Concentration, Risk* (New York: Springer Verlag, 1997).

39. Benoit B. Mandelbrot, *The Fractalist: Memoir of a Scientific Maverick* (New York: Pantheon Books, 2012) loc. 2349-2487, Kindle.

40. Taleb, *The Black Swan*, 33.

41. Joseph M. Juran, "Pareto, Lorenz, Cournot, Bernoulli, Juran, and Others," *Industrial Quality Control* 17:4 (1960): 25.

42. Arthur De Vany, *Hollywood Economics: How Extreme Uncertainty Shapes the Film Industry* (New York: Routledge, 2004), 214.
43. Duncan Thomas and Alfred Smith, eds., *Joint Agency Cost Schedule Risk and Uncertainty Handbook* (Washington, DC: Naval Center for Cost Analysis, 2014), 15.
44. S. Sobel, "A Computerized Technique to Express Uncertainty in Advanced System Cost Estimates," ESD-TR-65-79, MITRE Corporation technical report, 1965; Paul F. Dienemann, "Estimating Cost Uncertainty Using Monte Carlo Techniques," RM-4854-PR, The RAND Corporation research memorandum, 1966.
45. However, for some estimates, analytic approximation techniques provide similar results. A good example is the cost risk methodology included in the NASA/Air Force Cost Model: Christian B. Smart, "Cost Risk in the NASA/Air Force Cost Model," paper presented at the SCEA-ISPA Joint International Conference and Educational Workshop, Denver, CO, June 14–17, 2005.
46. This example was inspired by a brilliant presentation by Steve Book. My only issue with his presentation is that he appeals to the Central Limit Theorem, which does not apply in cost estimating. Source: Stephen A. Book, "Do Not Sum 'Most Likely' Costs," Presented to the Society of Cost Estimating and Analysis, New England chapter meeting, April 29, 2003.
47. Garvey et al., *Probability Methods for Cost Uncertainty Analysis*, 264–65.
48. The idea of a protect scenario is discussed in Garvey et al., *Probability Methods for Cost Uncertainty Analysis*, 396–97.
49. Garvey et al., *Probability Methods for Cost Uncertainty Analysis*.
50. David Hulett, *Practical Schedule Risk Analysis* (Burlington, VT, Gower Publishing Company, 2009).

Chapter 4
1. Campbell Robertson and Clifford Krauss, "Gulf Spill Is the Largest of Its Kind, Scientists Say," *New York Times*, August 2, 2010.
2. David A. Graham, "Rumsfeld's Knowns and Unknowns: The Intellectual History of a Quip," *The Atlantic*, March 27, 2014, https://www.theatlantic.com/politics/archive/2014/03/rumsfelds-knowns-and-unknowns-the-intellectual-history-of-a-quip/359719/.
3. Bent Flyvbjerg, Nils Bruzelius, and Werner Rothengatter, *Megaprojects and Risk: An Anatomy of Ambition* (Cambridge: Cambridge University Press, 2003), 79.

4. World Bank Independent Evaluation Group, *Cost Benefit Analysis in World-Bank Projects* (Washington, DC: The World Bank, 2010), 12.

5. Nassim N. Taleb, *The Black Swan: The Impact of the Highly Improbable* (New York: Random House, 2007), 193.

6. George E. P. Box and Norman R. Draper, *Empirical Model-Building and Response Surfaces* (New York: John Wiley & Sons, 1987), 424.

7. Some are from data I have collected over the years; the others are from: Bent Flyvbjerg and Alexander Budzier, "Report for the Commission of Inquiry Respecting the Muskrat Falls Project," August 2018, http://dx.doi.org/10.2139/ssrn.3251965; and John K. Hollmann, "Estimate Accuracy: Dealing with Reality," *American Association of Cost Engineering International Transactions*, November–December 2012.

8. This is based on modeling the event "exceeds 90% confidence level" as a binomial distribution. If accurate, the probability for one project is 10%.

9. Stephen A. Book, "Why Correlation Matters in Cost Estimating," presented at the 32nd Annual Department of Defense Cost Analysis Symposium, Williamsburg, VA, February 2–5, 1999.

10. Christian B. Smart, "Robust Default Correlation for Cost Risk Analysis," paper presented at the International Cost Estimating and Analysis Association Professional Development and Training Workshop, New Orleans, June 18–21, 2013.

11. David Hulett is the developer of the risk driver approach. See David Hulett, *Practical Schedule Risk Analysis* (Burlington, VT: Gower Publishing Company, 2009), 133–62.

12. Felix Salmon, "Recipe for Disaster: The Formula That Killed Wall Street," *Wired*, February 23, 2009, https://www.wired.com/2009/02/wp-quant/. See also Sam Jones, "The Formula That Felled Wall Street," *The Financial Times*, April 24, 2009.

13. Christian B. Smart, "Beyond Correlation: Don't Use the Formula That Killed Wall Street," paper presented at the International Cost Estimating and Analysis Association Professional Development and Training Workshop, San Diego, June 9–12, 2015.

14. Christian B. Smart "Covered with Oil: Incorporating Realism in Cost Risk Analysis," *Journal of Cost Analysis and Parametrics* 8, no. 3 (2015): 186–205, , doi: 10.1080/1941658X.2015.1096220.

15. William D. Ross, *Plato's Theory of Ideas* (Oxford: Oxford University Press, 2000).

16. Milton Friedman, *Essays in Positive Economics* (Chicago: University of Chicago Press, 1966), 3–16.

17. Daniel M. Hausman, *The Philosophy of Economics: An Anthology*, 3rd ed. (Cambridge: Cambridge University Press, 2007), 180.

18. William J. Baumol, *Business Behavior, Value, and Growth* (New York: The Macmillan Company, 1959), 45–53.

19. Jonathan Tepper and Denise Hearn, *The Myth of Capitalism: Monopolies and the Death of Competition* (Hoboken: John Wiley & Sons, 2019).

20. William J. Baumol et al., *The Cost Disease: Why Computers Get Cheaper and Health Care Doesn't* (New Haven: Yale University Press, 2012).

21. Baumol, *Business Behavior, Value, and Growth*, 6.

22. Tyler Vigen, *Spurious Correlations: Correlation Does Not Equal Causation* (New York: Hachette Books, 2015), 29, 47.

23. Stanislaw M. Ulam, *Adventures of a Mathematician* (New York: Charles Scribner's Sons, 1976), 286.

24. Nassim N. Taleb, *The Black Swan: The Impact of the Highly Improbable*, (New York: Random House, 2007), 63.

25. Andy Prince and Christian B. Smart, "Being Certain About Uncertainty: Part II," paper presented at the International Cost Estimating and Analysis Association Professional Development and Training Workshop, Phoenix, AZ, June 12–15, 2018, https://www.iceaaonline.com/phx18papers/.

26. E. C. Capen, "The Difficulty in Assessing Uncertainty," *Journal of Petroleum Technology* 28 no. 8 (1976): 843–50, doi: 10.2118/5579-PA.

27. Capen, "The Difficulty in Assessing Uncertainty."

28. Norman R. Augustine, *Augustine's Laws*, 6th ed. (Reston, VA: American Institute of Astronautics and Aeronautics, 1997), 50.

29. For more details on this process, see Christian B. Smart, "Enhancing Risk Calibration Methods." Paper presented at the International Cost Estimating and Analysis Professional Development and Training Workshop, Phoenix, June 12–15, 2018, https://www.iceaaonline.com/ready/wp-content/uploads/2018/07/RU06-Paper-Enhancing-Risk-Calibration-Smart.pdf. An Excel spreadsheet that implements the approach in the paper is also available at https://www.iceaaonline.com/ready/wp-content/uploads/2018/07/RU06-Enhancing-Risk-Calibration-Smart.xlsx.

30. This is an effective coefficient of variation that takes into account underruns, which happen occasionally. Some add 1 to average cost growth to avoid the problem of negative costs, but this underestimates the effective coefficient of variation as this approach assumes it is possible for costs to underrun to the point of being free. Values in this table are taken or derived from information in Smart, "Covered with Oil";

Prince and Smart, "Being Certain About Uncertainty: Part II,"; John K. Hollman, "Estimate Accuracy: Dealing with Reality," *Transactions and Cost Engineering Journal*, November–December 2012; Bent Flyvbjerg, Mette Skamris Holm, and Søren Buhl, "Underestimating Costs in Public Works Projects Error or Lie?" *Journal of the American Planning Association* 68, no. 3 (Summer 2002), American Planning Association, Chicago, IL; Mattia Lundberg, Anchalee Jenpanitsub, and Roger Pyddoke, "Cost Overruns in Swedish Transportation Projects," Centre for Transportation Studies Stockholm, CTS Working Paper 2011:11, 2011; Edward W. Merrow, *Understanding the Outcomes of Megaprojects: A Quantitative Analysis of Very Large Civilian Projects* (Santa Monica: The RAND Corporation, 1988), 32; Michael Popp, "Calibrating Software Cost Growth." Paper presented at the 39th Department of Defense Cost Analysis Symposium, Williamsburg, VA, February 14–17, 2006.

31. Duncan Thomas and Alfred Smith, eds., *Joint Agency Cost Schedule Risk and Uncertainty Handbook* (Washington, DC: Naval Center for Cost Analysis, 2014).

32. Interestingly, for 10 projects, the probability that at most one exceeds the 90% confidence level is approximately 74% (the probability is not 90% because 10 data points comprise a small set). These calculations are based on a binomial distribution.

33. William Feller, *An Introduction to Probability Theory and Its Applications Volume II*, 3rd ed. (New York: John Wiley & Sons, 1950), 256–57.

34. Prince and Smart, "Being Certain About Uncertainty: Part II."

35. Michael Mitzenmacher, "A Brief History of Generative Models for Power Law and Lognormal Distributions," *Internet Mathematics* 1, no. 2 (2003): 226–51.

36. Prince and Smart, "Being Certain About Uncertainty: Part II."

37. Bent Flyvbjerg, Nils Bruzelius, and Werner Rothengatter, *Megaprojects and Risk: An Anatomy of Ambition* (Cambridge: Cambridge University Press, 2003), 18.

38. Mark Aitken, "Experts Warn £414m Scottish Parliament Building Might Not Last 40 Years," *Daily Record*, September 17, 2017.

39. Dara Bramson, "Supersonic Airplanes and the Age of Irrational Technology: Was the Concorde a Triumph of Modern Engineering, a Metaphor for Misplaced 20th-Century Values, or Both?" *The Atlantic*, July 1, 2015, https://www.theatlantic.com/technology/archive/2015/07/supersonic-airplanes-concorde/396698/.

40. Aitken, "Experts Warn £414m Scottish Parliament Building Might Not Last."

41. Bent Flyvbjerg and Alexander Budzier, "Double Whammy: How ICT Projects Are Fooled by Randomness and Screwed by Political Intent," Said Business School Working Papers, August 2011.

42. Bob Hunt, "Estimating Agile Software Development," paper presented at the International Cost Estimating and Analysis Association Professional Development and Training Workshop, San Diego, CA, June 9–12, 2015.

43. Paul H. Cootner, ed., *The Random Character of Stock Market Prices* (Cambridge: MIT Press, 1964), 337.

44. Donald MacKenzie, *An Engine, Not a Camera: How Financial Models Shape Markets* (Cambridge: MIT Press, 2006) loc. 1521-1698, Kindle.

45. William Shakespeare, *Hamlet*, ed. Roma Gill (Oxford: Oxford University Press, 1992), Act I, Scene 5, page 35.

Chapter 5

1. Mark Twain, *Pudd'n'head Wilson and Those Extraordinary Twins* (New York and London: Harper & Brothers Publishers, 1899), 130.

2. Peter L. Bernstein, *Capital Ideas: The Improbable Origins of Modern Wall Street* (New York: The Free Press, 1992), 48.

3. Bernstein, *Capital Ideas*, 46–47.

4. Gerald M. Loeb, *The Battle for Investment Survival* (New York: Simon and Schuster, 1935), 119.

5. Harry M. Markowitz, "Portfolio Selection," *The Journal of Finance* 7, no. 1 (March 1952):77–91, doi:10.2307/2975974.

6. Peter L. Bernstein, *Capital Ideas: The Improbable Origins of Modern Wall Street* (New York: The Free Press, 1992), 47–50.

7. James J. Cramer, *Jim Cramer's Real Money: Sane Investing in an Insane World* (New York: Simon & Schuster, 2009) 72.

8. "Free Lunch in the South," *New York Times*, February 20, 1875, p. 4.

9. Daniel Breazeale, trans. Johann Fichte, *Fichte: Early Philosophical Writings* (Ithaca: Cornell University Press, 1993), 63.

10. Robert A. Heinlein, *The Moon Is a Harsh Mistress* (New York: G. P. Putnam's Sons, 1966), 129.

11. Milton Friedman, *There's No Such Thing as a Free Lunch* (Chicago: Open Court Publishing Company,1975).

12. Timothy P. Anderson, "The Trouble with Budgeting to the 80th Percentile," presented at the 72nd Military Operations Research Society Symposium, Monterey, CA, June 22–24, 2004.

13. Benoit B. Mandelbrot and Nassim N. Taleb, "Mild vs. Wild Randomness: Focusing on Those Risks That Matter," in Francis X. Diebold, Neil A. Doherty, and Richard J. Herring, eds., *The Known, the Unknown, and the Unknowable in Financial Risk Management* (Princeton: Princeton University Press, 2010), 47–58.

14. Alexander J. McNeil, Rudiger Frey, and Paul Embrechts, *Quantitative Risk Management: Concepts, Techniques, and Tools, Revised Edition* (Princeton: Princeton University Press, 2015), 16.

15. Department of Energy Performance Baseline Guide, https://www.directives.doe.gov/directives-documents/400-series/0413.3-EGuide-05a/@@images/file.

16. Bent Flyvbjerg, "From Nobel Prize to Project Management: Getting Risks Right," *Project Management Journal* 37, no. 3 (August 2006): 5–15.

17. Australian Government Department of Finance, "Defining P50 and P80 Manual," https://www.finance.gov.au/sites/default/files/2019-11/RMG500-Defining-P50-and-P80-Manual.pdf.

18. Infrastructure Risk Group, "Managing Cost Risk & Uncertainty in Infrastructure Projects: Leading Practice and Improvement," 2013, https://learninglegacy.crossrail.co.uk/wp-content/uploads/2016/02/1H-018_Managing-Cost-Risk-and-uncertainty-IRM-REPORTLRV2.pdf.

19. US Department of Transportation Federal Highway Administration, "Risk Assessment for Public-Private Partnerships: A Primer," January 2014, https://www.fhwa.dot.gov/ipd/p3/toolkit/publications/primers/risk_assessment/ch_1.aspx.

20. Bent Flyvbjerg and Alexander Budzier, "Report for the Commission of Inquiry Respecting the Muskrat Falls Project," August 2018, https://arxiv.org/ftp/arxiv/papers/1901/1901.03698.pdf.

21. David Hulett, *Practical Schedule Risk Analysis* (Burlington, VT: Gower Publishing Company VT, 2009), 122.

22. National Aeronautics and Space Administration, *NASA Cost Estimating Handbook version 4.0* (Washington, DC: NASA, 2015), Appendix J: Joint Cost and Schedule Confidence Level (JCL)Analysis, https://www.nasa.gov/sites/default/files/files/CEH_Appj.pdf.

23. Alexander J. McNeil, Rudiger Frey, and Paul Embrechts, *Quantitative Risk Management: Concepts, Techniques, and Tools*, rev. ed. (Princeton: Princeton University Press, 2015), 67–68.

24. Office of the Undersecretary of Defense for Acquisition, Technology, and Logistics, "Report of the Defense Science Board/Air Force Scientific Advisory Board Joint Task Force on Acquisition of National

Security Space Programs," May 2003, Washington, DC, http://www
.dtic.mil/docs/citations/ADA429180.

25. Anderson, "The Trouble with Budgeting to the 80th Percentile."

26. Flyvbjerg and Budzier, "Report for the Commission of Inquiry Respecting the Muskrat Falls Project."

27. Newton L. Bowers, *Actuarial Mathematics* (Schaumburg, IL: Society of Actuaries, 1997).

Chapter 6

1. Aaron Brown and David Einhorn, "Private Profits and Socialized Risks," *GARP Risk Review*, July/July 2008, 12.

2. Pablo Triana, *Lecturing Birds on Flying: Can Mathematical Theories Destroy the Markets?* (New York: John Wiley & Sons, 2009), 145.

3. Nassim N. Taleb, "The World According to Nassim Taleb," *Derivatives Strategy* 2 (December/January): 37–40, 1997.

4. James A. Connor, *Pascal's Wager: The Man Who Played Dice with God* (New York: Harper Collins, 2006), loc. 3182-3329, Kindle.

5. For a mathematical proof that the Gaussian is "riskier" than the lognormal at least up to the 84th percentile, see Christian B. Smart, "The Fractal Nature of Cost Risk: The Portfolio Effect, Power Laws, and Risk and Uncertainty Properties of Lognormal Distributions," *Journal of Cost Analysis and Parametrics* 5, no. 1 (June 2012): 5–24, dx.doi.org/10.1080/1941658X.2012.682922.

6. Phillippe Artzner et al., "Coherent Measures of Risk," *Mathematical Finance* 9, no. 3 (1999): 203–28, doi:10.1111/1467-9965.00068.

7. For a technical, concrete example that demonstrates that standard deviation and variance are not monotonic, see Smart, C. B., "Here There Be Dragons: Considering the Right Tail in Risk Management," *Journal of Cost Analysis and Parametrics* 5, no. 2 (2012): 65–86, http://dx.doi.org/10.1080/1941658X.2012.734752.

8. Alexander J. McNeil, Rudiger Frey, and Paul Embrechts, *Quantitative Risk Management: Concepts, Techniques, and Tools*, rev. ed. (Princeton: Princeton University Press, 2015), 69–70.

9. Carlo Acerbi and Dirk Tasche, "On the Coherence of Expected Shortfall," *Journal of Banking and Finance* 26, no. 7 (July 2002): 1487–1503.

10. B. John Manistre and Geoffrey H. Hancock, "Variance of the CTE Estimator," *North American Actuarial Journal* 9, no. 2 (2005): 129–56.

11. Damir Filipovic and Michael Kupper, "On the Group Level Swiss Solvency Test," *Bulletin of the Swiss Association of Actuaries* 1 (2007): 97–115.

12. Louis J. Lombardi, *Valuation of Life Insurance Liabilities: Establishing Reserves for Life Insurance Policies and Annuity Contracts* (ACTEX Publications: New Hartford CT, 2009), 271–78.
13. A. D. Roy, "Safety First and the Holding of Assets," *Econometrica* 20, no. 3 (July 1952): 431–49, doi: 10.2307/1907413.
14. For the technical details of the positive semi-deviation risk measure, see Christian B. Smart, "Cost Risk Allocation Theory and Practice," *Journal of Cost Analysis and Parametrics* 7, no. 2 (2014): 72–100, doi: 10.1080/1941658X.2014.922907.

Chapter 7

1. Christian B. Smart, "Cost and Schedule Interrelationships," presented at the NASA Cost Symposium, Denver, July 17–19, 2007.
2. Smart, "Cost and Schedule Interrelationships."
3. U.S. Congress, Office of Technology Assessment, *Reducing Launch Operations Costs: New Technologies and Practices* (Washington, DC: U.S. Government Printing Office, 1988) 14–16.
4. Rajeev Syal, "Abandoned NHS IT System Has Cost £10bn So Far," *The Guardian*, September 17, 2013, https://www.theguardian.com/society/2013/sep/18/nhs-records-system-10bn.
5. Alistair Maughan, "Six Reasons Why the NHS National Programme for IT Failed," ComputerWeekly.com, September 13, 2010, https://www.computerweekly.com/opinion/Six-reasons-why-the-NHS-National-Programme-for-IT-failed.
6. Oliver Wright, "NHS Pulls the Plug on its £11Bn IT System," *Independent*, August 3, 2011, https://www.independent.co.uk/life-style/health-and-families/health-news/nhs-pulls-the-plug-on-its-11bn-it-system-2330906.html.
7. Timothy Anderson, "Fifteen Undeniable Truths About Project Cost Estimates, or Why You Need an Independent Cost Estimate," paper presented at the International Cost Estimating and Analysis Association Professional Development and Training Workshop, New Orleans, June 18–21, 2013.
8. Christian B. Smart, "Cost and Schedule Interrelationships," presented at the NASA Cost Symposium, Denver, July 17–19, 2007.
9. Christian B. Smart and George Culver, "NAFCOM Improvements: Assessing the Impact of Phasing and Schedule on Cost: Final Report," prepared for NASA Headquarters, January 1, 2009.

10. Norman R. Augustine, *Augustine's Laws*, 6th ed. (Reston, VA: American Institute for Aeronautics and Astronautics, 1997) 275–78.

Chapter 8

1. Paul Raeburn and Kevin Zollman, *The Game Theorist's Guide to Parenting: How the Science of Strategic Thinking Can Help You Deal with the Toughest Negotiators You Know—Your Kids* (New York: Scientific American/Farrar, Strauss, and Giroux: New York, 2017), 4–6.
2. Andy Prince and Christian B. Smart, "Being Uncertain About Uncertainty: Part 2," paper presented at the International Cost Estimating and Analysis Association Professional Development and Training Workshop, Tampa, FL, May 14–17, 2019; Bent Flyvbjerg and Alexander Budzier, "Report for the Commission of Inquiry Respecting the Muskrat Falls Project," August 2018, https://ssrn.com/abstract=3251965.
3. NASA is considering using this method. See Marc Greenberg, "Calculating a Project's Reserve Dollars from its S-Curve," paper presented at the International Cost Estimating and Analysis Association Professional Development and Training Workshop, Phoenix, AZ, June 12–15, 2018.
4. For technical details see Christian Smart, "Cost Risk Allocation Theory and Practice," *Journal of Cost Analysis and Parametrics* 7, no. 2 (2014): 72–100, doi: 10.1080/1941658X.2014.922907.
5. Memorandum from the NASA Associate Administrator, "Joint Cost and Schedule Confidence Level (JCL) Requirements Updates," May 24, 2019, https://www.nasa.gov/sites/default/files/atoms/files/jcl_memo_5-24-19tagged.pdf.
6. This is adapted from an enterprise risk management framework set forth by the Casualty Actuarial Society, Enterprise Risk Management Committee, "Overview of Enterprise Risk Management," May 2003, https://www.casact.org/area/erm/overview.pdf.
7. James Lam, *Implementing Enterprise Risk Management: From Methods to Applications* (Hoboken: John Wiley & Sons, 2017), Chapter 1.
8. Nancy A. Nichols, "Scientific Management at Merck: An Interview with CFO Judy Lewent," *Harvard Business Review*, January-February 1994.
9. Norman R. Augustine, *Augustine's Laws* (Reston, VA: American Institute of Aeronautics and Astronautics, 1983), 250.
10. David Biron and Christian B. Smart, "Cost Risk for Firm Fixed-Price Contracts," paper presented at the International Cost Estimating and

Analysis Association Professional Development and Training Workshop, Atlanta, June 7–10, 2016.

11. Eric Olson, "Motorists Revel in Early Finish to Huntsville Highway," October 4, 2018, ConstructionEquipmentGuide.com, https://www .constructionequipmentguide.com/motorists-revel-in-early-finish-to -huntsville-highway/42169.

12. A standard reference is Leonid Hurwicz and Stanley Reiter, *Designing Economic Mechanisms* (Cambridge: Cambridge University Press, 2006).

13. Nobel Foundation, "The Sveriges Riksbank Prize in Economic Sciences in Memory of Alfred Nobel 2007" (press release), October 15, 2007, https://www.nobelprize.org/prizes/economic-sciences/2007/press -release/.

14. Alvin E. Roth, *Who Gets What and Why* (New York: Harper Collins, 2015).

15. By the Revelation Principle, any mechanism is equivalent to one that requires the contractor to reveal their private information. See Jean-Jacques Laffont and David Martimort, *The Theory of Incentives: The Principal-Agent Model* (Princeton: Princeton University Press, 2002), 26.

16. Martin Loeb and Wesley A. Magat, "A Decentralized Method for Utility Regulation," *Journal of Law and Economics* 22, no. 2 (October 1979), 399–404.

17. David P. Baron and Roger B. Myerson, "Regulating a Monopolist with Unknown Costs," *Econometrica* 50, no.4 (July 1982): 911–30.

18. For the technical details of the example, see Christian B. Smart and Brittany Staley, "Engineering the Acquisition Process: Using Mechanism Design to Achieve Better Value," paper presented at the International Cost Estimating and Analysis Association Professional Development and Training Workshop, Tampa, May 14–17, 2019.

19. Friedrich A. Hayek, *The Road to Serfdom* (Chicago: The University of Chicago Press, 1944), 71.

Chapter 9

1. Douglas W. Hubbard, *The Failure of Risk Management: Why It's Broken and How to Fix It*, 2nd ed. (Hoboken: John Wiley & Sons, 2020), 26–34.

2. Daniel Kahneman, *Thinking, Fast and Slow* (New York: Farrar, Straus, and Giroux, 2011), 20–121.

3. George Santayana, *The Life of Reason: Reason in Common Sense* (New York: Charles Scribner's Sons, 1905), 285.

BIBLIOGRAPHY

Acerbi, Carlo, and Dirk Tasche, "On the Coherence of Expected Shortfall." *Journal of Banking and Finance* 26, no. 7 (July 2002): 1487–1503.

Alvarado, Wilmer, Daniel Barkmeyer, and Erik Burgess, "Commercial-Like Acquisitions: Practices and Costs." *Journal of Cost Analysis and Parametrics* 3, no. 1 (2010): 41–58, doi:10.1080/1941658X.2010.10462227.

Anderson, Timothy P., "The Trouble with Budgeting to the 80th Percentile," presented at the 72nd Military Operations Research Society Symposium, Monterey, CA, June 22–24 2004.

Anderson, Timothy, and Raymond Covert, eds., *Space Systems Cost Risk Handbook: Applying the Best Practices in Cost Risk Analysis to Space System Cost Estimates.* Hampton, VA: Space Systems Cost Analysis Group, 2005.

Anderson, Timothy, "Fifteen Undeniable Truths About Project Cost Estimates, or Why You Need an Independent Cost Estimate." Paper presented at the International Cost Estimating and Analysis Association Professional Development and Training Workshop, New Orleans, June 18–21, 2013.

Apgar, Henry, "The Legacy of Parametric Estimating." Paper presented at the International Cost Estimating and Analysis Association Professional Development and Training Workshop, Tampa, FL, May 14–17, 2019.

Artzner, Phillippe, Freddy Delbaen, Jean-Marc Eber, and David Heath, "Coherent Measures of Risk." *Mathematical Finance* 9, no. 3 (1999): 203–28, doi:10.1111/1467-9965.00068.

Augustine, Norman R., *Augustine's Laws*, 6th ed. Reston, VA: American Institute of Astronautics and Aeronautics, 1997.

Australian Government Department of Finance, "Defining P50 and P80 Manual," https://www.finance.gov.au/sites/default/files/2019-11/RMG 500-Defining-P50-and-P80-Manual.pdf.

Baron, David P., and Roger B. Myerson, "Regulating a Monopolist with Unknown Costs." *Econometrica* 50, no. 4 (July 1982): 911–30.

Baumol, William J., *Business Behavior, Value, and Growth.* New York: The Macmillan Company, 1959.

Baumol, William J., Monte Malach, Ariel Pablos-Mendez, and Lillian Gomory Wu, *The Cost Disease: Why Computers Get Cheaper and Health Care Doesn't*. New Haven: Yale University Press, 2012.

Bernstein, Peter L., *Capital Ideas: The Improbable Origins of Modern Wall Street*. New York: The Free Press, 1992.

Bilbro, James W., "Systematic Assessment of the Project/Program Impacts of Technological Advancement and Insertion," in William L. Nolte, *Did I Ever Tell You About the Whale? Or Measuring Technology Maturity*. Charlotte, NC: Information Age Publishing, 2008.

Billings, Lee "Space Science: The Telescope that Ate Astronomy." *Nature* 467 (October 2010): 1028–30, doi:10.1038/4671028a.

Book, Stephen A., "Why Correlation Matters in Cost Estimating," presented at the 32nd Annual Department of Defense Cost Analysis Symposium, Williamsburg, VA, February 2–5, 1999.

Book, Stephen A., "The Morass of Software Costing," presentation to the Maxwell Air Force Base, November 14, 2001.

Book, Stephen A., "Do Not Sum 'Most Likely' Costs," presented to the Society of Cost Estimating and Analysis, New England chapter meeting, April 29, 2003.

Box, George E. P., and Norman R. Draper, *Empirical Model-Building and Response Surfaces*. New York: John Wiley & Sons, 1987.

Brown, Aaron, and David Einhorn, "Private Profits and Socialized Risks." *GARP Risk Review*, July/July 2008.

Burgess, Erik L., and Hany S. Gobreial, "Integrating Spacecraft Design and Cost-Risk Analysis Using NASA Technology Readiness Levels." Paper presented at the 29th Annual Department of Defense Cost Analysis Symposium, February 1996.

Calleam Consulting, Ltd., "Case Study: Denver International Airport Baggage Handling System—An Illustration of Ineffectual Decision Making," undated, http://calleam.com/WTPF/wp-content/uploads/articles/DIABaggage.pdf.

Capen, E. C., "The Difficulty in Assessing Uncertainty." *Journal of Petroleum Technology* 28, no. 8 (1976): 843–50. doi:10.2118/5579-PA.

Casualty Actuarial Society, Enterprise Risk Management Committee, "Overview of Enterprise Risk Management," May 2003, https://www.casact.org/area/erm/overview.pdf.

Connor, James A., *Pascal's Wager: The Man Who Played Dice with God*. New York: Harper Collins, 2006.

Cootner, Paul H., ed., *The Random Character of Stock Market Prices*. Cambridge: MIT Press, 1964.

Cramer, James J., *Jim Cramer's Real Money: Sane Investing in an Insane World.* New York: Simon & Schuster, 2009.

De Vany, Arthur, *Hollywood Economics: How Extreme Uncertainty Shapes the Film Industry.* New York: Routledge, 2004.

Dienemann, Paul F., "Estimating Cost Uncertainty Using Monte Carlo Techniques," RM-4854-PR, The RAND Corporation research memorandum, 1966.

Drezner, Jeffrey A., and Giles K. Smith, *An Analysis of Weapon Systems Acquisition Schedules.* Santa Monica, CA: RAND Corporation, December 1990, RAND Report R-3937-ACQ.

Fahringer, Philip, John Hinton, Marc Thibault, and Sam Savage, "The Flaw of Averages in Project Management." PMI Virtual Library, September 16, 2011, https://www.projectmanagement.com/articles/283939/The -Flaw-of-Averages-in-Project-Management.

Feller, William, *An Introduction to Probability Theory and Its Applications Volume II*, 3rd ed. New York: John Wiley & Sons, 1950.

Filipovic, Damir, and Michael Kupper, "On the Group Level Swiss Solvency Test." *Bulletin of the Swiss Association of Actuaries* 1 (2007): 97–115.

Flyvbjerg, Bent, Mette Skamris Holm, and Søren Buhl, "Underestimating Costs in Public Works Projects: Error or Lie?" *Journal of the American Planning Association* 68, no. 3, Summer 2002. American Planning Association, Chicago, IL.

Flyvbjerg, Bent, Nils Bruzelius, and Werner Rothengatter, *Megaprojects and Risk: An Anatomy of Ambition.* Cambridge: Cambridge University Press, 2003.

Flyvbjerg, Bent, "From Nobel Prize to Project Management: Getting Risks Right." *Project Management Journal* 37, no. 3, August 2006.

Flyvbjerg, Bent, Allison Stewart, and Alexander Budzier, "The Oxford Olympics Study 2016: Cost and Cost Overrun at the Games," University of Oxford's Said Business School Research Paper, July 2016.

Flyvbjerg, Bent, ed., *The Oxford Handbook of Megaproject Management.* Oxford: Oxford University Press, 2017.

Flyvbjerg, Bent and Alexander Budzier, "Report for the Commission of Inquiry Respecting the Muskrat Falls Project," August 2018, https:// arxiv.org/ftp/arxiv/papers/1901/1901.03698.pdf.

Freaner, Claude, Bob Bitten, Dave Bearden, and Debra Emmons, "An Assessment of the Inherent Optimism in Early Conceptual Designs and Its Effect on Cost and Schedule Growth." Paper presented to the Planetary Science Subcommittee, NASA Goddard Space Flight Center, MD, June 23, 2008.

Friedman, Milton, *Essays in Positive Economics*. Chicago: University of Chicago Press, 1966.

Friedman, Milton, *There's No Such Thing as a Free Lunch*. Chicago: Open Court Publishing Company, 1975.

Garvey, Paul R., Stephen A. Book, and Raymond P. Covert, *Probability Methods for Cost Uncertainty Analysis: A Systems Engineering Perspective*, 2nd ed. New York: CRC Press, 2016.

Goeller, Lawrence N., "Military Satellite Communications: Why So Many, Why So Hard?" Paper presented at the 42nd Department of Defense Cost Analysis Symposium, Williamsburg, VA, February 16–19, 2009.

Goldberg, Matthew S., and Charles A. Weber, "Evaluation of the Risk Analysis and Cost Management (RACM) Model," Institute for Defense Analysis, IDA Paper P-3388, August 1998.

Gould, Stephen Jay, "The Median Isn't the Message," *Discover* magazine, June 1985.

Gould, Stephen Jay, *Full House: The Spread of Excellence from Plato to Darwin*. New York: Harmony Books, 1996.

Gould, Stephen Jay, *The Mismeasure of Man*, revised and expanded edition. New York: W.W. Norton & Company, 2006.

Government Accountability Office, "Cost, Schedule, and Performance of NASA's Ulysses Mission to the Sun," GAO Report No. 88059, May 1988.

Government Accountability Office, "Weapon Systems: Concurrency in the Acquisition Process," Statement of Frank C. Conohan, Assistant Comptroller General National Security and International Affairs Division Before the Committee on Armed Services, United States Senate, May 17, 1990, GAO/T-NSIAD-90-43.

Government Accountability Office, Defense Acquisitions: Assessment of Selection Program, GAO Report GAO16-329SP, March 2016, http://www.gao.gov/assets/680/676281.pdf.

Government Accountability Office, *Defense Acquisitions: Assessments of Selected Weapons Programs*, March 2017, GAO-17-333SP, https://www.gao.gov/assets/690/683838.pdf.

Greenberg, Marc, "Calculating a Project's Reserve Dollars from Its S-Curve." Paper presented at the International Cost Estimating and Analysis Association Professional Development and Training Workshop, Phoenix, AZ, June 12–15, 2018.

Hacking, Ian, *The Emergence of Probability: A Philosophical Study of Early Ideas About Probability Induction and Statistical Inference*. Cambridge: Cambridge University Press, 2006.

Hamaker, Joseph W., "But What Will It Cost? The History of NASA Cost Estimating," in *Issues in NASA Program and Project Management*, ed. Francis T. Hoban. Huntsville, AL: NASA Marshall Space Flight Center, 1993.

Hausman, Daniel M., *The Philosophy of Economics: An Anthology*, 3rd ed. Cambridge: Cambridge University Press, 2007.

Hayek, Friedrich A., *The Road to Serfdom*. Chicago: The University of Chicago Press, 1944.

Hirschey, Mark, *Fundamentals of Managerial Economics*, 9th ed. Mason, OH: South-Western Cengage Learning, 2009.

Hofstadter, Douglas R., *Godel, Escher, Bach: An Eternal Golden Braid*. New York: Basic Books, 1979.

Hollman, John K., "Estimate Accuracy: Dealing with Reality." *Transactions and Cost Engr Journal*; Nov–Dec 2012.

Hubbard, Douglas W., *The Failure of Risk Management: Why It's Broken and How to Fix It*, 2nd ed. Hoboken: John Wiley & Sons, 2020.

Hulett, David, *Practical Schedule Risk Analysis*. Burlington, VT: Gower Publishing Company, 2009.

Hurwicz, Leonid, and Stanley Reiter, *Designing Economic Mechanisms*. Cambridge: Cambridge University Press, 2006.

Infrastructure Risk Group, "Managing Cost Risk & Uncertainty in Infrastructure Projects: Leading Practice and Improvement," 2013, https://learninglegacy.crossrail.co.uk/wp-content/uploads/2016/02/1H-018_Managing-Cost-Risk-and-uncertainty-IRM-REPORTLRV2.pdf.

Jones, Capers, *Quantifying Software: Global and Industry Perspectives*. New York: CRC Press, 2018.

Jorion, Phillipe, *Big Bets Gone Bad: The Largest Municipal Failure in U.S. History*. Bingley, UK: Emerald Group Publishing Limited, 1995.

Kahneman, Daniel, *Thinking Fast and Slow*. New York: Macmillan, 2011.

Keen, Steve, *Debunking Economics: The Naked Emperor Dethroned?* New York and London: Zed Books Limited, 2011.

Laffont, Jean-Jacques, and David Martimort, *The Theory of Incentives: The Principal-Agent Model*. Princeton: Princeton University Press, 2002.

Lam, James, *Implementing Enterprise Risk Management: From Methods to Applications*. Hoboken, NJ: John Wiley & Sons, 2017.

Lewis, Michael, *The Big Short: Inside the Doomsday Machine*. New York: W.W. Norton and Company, 2010.

Loeb, Gerald M., *The Battle for Investment Survival*. New York: Simon and Schuster, 1935.

Loeb, Martin, and Wesley A. Magat, "A Decentralized Method for Utility Regulation." *The Journal of Law and Economics* 22, no. 2 (October 1979), 399–404.

Lofgren, Eric M., "A History of Thought in Defense Acquisition." Paper presented at the International Cost Estimating and Analysis Professional Development and Training Workshop, Portland, OR, June 6–9, 2017.

Lombardi, Louis J., *Valuation of Life Insurance Liabilities: Establishing Reserves for Life Insurance Policies and Annuity Contracts*. New Hartford, CT: ACTEX Publications, 2009.

Lowenstein, Roger, *When Genius Failed: The Rise and Fall of Long-Term Capital Management*. New York: Random House, 2000.

Lundberg, Mattia, Anchalee Jenpanitsub, and Roger Pyddoke, "Cost Overruns in Swedish Transportation Projects," Centre for Transportation Studies Stockholm, CTS Working Paper 2011:11, 2011.

Lytras, Miltiadis D., and Patricia Ordonez de Pablos, eds., *Emerging Topics and Technologies in Information Systems*. Hershey, PA: Information Science Reference, 2009.

Mackenzie, Donald, *An Engine, Not a Camera: How Financial Models Shape Markets*. Cambridge: MIT Press, 2006.

Mandelbrot, Benoit B., *The Fractal Geometry of Nature*. New York: W.H. Freeman and Company, 1983.

Mandelbrot, Benoit B., *Fractals and Scaling in Finance: Discontinuity, Concentration, Risk*. New York: Springer Verlag, 1997.

Mandelbrot, Benoit B., and Nassim N. Taleb, "Mild vs. Wild Randomness: Focusing on Those Risks That Matter," in Francis X. Diebold, Neil A. Doherty, and Richard J. Herring, eds., *The Known, the Unknown, and the Unknowable in Financial Risk Management*. Princeton: Princeton University Press, 2010.

Mandelbrot, Benoit B., *The Fractalist: Memoir of a Scientific Maverick*. New York: Pantheon Books, 2012.

Manistre, B. John, and Geoffrey H. Hancock, "Variance of the CTE Estimator." *North American Actuarial Journal* 9, no. 2 (2005): 129–56.

Markowitz, Harry M., "Portfolio Selection." *Journal of Finance* 7, no. 1 (March 1952):77–91, doi:10.2307/2975974.

Merrow, Edward W., *Understanding the Outcomes of Megaprojects: A Quantitative Analysis of Very Large Civilian Projects*. Santa Monica: The RAND Corporation, 1988.

Merrow, Edward W., and Ralph F. Shangraw Jr., "Understanding the Costs and Schedules of World Bank Supported Hydroelectric Projects," The

World Bank Industry and Energy Department Working Paper Energy Series Paper No. 31, July 1990.

Mitzenmacher, Michael, "A Brief History of Generative Models for Power Law and Lognormal Distributions." *Internet Mathematics* 1, no. 2 (2003), 226–51.

McNeil, Alexander J., Rudiger Frey, and Paul Embrechts, *Quantitative Risk Management: Concepts, Techniques, and Tools*, rev. ed. Princeton: Princeton University Press, 2015.

Mumford, David, "The Dawning of the Age of Stochasticity." Paper presented at the Mathematics Towards the Third Millennium Conference, Accademia Nazionale dei Lincei, May 27–29, 1999, Rome.

Murray, Charles A., and Richard Herrnstein, *The Bell Curve: Intelligence and Class Structure in American Life*. New York: Simon and Schuster, 1994.

National Aeronautics and Space Administration, *NASA Cost Estimating Handbook* version 4.0 Washington, DC: NASA, 2015.

Nichols, Nancy A., "Scientific Management at Merck: An Interview with CFO Judy Lewent." *Harvard Business Review*, January–February 1994.

Office of the Undersecretary of Defense for Acquisition, Technology, and Logistics, "Report of the Defense Science Board/Air Force Scientific Advisory Board Joint Task Force on Acquisition of National Security Space Programs," May 2003, Washington, DC, http://www.dtic.mil /docs/citations/ADA429180.

Parkinson, C. Northcote, *Parkinson's Law and Other Studies in Administration*. Boston: Houghton Mifflin Company, 1957.

Popp, Michael, "Calibrating Software Cost Growth." Paper presented at the 39th Department of Defense Cost Analysis Symposium, Williamsburg, VA, February 14–17, 2006.

Prince, Andy, "Being Certain About Uncertainty: Part 1." Paper presented at the International Cost Estimating and Analysis Association Professional Development and Training Workshop, Portland, OR, June 6–9, 2017.

Prince, Andy, and Christian B. Smart, "Being Certain About Uncertainty: Part 2." Paper presented at the International Cost Estimating and Analysis Association Professional Development and Training Workshop, Phoenix, AZ, June 12–15, 2018.

Raeburn, Paul, and Kevin Zollman, *The Game Theorist's Guide to Parenting: How the Science of Strategic Thinking Can Help You Deal with the Toughest Negotiators You Know—Your Kids*. New York: Scientific American/Farrar, Straus, and Giroux, 2017.

Rebonato, Riccardo, *Plight of the Fortune Tellers: Why We Need to Manage Financial Risk Differently*. Princeton: Princeton University Press, 2007.

Roth, Alvin E., *Who Gets What and Why*. New York: Harper Collins, 2015.

Rotman, David, "We're Not Prepared for the End of Moore's Law." *MIT Technology Review*, February 24, 2020, https://www.technologyreview.com/s/615226/were-not-prepared-for-the-end-of-moores-law/.

Roy, A. D., "Safety First and the Holding of Assets." *Econometrica* 20, no. 3 (July 1952): 431–49, doi:10.2307/1907413.

Savage, Sam L., *The Flaw of Averages: Why We Underestimate Risk in the Face of Uncertainty*. Hoboken: John Wiley & Sons, 2009.

Scott, Judy E., "The FoxMeyer's Drugs Bankruptcy: Was It a Failure of ERP?" Proceedings of the 5th Americas Conference on Information Systems, Milwaukee, WI, May 13, 1999, 223–25.

Shetterly, Margot Lee, *Hidden Figures: The American Dream and the Untold Story of the Black Women Mathematicians Who Helped Win the Space Race*. New York: William Morrow, 2016.

Silver, Nate, *The Signal and the Noise: Why So Many Predictions Fail—but Some Don't*. New York: Penguin Books, 2012.

Smart, Christian B., "Exploring the Limits of Faster-Better-Cheaper with the Mission Cost Risk Assessment Model," presented to the Office of Management and Budget, Washington, DC, January 4, 2001.

Smart, Christian B., "Cost Risk in the NASA/Air Force Cost Model." Paper presented at the SCEA-ISPA Joint International Conference and Educational Workshop, Denver, CO, June 14–17, 2005.

Smart, Christian B., "Cost and Schedule Interrelationships," presented at the NASA Cost Symposium, Denver, July 17–19, 2007.

Smart, Christian B., and George Culver, "NAFCOM Improvements: Assessing the Impact of Phasing and Schedule on Cost: Final Report," prepared for NASA Headquarters, January 1, 2009.

Smart, Christian B., "The Portfolio Effect and the Free Lunch." Paper presented at The International Society of Parametric Analysts and The Society of Cost Estimating and Analysis Professional Development and Training Workshop, St. Louis, MO, June 2–5, 2009.

Smart, Christian B., ed., *Missile Defense Agency Cost Estimating Handbook* (Huntsville, AL: Missile Defense Agency, 2012).

Smart, Christian B., "The Fractal Nature of Cost Risk: The Portfolio Effect, Power Laws, and Risk and Uncertainty Properties of Lognormal Distributions." *Journal of Cost Analysis and Parametrics* 5, no. 1 (2012): 5–24, dx.doi.org/10.1080/1941658X.2012.682922.

Smart, Christian B., "Here There Be Dragons: Considering the Right Tail in Risk Management." *Journal of Cost Analysis and Parametrics* 5, no. 2 (2012): 65–86, http://dx.doi.org/10.1080/1941658X.2012.734752.

Smart, Christian B., "Robust Default Correlation for Cost Risk Analysis." Paper presented at the International Cost Estimating and Analysis Association Professional Development and Training Workshop, New Orleans, June 18–21, 2013.

Smart, Christian B., "Cost Risk Allocation Theory and Practice." *Journal of Cost Analysis and Parametrics* 7, no. 2 (2014): 72–100, doi:10.1080/1941658X.2014.922907.

Smart, Christian B., "Covered with Oil: Incorporating Realism in Cost Risk Analysis." *Journal of Cost Analysis and Parametrics* 8, no. 3 (2015): 186–205, doi:10.1080/1941658X.2015.1096220.

Smart, Christian B. "Beyond Correlation: Don't Use the Formula That Killed Wall Street." Paper presented at the International Cost Estimating and Analysis Association Professional Development and Training Workshop, San Diego, June 9–12, 2015.

Smart, Christian B., "The Signal and the Noise in Cost Estimating." Paper presented at the ICEAA International Training Symposium, Bristol, UK, October 17–20, 2016.

Smart, Christian B., "Enhancing Risk Calibration Methods." Paper presented at the International Cost Estimating and Analysis Professional Development and Training Workshop, Phoenix, June 12–15, 2018.

Smart, Christian B., and Brittany Staley, "Engineering the Acquisition Process: Using Mechanism Design to Achieve Better Value." Paper presented at the International Cost Estimating and Analysis Association Professional Development and Training Workshop, Tampa, May 14–17, 2019.

Sobel, S., 1965. "A Computerized Technique to Express Uncertainty in Advanced System Cost Estimates," ESD-TR-65-79, MITRE Corporation technical report, 1965.

The Standish Group, *CHAOS Manifesto: The Laws of CHAOS and the CHAOS 100 Best PM Practices*. Boston: Standish Group, 2010.

Stigler, Stephen M., *The History of Statistics: The Measurement of Uncertainty Before 1900*. Cambridge: Harvard University Press, 1986.

Strickland, Daniel, *Software Cost Estimating and Analysis Handbook*. Huntsville, AL: Missile Defense Agency, 2016.

Taleb, Nassim N., "The World According to Nassim Taleb." *Derivatives Strategy* 2 (December/January 1997): 37–40.

Taleb, Nassim N., *The Black Swan: The Impact of the Highly Improbable*. New York: Random House, 2007.

Tatarewicz, Joseph N., "The Hubble Space Telescope Servicing Mission," in *From Engineering Science to Big Science*, ed. Pamela E. Mack, 365–96. Washington, DC: NASA, 1998.

Tepper, Jonathan, and Denise Hearn, *The Myth of Capitalism: Monopolies and the Death of Competition*. Hoboken: John Wiley & Sons, 2019.

Thaler, Richard H., *Misbehaving: The Making of Behavioral Economics*. New York: W.W. Norton & Company, 1986.

Thomas, Duncan Thomas, and Alfred Smith, eds., *Joint Agency Cost Schedule Risk and Uncertainty Handbook*. Washington, DC: Naval Center for Cost Analysis, 2014.

Triana, Pablo, *Lecturing Birds on Flying: Can Mathematical Theories Destroy the Markets?* New York: John Wiley & Sons, 2009.

Tribus, Myron, and Edward C. McIrvine, "Energy and Information." *Scientific American* 224, no. 3 (September 1971): 179–90.

Tyson, Karen W., Bruce R. Harmon, and Daniel M. Utech, "Understanding Cost and Schedule Growth in Acquisition Programs," Institute for Defense Analysis research paper, July 1994, IDA paper P-2967.

Ulam, Stanislaw M., *Adventures of a Mathematician*. New York: Charles Scribner's Sons, 1976.

U.S. Congress, Office of Technology Assessment, *Reducing Launch Operations Costs: New Technologies and Practices*. Washington, DC: U.S. Government Printing Office, 1988.

U.S. Department of Transportation Federal Highway Administration, "Risk Assessment for Public-Private Partnerships: A Primer," January 2014.

Waldrop, M. Mitchell, "The Chips Are Down for Moore's Law." *Nature* 530 (February 9, 2016): 144–47, doi:10.1038/530144a.

World Bank Independent Evaluation Group, "Cost Benefit Analysis in World-Bank Projects." Washington, DC: The World Bank, 2010.

Wriston, Walter B., *Risk & Other Four-Letter Words*. New York: Harper & Row, 1986.

INDEX

Dams, 4, 13, 14*t*
De Moivre, Abraham, 80
Deep Blue, 8
Deepwater Horizon oil spill, xi, 105, 106
Defense sector, xi, 56, 233
Delta 180 project, 200
Demand, predicting, 50–53
Demand curve, 233–238, 236*f*
Denver International Airport, 44
Department of Defense, xv, 7, 9, 31, 32, 35–37, 46–48, 56, 211, 226
Department of Energy, 148
Dependencies, external, 50–55
Derivatives, 153–154
Development phase, 4
Diminishing returns, 47–48, 47*f*
Direct costs, 33
Discover magazine, 64
Disposal phase, 5
Distributions, probability (*see* Probability distributions)
Diversification, 143–163
The Doctrine of Changes (de Moivre), 80
"Drinking the Kool-Aid," 23
Ducats, transport of, 67–68, 69*f*

Economics, 120–121
Education costs, 121
80/20 rule, 86
Einhorn, David, 174
Elephants, 82
England, 58–59
English Channel tunnel, 12
ENIAC computer, 93
Enterprise resource planning (ERP), 18–19

Enterprise risk management, 228–229, 241–242
Entropy, xiii–xiv, 33
Ephesus, 229
Equivalent software lines of code (ESLOC), 12–13
Erasmus, Desiderius, 66
Estimates, rough-order-of-magnitude, 27
Estimation, errors in, 35–37
Euclidean geometry, 84
European Space Agency (ESA), 10–11, 16–17
"Everything Goes According to Plan" principle, 107
Exceptional variation, 173
Excess capacity, 51
Execution, cost/schedule growth due to poor, 32–35
Expected shortfall, 186–187, 186*t*, 219–221, 220*t*, 226, 248
and portfolio effect, 190–191, 191*t*
and tails, 184–189, 186*t*
Expected value, 64, 66–68, 70, 73, 76, 90, 178, 184
External dependencies, 50–55, 243
External factors, in cost/schedule growth, 22
Extreme events, 77 (*See also* Black swans)
Extremistan, 85, 86, 132, 137, 139, 156, 246
Exxon Valdez oil spill, xi

F-35 aircraft, 35–37, 43, 52
"Faster-better-cheaper" policy (NASA), 38–40, 200
Fat-tailed distributions, 86

Knight Capital, 43–44, 200
K-standard deviation events,
 83–84, 83*t*

Las Vegas Factor of Development
 Program Planning, 7, 9
Launch vehicle availability, 53–55
Law of Marginal Survival, 211
Leadership, 246
Learning (manufacturing), 51
Leibniz, Gottfried von, 1
Lemons (used cars), 232
Leverage, 72–73, 145, 153–154
Lewent, Judy, 229
Liberalism, 146
Littoral Combat Ship (LCS), 52
Lockheed Martin, 7
Loeb-Magat mechanism, 235–238,
 236*f*, 238*t*
Logarithms (logarithmic scale), 87,
 88, 87*f*
Lognormal distributions, 89–90,
 90*f*, 97–99, 97*f*–99*f*, 134–
 140, 135*t*, 151, 245
 and expected shortfall, 186–187,
 186*t*
 tails in, 170–171, 174–177, 175*f*,
 176*t*, 178–181, 179*f*, 181*f*
Lognormal paradox, 178–181, 179*f*,
 181*f*
Long-Term Capital Management,
 73
Losses, reactions to prospective, 26
Lotteries, 59

Magnus, Olaus, 166*f*
MAIMS principle, 3, 38, 216, 240
Mandelbrot, Benoit, 84–85,
 139–140
Manhattan Project, 94

Manufacturing costs, 51
"Margaritaville" (song), 105
Marginal cost, 234–238, 235*f*–237*f*
Marginal utility, 26
Market design, 233
Markowitz, Harry, 143, 144,
 147–148
Mars, manned missions to, 28
Massachusetts Institute of
 Technology (MIT), 140
Mean (statistical term), 2, 81, 86,
 91, 91*f*, 127
Measures of central tendency, 64,
 85
Mechanism design, 232–233
Median (statistical term), 2–3, 81,
 91, 91*f*, 127
"The Median Isn't the Message"
 (Gould), 64
Mediocristan, 85, 132–133, 137
Megaprojects, 6, 11–12
Mensa, 172
Merck Corporation, 229
Merrill Lynch, 174
Ming, Kong, 215
Minnesota Twins, 63
Misalignment of cost, schedule,
 and technology, 37–48
Mitigation, risk, 227
Mode (statistical term), 3, 81, 91,
 91*f*
Monopolies, 234–238
Monotonicity, 182
Monte Carlo simulation, 93–94,
 97, 125, 126, 151, 245, 250
Montreal Olympics, 13
Moon, manned missions to the,
 28, 43
The Moon Is a Harsh Mistress
 (Heinlein), 146

ABOUT THE AUTHOR

Christian Smart is the Chief Data Scientist with Galorath Federal, a leading international supplier of parametric cost models and data analytics consulting services. He supports NASA and the Department of Defense in the application of analytics for cutting-edge programs, including nuclear thermal propulsion for crewed space transportation and hypersonic weapon systems.

Dr. Smart's professional career has focused on parametric cost analysis and cost risk analysis of space flight and weapon system programs and related areas, such as machine learning, regression analysis, cost and schedule risk analysis, probabilistic risk assessment, and the project management policies that support best-in-class cost and schedule analysis. He led the development of a quantitative cost risk analysis capability for the NASA/Air Force Cost Model. Dr. Smart participated in the development of a probabilistic risk analysis for the Space Shuttle. He led and edited the publication of a cost estimating handbook for the Missile Defense Agency. Dr. Smart developed a joint cost and schedule quantitative risk analysis for the Ares I launch vehicle and served on the Review of United States Human Space Flight Plans Committee (also known as The Augustine Commission), for which he was awarded an Exceptional Public Service Medal by NASA in 2010.

Dr. Smart served as the Cost Director for the Missile Defense Agency for several years, leading a team of more than 100 estimators. He is a longtime member of and is certified by the International Cost Estimating and Analysis Association (ICEAA). Dr. Smart currently serves as the Vice President for Professional Development for ICEAA. He has written extensively about cost modeling,